THE
2025 REPORT
A Concise History of the Future
1975–2025

THE
2025
REPORT

A CONCISE HISTORY OF
THE FUTURE
1975–2025

NORMAN MACRAE

MACMILLAN PUBLISHING COMPANY

NEW YORK

Macmillan Publishing Company
866 Third Avenue, New York, N.Y. 10002

Library of Congress Cataloging in Publication Data

Macrae, Norman.
The 2025 report: a concise history of the future,
1975–2025.

Includes index.
1. Twentieth century—Forecasts. 2. Twenty-first
century—Forecasts. I. Title.
CB161.M32   1984   303.4′90905   84-20172
ISBN 0-02-579090-0

Macmillan books are available at special discounts for bulk
purchases for sales promotions, premiums, fund-raising, or
educational use. Special editions or book excerpts can also
be created to specification. For details, contact:

Special Sales Director
Macmillan Publishing Company
866 Third Avenue
New York, New York 10022

10   9   8   7   6   5   4   3   2   1

Printed in the United States of America

Contents

Contents

Author's Note

THE HARD WORK in this history of 1975–2025 was done by a computer expert and a scientist, whose professional forecasts I then edited to fit with my economic prejudices.

The computer expert was my son, Christopher Macrae, who lives in Paris and already telecommutes from there. The scientist he recruited proved by far the best writer of the three of us, and also wrote the most sparkling of the biographies. He did not want to be named because, as he explained at a book conference we sensibly held in the cheaper grandstand at Ascot: "As an atheistic moral relativist, I've been publishing stuff about another future, so I don't want to seem to be forecasting your Christian libertarian one at the same time." I suspect that, in his future, mad Christian libertarian economists like me blow the world up.

[vii]

Nevertheless, each of the three professionals—the scientist, the computerman and the economist—thinks the things here forecast in his field are technically likely to become feasible within the next forty years. Our disagreement is whether men will devise the best incentive systems to put them efficiently into operation. As we scrabbled over each other's copy, we began to cross out each other's best jokes because we eventually felt that we were writing a deeply serious book. This is the lovely future everybody under the age of fifty could have if only all democrats made the right decisions.

It was particularly nice for me that the book was accepted even in its then inchoate state by Sidgwick and Jackson in Britain; and now Macmillan is to publish it in America. When General Sir John Hackett wrote his brilliant work on *The Third World War*, there was an excellent arrangement whereby he did all the work and six of us who had written memos collected half the money. I said then that my difficulty was I didn't believe there would be a war, and that I had in the past decade written many articles in *The Economist* and delivered lectures in nearly thirty countries across the world saying the future should be much more rosy. Some of those who have read those articles and heard those lectures—mainly on the future organization of business and the coming decline of governments—will find similarities of expression here; if one wants to say the same thing at about the same length it is affectation to strive for second-best sentences. Any complaints about this or about the book's implausibility will be answered after 20 June 2025, when one of the two of us signing below is actuarially likely to be still alive. California's Institute for Contemporary Studies financed the work done up front by the computerman and the scientist, but it has no responsibility for our guesses on what is about to happen.

NORMAN MACRAE
(*Author*)

CHRISTOPHER MACRAE
(*Telecommuting author on computers*)

TC Key

THIS TRANSMISSION IS PROGRAMMED so that the reader may switch as required to subsidiary databases (open 15 June 2025) for extensive background information on all sources and statistics used by the authors. This includes (a) explanations of all words with no meaning in 2025 (like OPEC, EEC, mugging, nuclear disarmament, sexism, ministries of the interior); (b) full references for all quotations used; and (c) further material from the Biographical Institute of the University of the Caucasus at Borovskygrad, from whose unrivalled collection of twentieth and twenty-first century lives we have drawn during this transmission. We thereby avoid, in this concise history, what pre-TC historians called footnotes.

Prologue

WE HAVE BEEN COMMISSIONED to transmit on your telecomputing systems this examination of how and why the tumultuous history of the past half-century has come about. In 1975 few people believed mankind could quickly achieve today's comfort, ease, abolition of crime and freedom of living styles. Moreover, mankind very nearly didn't. This is an examination of why what happened did, and why what could have happened was mercifully avoided.

The first chapter is a brief summary of the thirty years before 1975. It may help explain why, during the youth of 2025's middle-aged and senior citizens, one of the fastest growing human diseases was something called a nervous breakdown.

20 June 2025
Tahiti

THE
2025 REPORT
A Concise History of the Future
1975–2025

1

1945-75:
The Age of
Quadrupling
Real Income

AT THE END OF THE SECOND WORLD WAR in 1945 the earth seemed a much more dangerous place than at the end of the First World War in 1918. In 1945 the dominating figure in Europe and Asia was a widely admired dictator who unfortunately was clinically insane. Marshal Josef Stalin had already killed more than 10 million of his own people who had in some way failed to worship him, and before his death in 1953 he wanted to execute his own doctors because they did not make him feel better on the increasingly frequent occasions when he went to bed roaring drunk. Into his hands during the 1940s a group of genuinely idealistic scientists had delivered the power to destroy the world. By 1953 Russia knew how to make a nuclear bomb which could soon release in one flash a greater destructive power than had been exploded by all the TNT in all the wars of history.

Economically, in 1945, Central Europe (especially West Germany) and Japan were devastated heaps of rubble. Among the economic forecasts made in 1945–8 were erudite prophecies that defeated Germany and Japan could never expect to re-attain their 1929 standards of living; and that war-devastated areas like Western Europe and Japan had better concentrate on agriculture and mining coal because they would probably need to ration basic materials and foodstuffs (and certainly luxury foods like butter) for the rest of the century. It was said that bureaucratic controls were needed to ensure fair distri-bution of supplies, and when West Germany dashed for freedom from some controls at the time of its deflationary currency reform in 1948 there were wide forecasts of misery, starvation and chaos.

Instead, continental Europe—led by West Germany—went into its fastest boom, marred mainly by wastefully rising moun-tains of unsalable butter. Across the world, Japan went into even faster boom, especially after it closed all its loss-making coal mines down. Although the victorious nations did slightly less well than the vanquished ones, real gross world product quadrupled during 1945–75. The soldiers demobilized after Hitler's and Tojo's war doughtily added, during this brief main quarter-century of their civilian working lives, three times as much to the world's productive power as had been added in all the previous millennia of man's history. By the late 1960s they therefore self-satisfiedly felt that they had passed on a rather good legacy to their by now teenage children, especially in the richer and freer countries.

Unfortunately, especially in the richer and freer countries, those teenage children were by the late 1960s in noisy revolt. They said they had been handed a world that was mortally dangerous, insufficiently compassionate, unspeakably boring and vulgarly materialistic. The only moderately successful leg-acy from their parents, they said, was the conquest of unem-ployment—which would always be easy but was of little use if people had unsatisfying jobs.

In 1974, amid much greater dissatisfaction, a decade and a half of high unemployment began.

2

Red Sunset

DURING MUCH OF THE SECOND HALF of the twentieth century young kids and old goats marched in demonstrations against the existence of nuclear weapons. Unfortunately they advocated isolationist pacifist policies which, we now know, came within an ace of causing such weapons to be used. In the same years the same groups marched first against the "ecological crime" of fast economic growth, and then against the unemployment which was naturally caused when growth was slowed down.

For most of the second half of the twentieth century it seemed more than 50 per cent likely that the world would blow itself up. After the achievement of nuclear fission in 1945, mankind could soon count how many hydrogen bombs or cobalt bombs would be required to destroy the planet.

Our grandfathers at this period were strangely allowing

[3]

themselves to be bossed around by three sorts of excessive government, misleadingly called the "rich democracies," the "communist powers," and (somewhat contemptuously) the "Third World." Each was in a dangerously unstable state. Today psychology is recognized as the science concerned with diverting humans in an unstable state to a more comfortable one, but psychology played little part in the last century's conduct of foreign policy or any other policy.

In the rich democracies, this was the age of limited-channel television, which was very different from the free-as-air telecommunicating computer terminals (TCs) of our time. Under that limited-channel television, for the first time since the days of Pericles, democratic electors could regularly see and hear in their own living rooms those whom they were asked to vote for. Democracy thereby became a system of picking men with the characteristics of good television actors—that is, prima donnas skilled in dissembling—and then putting them into the kind of antagonistic work environment which would turn a poodle into a paranoiac (listen to the tapes we still have of congressional committees vetting American presidential appointees or of the daily, shouted question times in the British House of Commons). The rulers who emerged through this system were then allowed, amid an atmosphere of power and egomania (but also occasional appallingly unjust personal slander), to spend half their people's money for them, until somebody heard some tape of what they had been saying casually to their own staffs in private, when there arose a great clamour to put them in prison instead.

And this was the most civilized of the three contemporary systems of over-government. In 1974 it applied to about 40 of the 165 governments of the world. In most of the 125 non-democratic countries the head of government went to bed each night in some way afraid that he might be killed together with his family in a *coup d'état* before breakfast tomorrow morning. This did not lead to a relaxed frame of mind in what was to become the nuclear trigger-minders' profession.

The first nuclear power among what might be called the *coup d'état*-terrified states was communist Russia. It was thus the first power that looked as if its system of neurotic over-government might destroy the planet. It was also the first to disappear, and it is interesting to see how this came about.

Through most of the second half of the twentieth century around a third of mankind was ruled by communist governments, including the peoples of China and Russia. All of the communist governments had come to power by force. None had been elected by its people, and communism was proving to be a system of over-government that had no prospect of bringing adequate prosperity or liberty to its subjects.

In 1913 tsarist Russia had a higher income per head than imperial Japan. After sixty years of communism in the late 1970s Russians had a lower income, lower life expectancy and a lower range of choice than the Japanese at every level of their society. By 1970 there was no communist country in which a majority of the workers would willingly have voted for the government in power. From then until 1991 communism was therefore dying, as so many other failed religions and failed governing systems had so frequently and so bloodily died before.

Two recent similar failures were everywhere in men's minds. Any fifty-five-year-old Russian in 1949 had been aged twenty-three in 1917, when the privileged families who ran the scattered estates and towns of the Tsars' Russia—a vast country with practically no communications—had been overthrown and often horribly done to death in a few months. By 1949 the scattered towns and collective farms of the Soviet Union were run by a communist party privilegentsia whose understandable, if neurotic, obsession was not to suffer the same fate. Most of these local communist leaders were cautious men, instantly obedient to Moscow's authority. Any who had been incautious or idealistic, intent on building socialism without quite knowing what it meant, had been murdered in Stalin's purges. If in 1949–53 Stalin had ordered the world to be destroyed by nuclear bombs on the grounds that only this could make it safe for communism, few local or national leaders of the Soviet communist party would have dared to say him nay.

Horrified observers could look back only a few years to the last European governing system that had collapsed in Wagnerian epic. When Adolf Hitler had been driven back to his bunker in 1945 his propaganda minister Goebbels had cried on the radio, "If our National Socialist Germany is to go down, we will slam the door on history so loud that it will remember us for ten thousand years." Hitler's Nazism mercifully could not fulfil that threat, because it did not possess the nuclear bomb. Soviet communism, which was as plainly due to die either epically or otherwise, did possess it.

In the ailing Stalin's last years, nobody knew who would succeed him. If anybody had known, Stalin would have known, and he would have bumped him off tomorrow. When Stalin had his last heart attack in March 1953 his housekeeper called in the main members of his government, but none of them dared to summon a doctor. If Stalin had recovered but in a dilapidated state, he would have blamed the doctor and the politician or house servant who called him in. So Stalin lay through the night on his living room floor, until his family next day sent him to the hospital, already clearly dying.

"With the passing of Marshal Stalin," said the London viewspaper *The Economist* that week, "the world is a healthier but not a safer place." This proved to be wrong reporting. The world became a slightly safer place from the instant of Stalin's death. Up until then war could have come through madness in the Kremlin. Thereafter it could spring only from miscalculation in the Kremlin, but muddled Western policies and communism's own unstable dynamic meant that the opportunities for miscalculation were about to increase.

The principal destabilizer was the lack of a free-market mechanism in the communist system, which ensured that Soviet economic policy in a technologically advancing world would go more and more awry. At the same time the growth of education in Russia meant that the Russian people could see ever more plainly that they were not getting richer or freer at anything like the pace they could. Only the parts of national policy which did not depend on the existence of any free-market mechanism even in other countries—such as foreign policy, defense policy, police organization, internal relations within the bureaucracy—proved as adept as equivalent policies in the West.

The change in relations within the bureaucracy started on the morning after Stalin's death. The men at the top of the government had lived until then under daily fear that Stalin might decide to execute them, so they met in sensible conclave and promised each other that from now on no Russian politician was going to order the secret police to kill any other politician any more. One of those who made this promise was lying through his teeth. Unsurprisingly, he was the man in charge of the secret police. So the others banded together and shot this Beria, but from then on the no-fratricide promise among top men was generally kept. Internal machinations continued as before, but all those thereafter toppled (in 1954–64, Malenkov, Molotov, Bulganin, then Khrushchev) were retired to positions of moderate comfort instead of to the firing squad.

When Stalin died at the age of seventy-three and Khrushchev was removed at the age of seventy, most Politburo members were ten to fifteen years younger. At Khrushchev's deposition in 1964, the organizing deposer, Brezhnev, was fifty-seven, and he learned from the easiness of his own deed. As the leading young Turk of 1964, Brezhnev's principal determination from then on was that there should be no young Turks on his Politburo lest they organize to depose him. By the beginning of the 1980s twelve of the fourteen voting members of the Politburo were over sixty-five, and at least three were known to be gaga.

This was annoying for the younger apparatchiks kept waiting in line, but there was nothing much they could do. While the leader of a democracy was in those days usually picked by his people as the less bad of two party-caucus-selected candidates whom most of the people did not want, the leader of Russia was picked for the Russian people out of candidates of whom most knew less than nothing by a secret cabal to which efficient young people were not allowed to belong.

When Brezhnev died in 1982 the cabal plus the Red Army chose in his place the sixty-eight-year-old Yuri Andropov, the former head of the secret police. He was an old, ill, gray man. Some Western journalists said hopefully that he might move to implement Hungarian-style economic reforms in the Soviet Union; Hungary had become a freer country when a partly market-oriented economy had been introduced there. But Andropov's idea of economic reform proved to be to put black marketeers in prison.

When he died, in February 1984, he was succeeded by a man three years older than himself. It soon became clear that Konstantin Chernenko's appointment had merely delayed the real battle for succession in the Soviet Union—and not for very long. Chernenko spent most of his short chairmanship in his sickbed. His nominated heir, Mihail Gorbachev, was in the mild mould of Malenkov (brief successor to Stalin) and Hua (brief successor to Mao)—a caretaker very willing to bow out in favour of any more forceful character who seized control of the party, and who was willing to pension, instead of kill, him off. The sacking in 1984 of Marshal Ogarkov and the death of Marshal Ustinov meant that a struggle for power in the Red Army was proceeding at the same time. In 1988 rumors began to circulate in the West that Colonel-General Yuli Lermontov, the chief political commissar for the Red Army, was making a bid either for the leadership or to be a new Soviet leader's left-hand man. And the policy reportedly advocated by Lermontov sounded very frightening indeed.

3

1988:
The Lermontov
Assessments

SHORTLY AFTER GARY HART was elected as President of the United States in November 1988, he sent a worried memo to the brain trust he had gathered around him:

I have just had my first in-depth briefing from the CIA and it leaves me very disturbed. It is agreed that the apparatchiks at present controlling the Soviet Union can best be divided into three groups: the men in charge of Russia's successful foreign policy, the men in charge of Russia's untried defense forces, and the much larger body of men deriving corrupt sustenance from running an economy which is spinning downward out of control.

Into these three groups a Colonel-General Yuli Lermontov—who is described as the most political of the Soviet

generals, and therefore a man with a foot in all three camps—
has been pounding the most bellicose memos in the history
of the Soviet Union. After taking extensive opinion polls within
the Red Army, Lermontov is advocating that during the current "window of opportunity"—the period when we could
not beat the Soviet Union in nuclear war—Russia should do
its utmost to humiliate my very inexperienced administration. It should trail its coat for war, feeling confident that
we will run away from it.

I want your assessment of how each of the three groups of
apparatchiks in the Soviet Union is likely to respond to this.

Each report should (a) assess the present mood of the group
of apparatchiks you are studying; (b) say how they are likely
to respond to Lermontov; and (c) say what mistakes of policy
we have been making in regard to each group, so that we
can immediately correct those mistakes. All reports to me
before 10 December, please.

1988 Report: Russia's Foreign Policy Makers

The apparatchiks in charge of Russia's foreign policy in
1988 are very nationalist, only superficially communist, cocky
as hell, determined to make Russia number one, well aware
that they are the only group in their society who have enjoyed
success in the past dozen years. In the first nine years after
their *annus mirabilis* of 1975 they placed eight pro-Moscow
governments in power by armed force (South Vietnam, Laos,
Angola, Ethiopia, Afghanistan, South Yemen, Kampuchea
and Nicaragua).

It was in 1975 that they got agreement to their policy: "Do
not let us defend the fatherland merely by preparing to crush
counter-revolution in Poland and other neighbors (if we stick
to that reactive policy we will probably lose); let us take the
offensive by imposing pro-Soviet governments thousands of
miles from our borders." In a brilliant logistical feat to start
this process, 15,000 Cuban troops were moved in a fortnight
across the Atlantic into Africa, in order to maintain or impose

in that unhappy continent governments which the local people clearly did not want. The West did not utter more than a deprecatory cough.

This interventionist policy has since been extended across the Third World à la carte. Cuban troops, accompanied by East German advisers and North Korean construction workers, have appeared in other poor countries in Asia, the Caribbean and Latin America. Except in the case of Grenada (1983), the West has allowed Russia's post-1975 Third World policy to proceed. This has been an extraordinary triumph for the sophisticated foreign policy apparatchiks in Moscow, who had prophesied precisely that non-reaction.

Since 1975 if a new dictator succeeds to power in a poor country by murdering some other leader who was the previous dictator, he has been wise to call himself a left-wing idealist. If he does, Russia will help him in tough security measures against whatever next leader is currently plotting to murder him. One such dictator recently shot the top dozen of his political opponents on a football field before 10,000 spectators, including the victims' families who were obliged to turn up and cheer.

By contrast, if the successful murdering leader calls himself an ally of the West, and starts to guard his own neck through what he regards as the only viable security policy (i.e., a fairly nasty one), then much of the Western media and professoriat will decently hound him for permitting imprisonment without trial when he puts under house arrest the rival "progressive" politician who has clearly been organizing bomb attacks against him. In those circumstances the West-supporting dictator feels forced to allow the rival to emigrate on a state pension to Paris or Harvard, in which former (though not yet latter) place he augments his pension with Russian and Libyan money as he plans the planting of more bombs back home.

The Russian-supported dictator also has economic advantages. In the mid-1980s one of them "parastatelized" (which meant confiscating for his wife) his island's most luxurious hotel for a compensation payment of one rupee. Generally, the cronies of a left-wing government will seize control of most scarce goods and all imports, so that ministers' families grow fat by selling these goods internally at a profit, while "controlling inflation" by giving local farmers such low prices that they stop producing food. American aid has continued to flow to many such countries.

By contrast, a right-wing Third World government will usually impose import licensing rather than state monopoly purchasing, and only when goods are needed fast (as soaring market prices of them show) is expedition of the licenses bought off some civil servant or the second cousin of the president's wife. After 1976 any U.S. company executive who economically expedited trade in that way has been liable to be sent to prison, so the free world's trade has expanded faster since 1975 with totally corrupt Moscow-run tyrannies than with venal but freer-market ones.

Since three-fifths of the world's governments are installed by *coups d'état*, this system has meant that three-fifths of the world's heads of government are logically finding it securer for their peace of mind to sound stridently anti-American. Unsurprisingly, therefore, during the 1980s Russia's able foreign policy apparatchiks have continued to place more governments friendly to themselves in power in more of Latin America, Africa and Asia, even as their East European allies (such as Poland and East Germany) and indeed parts of their Soviet homeland have simmered nearer and nearer to revolt.

Surprisingly, Moscow's foreign policy apparatchiks have not so far tried to stir coups in Saudi Arabia and the Gulf, although reports are rising that they have prepared for possible action there and also in China, where a coup by old-guard communists against the Dengists (divided after Deng's death) has long seemed conceivable.

The most alarming scenario is that coups in China and the Gulf might be organized to take place at the same time as a Russian army invades Pakistan from Afghanistan and perhaps as Soviet "volunteers" are landed in black southern

Africa for a war of liberation against white South Africa. Under the so-called "Lermontov strategy" favored by some political commissars in the Russian armed forces, the only way to discourage revolts in countries such as Poland and Czechoslovakia is deemed to be for Soviet forces to undertake aggressions far from their borders, to which the West would be too weak to respond. By thus recapturing the initiative Lermontov's group thinks that the Soviet Union could show Poland and the other restless East Europeans that national revolts are hopeless.

It is not certain that all forces even in the armed services incline to Lermontov's line. Oddly, more of the home policy apparatchiks might favor it. The views of both these groups are discussed in more detail in separate reports below. The task given to the compilers of this report was to gauge whether the able foreign policy apparatchiks in the Soviet Union are likely to favor an extreme Lermontov strategy.

Our majority view is that they are not. Precisely because they have been so successful, this group of foreign policy apparatchiks has attracted into its ranks some of the ablest men and women in the Soviet system. Theirs is a nice job to have and some of the leaders of this group (such as young Andrej Borovsky) are men who would have risen in any society. Large parts of the Soviet establishment now have something to lose and do not intend to lose it. We believe that ultimately such men will be intelligent enough to conclude that the Soviet Union has more to fear than to hope from steps that could increase the chance of war.

1988 Report: Soviet Armed Forces

This memo will compare the 1988 Soviet military with the 1988 U.S. military in the four main fields of (a) combat planning, (b) available troops, (c) available equipment, and (d) recent good or bad political fortune. Up to 1988 the Soviet military have had advantages in most of these four respects, but the Soviet marshals think their advantages may be about

13

to peter out. This could make more of them favor the Lermontov strategy of chancing their arms round the world at a time when the "window of opportunity" from 1988–94 means that both Russia and the U.S. still think that Russia would win any early all-out nuclear struggle—so that the Russians assume the U.S. would not dare to enter one.

(a) Combat Planning It was a mistake thirty-five years ago for the U.S. chiefs of staff to be set up apart from the operational commanders. The chiefs are now experts in equipment, rather than in drawing up contingency plans. There are now not enough contingency plans, compared with the many places where Russia might strike.

The Russians have had the advantage that they can spend their time planning possible attacks on any place in the world. They then ditch those that do not look hopeful, while slowly moving up to the top of a contingent hit list those that would probably work.

They have the problem that most of their equipment is geared to blitzkrieg. Their navy would be good at sudden Pearl Harbor type attacks or the quick transport of troops anywhere, but is not fitted to stay long at sea. The same is true of their army, which is now particularly ill-fitted for the tasks Soviet politicians have put on it, such as long-time occupation of Afghanistan, or garrisoning troops in Poland and even parts of the Soviet Union where disaffection might spread. So the Soviet marshals might be inclined to say, "Let us deter revolts in the Polands by showing how mighty the Soviet forces are by gaining glorious victories in places thousands of miles from the state borders of the Soviet Union. We have a viable plan for swiftly transshipping a Soviet expeditionary force to help the front-line black African states wage a war of liberation against white racist South Africa . . ."

(b) Available Troops We in the U.S. have the finest officer corps in the world, but until the beginning of the 1980s our rank-and-file troops were rudely described as "an army of

14

unemployables, half the time on pot.'' As late as 1979 about 45 per cent of the recruits in the U.S. Army were classified in the lowest intelligence category 4 (which means dummies). Over 60 per cent of the Army's recruits then came from the 11 per cent of American adults who did not have a high school diploma. In 1979 around 98 per cent of the U.S. Army's tank repairmen failed in proficiency tests for their own military jobs, as did 91 per cent of its aviation maintenance personnel (which helps explain why some new aircraft then spent most of their time being mended). Only three of the U.S. Army's job categories passed their tests 100 per cent in 1979, one of which was the Army's three bassoon players.

Since 1981 this situation has begun dramatically to improve. Higher armed services' pay and higher civilian unemployment have greatly increased the quality of U.S. service recruits. There has been a professional public relations campaign against drugs, like the Fleet's poster of a marijuana plant saying, "Not on my watch, not in my ship, not in my Navy." In the past two years we have also begun to draw sensible deductions from the awkward fact that we are the first world leader without a colonial army to do part of our job for us.

If the *pax Americana* was being enforced by a conventional empire the obvious course in the past decades would have been to put our superb officers in charge of mercenaries drawn from the Third World's tens of millions of underemployed twenty-year-olds. Since 1986 we have at last taken some half-steps towards this: the offer of immigrants' visas to picked young Mexicans and others who will join the U.S. colors, the recruitment of more Filipinos and Cuban *émigrés*, the beginning of a U.S. equivalent to Britain's Gurkha troops, the training of some Third World allies' armies with a lien on their use.

While our forces are thus on the mend, Russia's are deteriorating. In the past twenty-five years the Soviet Union's 210 million Europeans have grown more educated, more alcoholic, more prone to massive absenteeism from work, less willing to breed children, more prone to fissiparous nationalisms (Jews, Lithuanians, Volga Germans, and Ukrainians could soon be throwing bombs about) and more racist against the Soviet Union's 60 million Asians. These Soviet Asians numbered only 17 per cent of the population in the late 1970s, but by the late 1990s they will be around 45 per cent of the Soviet Union's nineteen-year-olds (and hence of its army conscripts). Partly because these young Asians are already providing an influx of muggers into Moscow, they are unpopular with most of the increasingly racist European Russians.

Present racism in European Russia may bring terrible revenge. By 1996 some 45 per cent of the Soviet privates carrying the guns held ready to put down civilian dissatisfaction at home and in countries such as Poland will be from these Asian hordes. The Soviet marshals are already terrified of being tarred with this brush. They also fret that Soviet army training manuals (including those on crowd control) will have to be written in languages like Uzbek, which the officers do not understand.

The Deputy Chief of Staff of the Red Army wrote in a recent intercepted document: "If we are ever going to adopt a Lermontov strategy of putting our forces to the test far from our own homeland, it had better be done before most of our Army recruits become Third World people themselves. The deduction from Lermontov is that only such distant drums for adventure may save us from having to launch our army in the 1990s against our own people and the people of our socialist allies. I must state plainly that if the Army thus deployed was by then largely Asian there could be refusal to shoot self-styled nationalists such as Poles or Ukrainians even by our European (but insufficiently communist) officer corps." It looks as if this was one vote for Lermontov.

(c) Available Equipment   The production of military equipment in the United States is just about the only form of manufacturing production that is not made efficient by market forces, which in the past generation for civilian (but not

military) goods has usually meant made efficient by Japanese competition.

Mainly because of that Japanese competition, productivity per manhour in producing civilian automobiles in the free world has increased by 700 per cent over the period 1957–87; the time taken to build civilian supertankers has fallen by three-quarters; and consumer electronics have grown actually cheaper in recent years, while increasing extraordinarily in quality. By contrast, productivity per manhour in producing Army tanks has grown by only 2 per cent over the period 1957–87; the time taken to build aircraft carriers has doubled; defense electronics have multiplied astronomically in cost, and are wrongly said to be "on the frontier of man's knowledge" while becoming less reliable when under stress. When the Soviet Union wanted to beat the ban on the Western export of weapons aiming systems, it instructed its military attaché in Washington to buy one of the successors to the computer game called "Space Invaders," and found that in the software program underlying it he had bought a more modern computerized aiming system than half of NATO's anti-aircraft guns possessed.

It has been a mistake to allow the U.S. chiefs of staff to set detailed descriptions of requirements for their own weapons. This is equivalent to allowing newspapermen to design their own typewriters. Most writers would then choose one that included a lot of ingenious extra gadgets, but these would make the typewriter a hundred times more expensive and also ensure that it did not actually work.

U.S. military equipment, after being hampered in this way, is then also bedevilled by political corruption. A weapon may be rejected in favor of some other one that is less efficient but brings jobs to the home constituency or state of some congressman or senator from whom the administration wants to wheedle something else. Since this game of politics means that young Americans are more likely to be killed by being sent into battle with inferior weapons chosen so as to create a few hundred jobs in the umpteenth congressional district

17

of Wyoming as a reward for a vote against his conscience by its congressman, one might have supposed that the citizens of Wyoming would swear never again to vote for those who disgrace them by such porkbarrelling. But during the present era of over-government the trends in voting do not so far seem to be that way.

As in the United States, the production of military equipment in the Soviet Union also does not benefit from a free-market system, but then no part of Soviet production does. In absolute terms Soviet military production is therefore as inefficient as American military production, but there is a great advantage for the Soviets in that an able Russian technician will have a more satisfying job making aiming systems for guns than making video games, while for an able American technician the reverse applies. The Russian making video games is generally dependent for next week's supply of raw materials on the whim of some planner who is not likely to favor video games. The Russian making aiming equipment has a priority in getting supplies; while the American making aiming equipment might actually get slightly lower-quality spare parts because of some politician's need to mop up unemployment in Ohio. The Russian maker of guns is not thwarted by the member for Omsk.

The American making guns often has his plans uneconomically changed because one of the chiefs of staff has been infected with some new technological idea, quarter-baked during a seminar at one of the learned institutes in Washington. The Russian chiefs of staff are making contingency plans for invading new Afghanistans, and the people whom they meet daily are not trying to sell them pseudo-intellectual (but actually porkbarrel) gee-whiz technological ideas. The able Russian technician making guns has a better chance than the able Russian technician making video games of achieving the largest step-up in his society (the step-up to being allowed to buy goods in the privilegentsia's shops). The American making video games has a better chance than the American military technician of becoming a millionaire.

For all these reasons we believe that the brightest technicians in Russia have for some time been moving into the military equipment industries, while the brightest technicians in American have been moving out of them. There was a brief period in the 1960s when the excitement of "bridging the missile gap" and putting a man on the moon flooded intelligent people into U.S. defense programs, but it is Russia which has that advantage today.

Oddly for the subject of this memo—namely whether Russia might adopt a Lermontov strategy—this particular instance of Russian superiority is cheering. We do not think the intelligent military equipment devisers of the Soviet Union want war. This is because (a) they are at present enjoying a reasonable and prestigious life, but are quartered in huge military-industrial compounds on to which U.S. missiles would home in the first few seconds of any nuclear war; and (b) they are making equipment which at present does not have to be used, and when used it could still (they themselves don't know) prove pretty inefficient.

(d) Recent Good or Bad Political Fortune We fought the last stages of the failed Vietnam war on the cheap, by slowing the development of sophisticated weapons not needed against the Vietcong. At the end of the Vietnam war the American people (and candidate Carter on the 1976 hustings) therefore demanded a peace dividend which did not exist. In office President Carter at first slowed military nuclear expenditure, citing the mutually-assured-destruction (or MAD) doctrine that, "Just one of our relatively invulnerable Poseidon submarines [which then carried 160 nuclear warheads] would deter Russia since each of these warheads could be targeted to attack a Soviet city."

This was the argument that Russia's able foreign policy apparatchiks were sedulously financing and spreading among the peace movements and within the left wings of Helmut Schmidt's and Michael Foot's European Labor parties. In the early 1980s the argument was rubbish—on a par with saying

19

that all four-and-a-half billion people in the world would die if they would queue up to take one lick each from a twelve-foot-square slab of the most virulent botulism poison available, so no nation need spend more on defense than the cost of culturing such a slab.

The cross-elasticities of substitution involved when an aggressor plans in advance how to neutralize his adversary's potential power to launch missiles unfortunately find themselves governed by equations a little more complicated than those assumed by the critics of overkill.

In 1988 the present "best-case" Russian assumption is that, in an all-out first-strike nuclear war, the Soviets might kill up to half of the present 240 million U.S. citizens, while losing less than the 20 million Russians who died during Hitler's war (from which Russia recovered very quickly). This does not mean that Russian decision-makers are eager for a nuclear war. They know (a) the estimate is subject to a huge margin of error; and (b) any missile that did get through would likely be targeted on the places where the decision-makers live. The decision-makers themselves are among the "mere" 20 million Russians who would probably be killed. But it is here that the argument about a "window of opportunity" arises.

Because he was an entirely honest man, President Carter abandoned his belief in the mutually-assured-destruction or MAD doctrine once he understood the devastating criticisms of it that arrived on the Oval Office's desk. The Reagan administration continued the increase in sophisticated military spending which Carter started after 1978–9, although this has not closed the gap behind the Russians as was first forecast. But we know from another intercepted message that one Soviet marshal was recently (June 1988) minuting: "It is clear to both the U.S. and the Soviet Union that we Russians are likely to win any nuclear war tomorrow, so the Americans would run away from any early threat of one. After about 1992–5 they may be reporting to themselves that we in Moscow must fear that the Soviet Union might likely lose any nuclear war. So the Americans will be more willing after 1992–5 to stir uprisings in areas such as Poland or even the Ukraine. If we decide to push the area of global conflict several thousand miles from the state borders of the Soviet Union, we should make our move before 1992 at the latest." It seems that this was another vote for Lermontov.

1988 Report: Soviet Domestic Rulers

The entire domestic Soviet privilegentsia is in a state of escalating neurosis. The social and economic system is breaking down in the Soviet homeland as well as in Poland, East Germany, Czechoslovakia, Hungary, Rumania and Bulgaria. For each country the computers chant, "Emergency erupting, emergency erupting, emergency erupting."

The riots may start in the Soviet colonies like Poland and North Korea first, but they could then explode across the entire urban and rural Soviet Union which is tinder dry. The local privilegentsia will not want to put down these insurrections by bringing in Soviet conscript soldiers carrying guns, because the guns might then be turned against themselves. They may not even want Soviet conscripts to be sent into the colonies because there is a growing probability that the insurrections in countries like Poland might succeed and the abashed Soviet conscripts might then return to Mother Russia carrying both guns and ideas.

The discontent across Russia is not due to starvation or even falling real incomes. Revolutions do not break out at moments of greater misery, but when people see that they are not getting richer and freer at the pace and with the evenness of rewards which they could reasonably expect. The period immediately before 1913 was one of fast increase in Tsarist Russia's real gross national product, but the fruits of advance were not coming through to non-aristocrats as smoothly as in Kaiser Wilhelm's neighboring imperial Germany. The period immediately before 1789 was one of advance in real income for most Frenchmen, but neighboring

Britain was handling its industrial revolution in more egalitarian and efficient fashion. Pre-1789 France's GNP growth and income-distribution compare interestingly with those in the Soviet Union right now.

The main aim of Soviet economic policy during the 1980s has been to raise wages faster than the supply of goods, but to try to check the resultant inflationary pressure by price controls and state management of the distribution system. Since this means there is no direct link between increased demand for anything and increased production of it, desperate shortages have appeared, especially of the goods that are most wanted. Higher supplies of these are then diverted to the special shops from which only the privilegentsia are allowed to buy. Ordinary people either have to start standing in line outside the ordinary shops at 5 a.m. on a cold Siberian morning, or else they buy the goods they really want at black market prices—either from corrupt warehouses or from the privilegentsia who have already bought them cheaply and at leisure in their own shops. This is an infuriating system for ordinary Ivan.

At various places in the planning mechanism sit apparatchiks whose job is to allocate raw materials to factories which are requisitioning for them. These apparatchiks get their main job satisfaction from saying "no" to factories which want more materials because there is a high demand for their products. Similar officials distribute supplies of finished goods to particular areas and retail outlets. If they distribute them "fairly" (that is, equally) between areas, they cause chaos, with long lines outside shops in the more affluent towns. These are eventually fed by re-exports from the poorer towns where some Georgian or Leningrad entrepreneur has found that he can buy the goods from overstocked shops at near the official price. If (which is more usual) the apparatchiks distribute the goods corruptly, by selling them to the highest bidder in whichever area has the biggest black market price, then the system works more smoothly, but it still causes resentment.

There is not nowadays a shortage in the Soviet Union of the absolute essentials of life, but the grain crop has consistently been too low to feed the cattle herds, so there is a shortage and rationing of meat. The ration varies from area to area, and in some places one stands in line for hours without ever being able to buy meat (and then resorts to buying it at black market prices from those who have stuffed themselves with surplus at the privilegentsia's shops).

This year's poor grain crop in the Soviet Union has as usual been attributed to what Michael Novak has called the country's 71st successive year of unusually bad weather, but the real reason is that younger people have fled the farms to escape what Marx called the idiocy of village life. The old people left on the farms could not work hard if they wanted to, and most do not want to because of the disincentives built into their pattern of earnings.

A Russian peasant pays 0 per cent income tax on anything he sells on the black market from his private plot, but he pays the equivalent of 100 per cent income tax on any work he does garnering the grain crop on the state farm. He just gets a wage from the state farm, which nowadays tends to be paid whether he turns up for work or not. He once had an incentive to turn up because a bonus is paid if production exceeds the state farm's quota, but nowadays in crops like grain it never does.

Unsurprisingly, private plots produce 40 per cent by value of Russia's food, even though they take up only 3 per cent of the agricultural land. There are other reasons why the Soviet Union state farms are underproducing. One state fruit farm did gather a good fruit crop recently, but was unable to ship it to market before it rotted. The farm was not allocated sufficient nails to close the packing cases.

There are supposed to be controls to prevent young people from flocking away from Soviet farms towards the towns, but these are breaking down. Permits to live even in Moscow are easily purchasable on the black market, and the price of these is at present falling because the secret police are no longer harassing those who sell them, unless they are bought by young Asian Russians, against whom Moscow policemen are racist.

During the 1960s and 70s the top men in the Soviet Union thought that Asian Russians were among their most loyal Uncle Toms. Soviet Uzbeks were richer than most Afghans or Pakistanis across the border, though not richer than Asians in the oil lands. Comfortable whites in the south-eastern United States thought the same about black people in the early 1950s when the southland claimed it was carrying through "the first enlightened industrial revolution in history." Britons in the 1950s enthused about the first generation West Indian and Pakistani immigrants ("marvellous chaps, a lower crime rate than among the British working class as a whole"). But the children and nephews of those Uncle Toms in both countries were building up resentment at their disadvantaged status in society. In the 1960s and 70s they exploded.

The same thing is happening in the Soviet Union now. Because disillusioned European Russians dropped their birth rate so dramatically twenty years ago, a large number of the fifteen- to twenty-year-olds who are flocking off the farms in 1988 are ex-rural Asians. They are streaming into the towns as drug-ridden illegal migrants, sometimes as deserters and draft dodgers from the army, sometimes as drug-carrying muggers into Moscow. They are hungry for Moscow girls, especially since the strange revival of the Muslim religion in Soviet Asia has caused girls to be locked up back home. They come from regions where the opium poppy grows. The police are trying to ship them back to Asia, while at the same time allowing white youngsters to stay in the towns without permits. A sort of pass law for Asians is operating in Moscow and Leningrad not unlike that in Johannesburg, and pass laws lead to civil war.

In industry, as in agriculture, bonuses are paid to Soviet workers only if they exceed their production targets. Some industries, like the coal mines, never come near those targets, so with the rise in black market prices after 1980 coal miners' real earnings went down. Some coal miners therefore went on strike. The Soviet authorities reacted in a very Soviet way, shipping the strike leaders off to lunatic asylums but giving the rest of the strikers large wage raises.

The large wage raises were not matched by the distribution of more consumer goods to the coal mining areas. With more money chasing the same volume of goods, shortages grew. As shortages grew, more goods were diverted to the privilegentsia's shops—and then sold secondhand out of them by the privilegentsia at ever higher black market prices. The higher-paid miners are now worse off than before the wage rises, and there have been some rioting and looting of the privilegentsia's shops. There is also sabotage in the mines. State property is nobody's property, and is being vandalized.

What is the likely reaction of the domestic-policy apparatchiks to this? Our impression is that they are very frightened men. The entire Soviet privilegentsia is rife with mistrust and fear.

It is difficult to say whether this will incline them to a Lermontov strategy. We know that some of the dimmer Soviet economic planners are saying, "We should seize Saudi Arabia from the feudalists, so as to add its oil wealth to our Soviet system," without understanding that economics does not work in that mercantilist way. Other domestic apparatchiks would accept a plunge by the Soviet Union into "popular little distant wars" as a useful diversion—but the emphasis would be on "distant." They do not want anybody except their own families to be carrying guns nearer home. The domestic apparatchiks are in a state of collapsed morale.

These reports were handed to the President-Elect of the United States in December 1988. They worried him sick, until he received the Borovsky Letter.

4

1989:
The Borovsky
Letter

SHORTLY AFTER THE NEW PRESIDENT of the United States was inaugurated in January 1989, a communication arrived at the White House which had been transmitted from within the Soviet Union along a route that showed it was from a high source. This became known as the Borovsky Letter. It ran:

From Andrej Borovsky, Candidate Member of the Politburo

It would be absurd to mark this as merely "confidential." If any mention of it seeps back to the Soviet Union, I will be eliminated as a traitor. You on your side will be investigating lest it be a Soviet trick, but please see that the investigators do not have deep throats to the *Washington Post*.

My name is Andrej Borovsky. I was born in 1942 into the

Soviet privilegentsia as the youngest son of an official who survived under Stalin, and who rose to fairly high office under both Khrushchev and Brezhnev, though not to my own present height. My grandfather and four uncles were also early members of the Communist Party, and only one was lost in the purges. I went up the usual accelerated escalator for a member of the privilegentsia, and after a brief period in Cuba was engaged in what you would call subversive work in Central America and Africa.

I was successful at this and was brought back to Moscow to head the institute which supervises most such operations. You have plenty of files on me for that period (my agent in the CIA has ensured that I have seen them). At the early age of forty-four I was appointed a candidate member of the Politburo, and am thus one of the top thirty men in the Soviet Union.

Like a substantial minority of those top thirty, I am terrified about the prospect ahead. A counter-revolution is coming in my fatherland. In an attempt to avert it the majority of my colleagues on the Politburo want to take steps that could lead to nuclear war.

To escape from this it is essential that sensible people near the leadership of the Soviet Union and ruling people in the United States run the next lap together. This is the situation:

1 Revolts like the Polish Solidarity riots of 1980–1 are about to erupt across Poland, East Germany, Czechoslovakia, Hungary, Rumania and Bulgaria. If they are not put down firmly, they will spread to the Soviet Union. The *total* preoccupation of the Soviet privilegentsia—by which I mean the top 1 per cent, or two-and-a-half million people, in the country—and especially those in our scattered small towns—is that they should not have their own throats cut.

2 There will be no prospect of "doing a Jaruzelski" against these simultaneous revolts in the socialist allies, nor of invasions by Soviet groups as in Hungary (1956) or Czechoslovakia (1968, when other socialist troops accompanied us). Soviet conscript soldiers in 1968 felt they were putting down

middle-class dissidents in Czechoslovakia, but recognize that invasions against Solidarity-type revolts would be oppression of the local working class.

3 A recent in-depth study called "Operation Lermontov" was undertaken by political commissars throughout the Soviet conscript army. Like presidential candidates' opinion polls in the U.S., these are pretty bogus. Like yours, they are believed. Most of my Politburo colleagues regard them as gospel. A scientific sample of soldiers was probed for attitudes when asked to suppose that "the Soviet Union took the initiative to free Saudi Arabians from their feudal rulers, in what could be quite a nasty little desert war."

The responses were enthusiastic and patriotic, and not just by soldiers anticipating opportunities of loot and rapine. There was the same loyal response to other scenarios which postulated "easy liberation" wars in other parts of the world. Say the authors of Lermontov, "The Soviet people would rally to the Soviet government during any small and successful war—with the same enthusiasm as the lower-middle-class Argentines rallied to Galtieri when he retook the Malvinas in 1982, and then as the lower-middle-class British rallied to Thatcher when she retook the same Falklands two months later."

Lermontov then asked for attitudes if the Soviet government deemed it necessary to mount an invasion of socialist neighbors, to put down counter-revolutions there. The response was overwhelmingly negative. The average twenty-year-old Soviet conscript identifies with bodies like Poland's Solidarity, and against the socialist privilegentsia, in these lands. Lermontov has drawn up a scenario that has driven most of the top Soviet privilegentsia neurotic. "Mass desertions . . . many Soviet soldiers helping to overthrow the local socialist regimes instead of supporting them . . . some soldiers shooting their officers and bringing back guns to overthrow their Soviet small-town bosses as so suddenly in 1917 . . ."

4 In consequence, a majority of my colleagues in the Politburo have made a planning decision that "the Soviet Union

should take the initiative in shifting the next areas of conflict far beyond the borders of the Soviet Union before it is too late."

5 This initiative will consist of (a) a counter-coup in China (preparations for which are well-advanced, in alliance with Peking mandarins frightened by the spread of slow—therefore unsuccessful but to them threatening—Western economic liberalization in that country); and (b), after completion of an "aggression pact with China," some deliberate challenge to an unprepared Western world.

6 The "deliberate challenge" could be one, or more probably several (but certainly not all), of the following: (a) the seizure of the Middle East oil jugular by the invasions of Iran, Iraq, Saudi Arabia and the Gulf sheikhdoms, after telling Western payroll politicians to spread the story that there had been local anti-feudal uprisings in the last three, but probably getting an Iranian invitation into the first; (b) a joint invasion with China of India to help Pakistan (or more probably vice versa) or maybe Hong Kong, followed the same dawn by Taiwan (Soviet Navy useful here) or South Korea, accompanied by the offer of a non-aggression pact to the frightened Japanese (possibly baited by "discussion" of yielding back to Japan some of the southern Kurile Islands); (c) a Soviet task force, supported against any intervening navies by Soviet nuclear submarines stationed outside NATO ports, to be landed on neighboring friendly territory to invade South Africa or the "worst" Latin American or South-East Asian "fascist" dictatorship (maybe the Philippines) especially if it was "oppressing" overseas Chinese; (d) most daringly, a similar invasion of somewhere in Western Europe (Iceland?) with threats of nuclear retaliation if the West reacted.

7 The object of any of these moves would not merely be to stir a Falklands or Malvinas populist reaction in Russia. My Politburo colleagues think the West would abjectly surrender before such unexpected threats if there was fear of nuclear war. The potential rebels in the East European socialist countries would then realize the West will always sur-

render allies to their fate, and the Solidarity-type revolts would be less likely to take place.

8 The alliance with China would be especially dangerous because some Chinese think a nuclear war is acceptable. Soviet army commanders able to hide in east Soviet Siberia might feel the same way.

All of this communication so far may sound very glum, and you may think I am in despair. On the contrary, I think we now have the greatest opportunity in history. The best escape route is that the group which shares my views should win power in the Soviet Union by democratic centralist decisions, although not under me. I have none of the talents of political or bureaucratic leadership, which your western democratic politics probably require, and I am acting as the conduit to you from our like-minded group principally because my institute has unrivalled facilities for sending secret messages abroad. We are each day sending secret messages to our Soviet agents in more than 150 governments round the world, including incidentally in your own White House Executive Office Building.

Probably when our group gains the leadership of the Soviet Union we will set up as a figurehead president some Nobel prizewinning semi-dissident novelist or scientist or (best choice?) musician, but our group will have a quite clear policy to implement. We will need your help in the process, and I am revealing the six main priorities to you now, starting with the easiest and least important.

1 It is going to be very easy to make the Russian economy boom. In European Russia we have a highly educated population, but with the lowest productivity (and hence lowest living standards) of any white people on earth. The situation (hopeless overdemand, near-total reliance on black markets) is most analogous to that of West Germany in 1947. West Germany's economic policies then have been much studied here ever since economics became a matter of playing games with computer models. We recognize that when West Ger-

many dashed into freer markets after 1948, it dashed all the way into becoming one of the richest and nicest societies on earth; the Germans under the Bonn government have behaved better than Germans have done for centuries. We in the Soviet Union are more efficiently educated than the Germans were in 1947, have a more advanced scientific base, can emerge through the problems immediately ahead with higher morale than 1947 Germany. Our group is determined to dash for economic freedom as dramatically as Erhard did: no half-measures like the Chinese and Hungarians have tried, which don't work.

There will be difficulties about full freedom of labor movement because Asian Russians, used to lower living standards, would with full economic freedom flock to the factories of European Russia, and the Soviet system has made our Russian European people nastily racist. But we will handle even that better than you have done so badly in Detroit.

We will need sympathetic international economic policies from you in the transition, by which I do not mean aid. The place played by Marshall Aid in the recovery of West Germany was greatly overstated, because it was the do-gooders' best excuse for explaining why brutal free markets worked.

But West Germany and Japan were helped in their astonishing post-1947 recoveries by the fact that both were allowed to keep such a very low exchange rate. It was absurd to pretend that the exchange rate deemed suitable for the Tokyo and Rhineland rubble of 1949 should have been deemed suitable for the great Japanese and West German exporting machines twenty years later. But that is what happened, and that is why they became successful exporting machines, and entered the ranks of civilized peacekeeping folk in consequence. You must allow the same dispensation for my Russia, please, and you will be very inefficient at running the free-market capitalist economy which you espouse if you cannot do even this for us.

2 You will ask next whether my group will move quickly to restore voting democracy in Russia. The answer is, "Of

course not." If we set democratic political parties free to seek votes on the hustings, all those worth their salt would start demanding impeachments for the corruption, robbery and some murders tolerated or committed by everybody who has been in authority during Soviet Communism's seventy inglorious years. I cannot allow that to happen. At each stage of restoring this society to decency, my group will need the co-operation of some part of the pre-existing Russian power structure, especially as it has been leavened with the most able people in the country as well as the sons of the privileged (and these are most often the same thing). I will need your help in this, particularly in what will be the ex-socialist states, such as Poland, Hungary and East Germany.

Solidarity-type governments will be doing their thing there before my group is fully established in the Soviet Union, and the Poles will want to string up and imprison the worst of their communist scoundrels. You in the United States must not allow this to happen. Fortunately, they will heed what you say, because they will wrongly think they need Marshall Aid from you; they are not as sophisticated economically as my group is. It is important that you make a loud noise saying that the transition from communism must be made without any revenge being taken on members of the old regime—a noise loud enough to be heard by my cousins who are the corrupt and frightened privilegentsia of Omsk. This will lose you some votes at home, but you can afford to risk votes for an election now four years away, especially since every member of my group is already risking his life in each hour.

3 My next requirement from you concerns China. There must not be a coup by what I will call the old Bolsheviks there. The preparation of that coup is already well advanced, but fortunately the preparation has been done by the institute under my leadership. I can therefore tell you each nuance to play on, each official to bribe and unbribe.

You should go to China yourself and make instant concessions to the Dengists about wording on Taiwan (they really don't intend to enslave it), about some other matters where you Americans have insulted prickly Chinese pride—remember, you are dealing with a 3,000-year-old bureaucracy that is neurotic. You should also get your corporations for a while to bribe the old Bolsheviks to allow American factories to be put in the inefficient areas they control. At present the Americans are putting plants only in the more efficient places run by the Dengists, and the majority of Chinese provincial governors and army chiefs who are not efficient think this is most unfair. I do wish you would show more Oriental cunning. But you must also, I beg, now show an unwonted degree of Western resolve.

You should, while in Peking, announce a full military alliance with the still Dengist post-Deng government. You should let it be known that you will be obliged to declare war on the Soviet Union if the Soviet Union infringes China's sovereignty either by invasion or by an internal coup manufactured from Moscow. Make nuclear threats as you sign that alliance.

4 We approach in that last sentence to the most difficult part of what history will be requiring of you in these next crucial months. You must make Moscow think that, as new President of the United States, you would resist any Lermontov-type expansion by resorting, if necessary, to nuclear war. You should guarantee with nuclear pledges the frontiers in the Middle East, Indo-Pakistan and all the other areas which I will designate to you. If you do, then the majority middle part of the Politburo will come over to my group's side. Most of the Politburo does not want to risk the start of the sort of nuclear war that would bring rockets homing in to whatever place they would personally be hiding in. They would in such circumstances quickly agree to send all the present hawks off to manage power plants in Outer Mongolia, particularly if they were simultaneously reassured that the counter-revolution which is about to engulf my homeland will not bring revenge by guillotine on them and their families.

5 I can help in making this toughness politically easier for

you. I can deliver to you documents setting out Soviet contingency plans for invasions and coups in all the threatened places. You can publish them in staggering detail—from Xerox copies because our Russian computers are so inefficient that we have not yet advanced to the paperless office. Within your own country, most of those in your peace movement are what Lenin called "useful fools"—sincere students and schoolteachers whose naïveté towards the Soviet Union confirms to me how inefficient your American and West European education systems have been. But, of course, much Soviet money and sexual entrapment have also gone into financing and blackmailing into their present postures some of that peace movement's less bright lights. There has been pandering to paedophiles and every other aberration. I can provide lots of lush headline material for your disgusting right-wing Press.

By good fortune I have been in charge of financing and arranging for these entrapments of disloyal citizens of the United States. I will now get some of my agents in America to defect carrying the appropriate documents. Do not, I urge again, lock up your traitors as this news pours out. Better to get lots of lachrymose confessions on television, declarations of amnesty for those who confess quickly during these days of greatest international crisis. This burst of information, together with your accurate details on the contingency plans for Chinese coups and Indo-Pakistan invasions, will depress those in the Soviet Union who are already suspicious of the hawks' inefficiency in not safeguarding intelligence. It will bring more of the doubters over to my group's side.

When we assume command I will send an official message to you, with drumbeats. "At this crucial hour, as a new government is set up in Moscow, I address you across a chasm that could have led to nuclear annihilation . . . It is clear that some monstrous things have been done both here and in the United States . . . many mistakes on both sides . . . Our policy is absolute on one matter: no revenge for the past, because men have been doing what they deemed mistakenly to be their duty to their countries or their consciences . . ." We can arrange the wording in advance so as to make it politically convenient for both of us.

6 When you and I have won, there will still be problems and some arguments between us. A big problem will be the poor two-thirds of the world, where over 100 unbalanced and quarrelsome dictators may soon have nuclear bombs to throw around. My guess is that Russia and America together will have to revive gunboat diplomacy against them, and we will probably disagree on who are the worst lunatics to leave ruling which banana republics where. In at least five Latin American states I have frankly thought that the unpleasant would-be dictators whom we in the Soviet Union have been financing would be less bad for their unfortunate people than those whom you have been financing; and in a sixth I discovered that you and we were financing the same crook who had in secrecy sworn eternal fealty to each of us against the other—a situation which I found useful, but that fool Chernenko got him bumped off. Still, we can solve these problems at leisure, when and if leisure comes. We face exciting months ahead.

Some cautious people in Washington argued that this letter ended very abruptly; that it contained no timetable for the President; that any collaboration with an alleged secret group within the Kremlin which urged America to make loud nuclear threats could be a rather obvious trap to make a tyro President look a dangerous fool; that any supping with the Borovsky group should be undertaken only with a very long spoon. Luckily, President Hart was the first American president since Kennedy who was not disposed to caution even on his Inauguration Day. By private message and public deed, he indicated across the divide that his administration and the Borovsky group did indeed intend to "run this next lap together." All history has had reason to welcome the results.

As one re-reads the Borovsky Letter for the hundredth time, one is amazed at how closely the things he foretold came to

pass. This has been obscured by some modern historians because of the eventual disappointment about Borovsky himself.
Most of the few Americans who knew of his letter in those
critical early months of 1989 were lost in admiration of him.
They waited for him to appear out of the mists of the glorious
and almost bloodless Russian counter-revolution of 1989–90.
They expected a hero on a white horse.

Instead the Borovsky who eventually appeared was a
taut and nervous alcoholic. He was clearly an embarrassment in the ranks of the impressive new Russian government which signed the U.S.-CPDR Treaty of Friendship in 1991,
and made only one independent initiative thereafter, when
he advocated a closer union of the seventeen successor states
of the old Soviet Union than those states were willing
to accept.

It is not clear what government office Borovsky held by June
1995, when he took off, piloting his own aircraft, after the cel-
ebrations which marked the enrollment of Georgia as the fourth
semi-autonomous member of the new Confederation of People's
Democratic Republics (CPDR). He crashed into a hillock a kil-
ometer from the runway. Nobody knows whether his death was
suicide or murder or accident or alcoholic mischance, but as
a best guess it was some mixture of all four. Those were
the days when the two permitted social drugs (alcohol and
marijuana) were incompatible even with driving a motor
car.

After his death, stories began to appear of the horrors that
Borovsky had committed while a Soviet official. Bestsellers
have been put on the TC system alleging that he was pushed
into writing the 1989 letter by wiser heads, who could black-
mail him (some of his crimes were illegal even under Soviet
law) to stick his neck out first. Their calculation was that they
could then deny all knowledge of what was happening if the
negotiations with the American President either leaked prematurely or broke down.

This book will not demean itself by casting judgment on that.
For the first forty-six years of his life he played the usual role

of a tense but intelligent young member of the old Soviet privilegentsia. During his last seven years he played his part in a
great heroic, and those who today live in freedom and joy have
no right to cast stones at Andrej Borovsky.

He delivered us.

5

1991-2005:
The Gunboat
Years

IN HIS 1989 LETTER Andrej Borovsky had referred to the big problem of "the poor two-thirds of the world, where over 100 unbalanced and quarrelsome dictators may soon have nuclear bombs to throw around." In 1990 more than 3.5 billion of the world's total population of 5 billion lived in countries with a median per capita income of below $750 a year. The United States, West Europe and Japan at this time had median per capita incomes above $15,000 a year. This ratio of 20:1 between the rich and poor was greater than the ratio of income between *aristos* and *sans culottes* in France at the time of the 1789 revolution. The 1990 dividing line between rich and poor also happened to be drawn embarrassingly closely along the line of skin color—an even more emotive grouping than that of social class. This made a world-wide 1789 seem quite likely.

Good-hearted people in the rich West said this should be tackled by their countries' governments giving money to poor countries' governments. As many of those poor countries' governments were precisely the dictators whose internal despotism was bringing most misery to their peoples, and whose over-swelling of local money supply was causing most inflation, this notion of propping up despots by further increasing their local money supply did not seem very liberal or bright.

There was, however, one emerging opportunity. Earnings per head in the Third World countries were low in 1990 partly because so much of their population was too young to earn. There were 2 billion people aged less than nineteen in the Third World in 1989 because of the happy recent fall in infant mortality. The number of children who died before the age of one in south Asia was over 150 per 1,000 in 1950 and below 30 per 1,000 in 1993. The biggest improvement had occurred in the 1970s, so in the 1990s the age bulge in the poor countries was about to move from teenagers to human beings.

Did this mean the poor countries were about to have a glut of parents (and thus still more children) or a bulge of healthy young workers? By 1990 the high sales of subsidized contraceptives made it clear they were not eager to become overburdened parents. Although world population continued to rise for a while as the poor world's people bulge reached peak childbearing age, it became clear that girls who had been in school at first menstruation (as most of this new generation had been) had no intention of bearing the average 2.1 children per female tummy which alone keeps world population constantly rising. Your TCs will tell you that world population peaked at 8,103,169,747 human beings on 5 June 2012, and since then has been moderately declining.

The 1990s were therefore due to be a period when the poor countries would have a peak inflow of young workers at the height of their physical and mental earning power. A great deal depended on whether the most flexible sorts of business organization could be created in these countries to provide jobs for them.

During most of the second half of the twentieth century the prospects for this looked glum. At the end of the 1939–45 war the colonial powers of Europe had still held one-quarter of the world in fee. They spent the next thirty years decently giving it back, but generally to unrespectable people. The foolish and wicked colonial age gave way to the equally foolish and wicked immediate post-colonial age. The biggest imperial power, Britain, said there must be a breathing space in each country while elections to less-than-independent legislative councils were held and while Britain laid the foundations for democracy. The effect of this policy was to pave the way for violent demagogocracy. At a time when the remaining colonial overlords were comprehensively hated, the elections to the legislative councils were won by whichever extremist (say, a Socialist miseducated at the London School of Economics) started the most riots as he demanded independence a week ago last Tuesday. If the riots were bloody enough to earn him a few comfortable weeks in jail, he could expect to be prime minister of his independent state at some age like twenty-eight. He would then replace the British major-general who was running his armed forces by a Sandhurst-trained native officer, who would shortly thereafter overthrow him in a *coup d'état*.

While there had been few rulers less suitable for the first half of the twentieth century than upper-class colonial Englishmen, there were no rulers less suitable for the second half of it than London School of Economics Socialists and Sandhurst generals. These two proceeded to fight civil wars against each other over the parts of the globe previously colored British imperial red.

The French colonial system (broadly, persuade the local élite to enjoy themselves like Frenchmen, and then pay them twice the world price for their peanuts) had slightly less damaging consequences, but it and all other European colonial muddles left behind the two great problems that had also caused Latin America's lost century since Bolivar—namely, underentrepreneurship and overreliance on military and political power. In all former European colonies, except only those East Asian ones that had been occupied by the Japanese without subsequently falling under communist or socialist control, there was no establishment of prosperity because individuals could not generally advance themselves by becoming businessmen but only by becoming politicians. And there was no establishment of security because politicians' private armies were killing each other (and whole tribes of their opponents' supporters) as they struggled for lucrative power in countries where governments frequently spent more than one half of the above-subsistence proportion of GNP.

After the 1991 U.S.-CPDR pact the two united superpowers met the problem of Third World insecurity by wielding the stick of gunboat diplomacy, and they met the problem of Third World poverty and underemployment by the brilliant carrot of the Centrobank scheme.

The gunboat diplomacy of 1993–2005 was widely condemned as a return to neo-colonialism, chiefly because it clearly was. The Russians were less mealy-mouthed in admitting this than the Americans, who were fearful during the gunboat period of being called racist. The government team that emerged from Moscow in 1990 was composed of impressive technocrats who said they believed in a collective leadership, as Russians had also said just after Stalin's time. Borovsky had talked of finding some internationally known musician to be prime minister, but there was then no leader of their band. As had also happened after Stalin's day, a leader soon emerged, and in familiar guise. Anatoly Berisov, who became prime minister of the CPDR in 1993, was an amiable, earthy, extrovert, hugging bear of a man. He believed that all citizens of his confederation should be encouraged to undergo the psychoanalytical process known as PET scanning. He was hugely amused, and nobody else was surprised, when his own PET scan showed that parts of his mind worked much as Nikita Khrushchev's had done.

Because he was more educated and (up to a cut-off point) more libertarian, Berisov's policies were not Khrushchev's. He believed in a dash for free-market economics, though he did

41

not intend to impose this on states in his confederation who did not vote for it. He thought each of the successor states of the old Soviet Union should be allowed to run its own economic and social policies, with only foreign policy and defense policy run from Moscow. Andrej Borovsky believed in a tighter federation, and it may not be wholly coincidence that, after the two men's most open row on this, Borovsky's aircraft crashed.

Berisov sometimes shocked the Americans by his reasons for wanting only a loose confederation. "I am all in favor of the Uzbeks running their own show, because that might make it easier for me to keep those Uzbeks out of Moscow." Berisov was sufficiently populist and brash to be able to say such things without causing enormous offence in his own country. He was also remarkably frank in explaining his defense policy. "We have inherited far too large an officer corps from the old Soviet Union, but I am not going to sack them all or they might mount a coup against me." He was determined that army officers should stay in Moscow, and not become powerful forces in the separate republics: "If they spread out across the CPDR, they really could mount coups against some of the state prime ministers who unfortunately, unlike me, deserve it." He used his internal power mainly to enforce a policy of "no revenge for the past." "I am not going to have inquests on what people did in Chernenko's time," he said at a long, drunken dinner of farewell to Marshal Lermontov, who was retiring to live in Wimbledon, "or else people might start inquiring what both Borovsky and I did in those days."

In international affairs his undiplomatic talk was rather more worrying. In February 1997, shortly after President Kemp won the American presidential election of 1996, Berisov made his most famous after-dinner oration: "Most of the black and brown heads of government in the world came to power through violence, and live in constant fear of being overthrown by violence. As the spread of nuclear power means that these violent men and their violent tribal enemies will some day get nuclear bombs, the CPDR and the U.S. are going to have a duty to see that the most dangerous kooks are disarmed and sometimes deposed."

42

Mr. Berisov made it clear that Russia was even more frightened than America that the "poor south of the world might some day rise in a nuclear version of what they will probably, most muddlingly, call their Great October Revolution against us in the rich north."

The danger of nuclear holocaust was reduced because former U.S. President Reagan's much-maligned anti-missile missile initiative of 1983 bore fruit just when he said it would: at around the turn of the century. In 1983 Mr. Reagan's critics had supposed missiles could be stopped only by zapping them in space-invaders fashion by laser beams. Since this could never be 100 per cent effective, it was called a wildly expensive waste. Critics said any hot war enemy would merely be encouraged to launch hundreds of missiles, in the knowledge that some would get through. Happily, the eventual zapping was done not with laser beams but with telecommuted beams which turned the missiles round.

In 1999 President Kemp and Prime Minister Berisov put on a television show during which the Russians launched some unarmed missiles from Siberia, and computer messages tele-commuted from the U.S. made them crash back either on ex-actly the spot from which they had taken off or on some agreed map co-ordinate some hundreds of miles distant ("Which could be the palace of any president who had launched the missile," pointed out Mr. Berisov). The Russians confirmed that the Americans had given them the technology, "so that we too can and will return any armed missile from space to what I believe you Americans call home base." This telecommuted "reverse course" or RC beam was expected to be about 90 per cent effective, and that was quite enough. Nobody henceforth was likely to launch a nuclear warhead which had a 90 per cent chance of landing back most precisely on his own head.

After this demonstration President Kemp made his famous declaration that "Man's half-century of nuclear nightmare is now over," and devotees of the campaign for nuclear disarm-ament agitated for all nuclear warheads to be destroyed. Prime Minister Berisov flatly refused this, and said that both the United

States and Russia must keep their weapon stocks. Otherwise, said this loquacious Russian, "There is a danger that some savages in the poor South may launch a war against the richer North, maybe a non-nuclear but still nasty one, maybe even nuclear via terrorists carrying bombs into our countries in suitcases. The two superpowers need to maintain a nuclear policeman's role against that threat."

Some subsidiary nuclear powers like Britain and France did destroy their own nuclear warheads, and declared that they were only too happy to accept America and Russia as the policemen. The policemen kept satellite watch over everybody else's troop and weapon movements—and made each movement public.

The Soviet Russians had been skilled and assiduous spies, willing to break every international convention. Mr. Berisov's post-Soviet Russians continued this tradition in a way that U.S. allies sometimes found undiplomatic. Moscow was happy to publish the private pillow talk of Third World leaders, which can only have been picked up by Russian bugs in the bedrooms of their palaces. When, in 2003, Prime Minister Berisov launched the operation in southern Africa that toppled President Mbogo, there occurred the most dramatic incident of those gunboat years. Let us draw from the Biographical Institute of the University of the Caucasus at Borovskygrad the short biography of Mario Mbogo (1961–?).

Mario Mbogo was born in 1961, in what was then a Portuguese colony in southern Africa. While it was still a colony it was growing fast enough to breed a new African middle class who bitterly resented their colonial overlords. One of the resenters was Mario's father, who had been given a mission-school education but was now a devotee of voodoo. In 1962 the twenty-eight-year-old father's religious practices and political passions made it desirable for him to move with one-year-old Mario and a six-year-old brother out of the capital into a new profession in the bush.

The new profession of Mr. Mbogo was as bandit leader. His

gang got their food, women and fun by regularly raiding the poorest villages. They got most of their money by operating a protection racket against Portuguese-owned estates. The band would send an ultimatum, demanding some sum like $10,000. If none of this was paid, the Mbogo gang tried to murder somebody in the estate-owning family. If part of it was paid, the Mbogo gang would merely kill some in the families of poorer estate workers who were less carefully guarded.

When the revolution against the Portuguese succeeded, the Mbogo gang was saluted as heroic former guerrilla fighters. Mr. Mbogo became a government minister. He strengthened his position when he supported the faction of the cabinet which welcomed the Cuban occupation troops who entered the country in 1975.

Mario's elder brother disliked leaving the excitements of life and murder in the bush, so he started a gang which committed voodoo murder against poorer people in the towns and demanded protection money from white businesses and individuals there. The brother brought Mario into some of these escapades, but the East German, Russian and Cuban advisers objected because some of the harassment was being committed against them. Minister Mbogo, who was anyway by now starting a new family with a younger and prettier wife, therefore executed his elder son, and punished Mario by sending him to study at South Liverpool Polytechnic in England.

Mario Mbogo had none of the educational qualifications nominally required for study at a British polytechnic, but the British Ministry of Overseas Development gave him a scholarship at British taxpayers' expense. The British Foreign Office's file said Mario Mbogo was the favorite son of a very important political family in his homeland, and that it was diplomatically important that he should learn to love England by going to study at the horrible South Liverpool Polytechnic.

On Merseyside Mario learned to hate England almost as viciously as he now hated his father, but he had two self-satisfying moments there. One was when a well-briefed communist cell in Britain contacted him, and said that the Soviet Union had appointed a Cuban undercover agent called Captain Ramon Leonardo as his guardian angel; Leonardo would help Mario to murder his father when he got back to his homeland. Mario's other good moment in Britain was in the Liverpool race riots in 1981 when he emerged as a natural leader of one group of both white and black teenage hoodlums who threw petrol bombs at the police, killing one of them.

The British authorities arranged to return this unpromising taxpayer-supported scholar to his homeland. Mbogo's communist cell contacted him with the warning: "Your father intends to kill you as soon as you reach home, so Captain Leonardo will meet you in the transit lounge at the aircraft's first stop." What happened in the transit lounge is not clear, but the bewildered West African drunk who arrived at the aircraft's final destination clearly was not Mario Mbogo. Minister Mbogo executed him just the same. Mario himself appeared in the bush a few months later, in his father's old trade as brigand leader, but this time against his father's government.

The Russian and Cuban advisers, who were displeased that the father's government was not sufficiently welcoming to the Lermontov plan to use the country as a base for a liberation war against white-ruled South Africa, refused to allow military operations against Mario's gang. In 1987 they turned to actively supporting it. The country's existing cabinet ministers, including Mario's father and common-law stepmother, were murdered in a *coup d'état*, and the new president of the country became the twenty-six-year-old Dr. Mario Mbogo (he called himself doctor, although he had not passed even his first year's exam at the poly).

In 1987–8 the new Mbogo government imported an enormous quantity of sophisticated weapons. The intention was that they should be used by the Russian expeditionary force which Colonel-General Lermontov planned to send to start invading white South Africa in 1989 or 1990. The Russian expeditionary force never arrived because Borovsky defeated Lermontov in Moscow in the meantime. The existing Cuban troops were withdrawn. Captain Leonardo, saying he had deserted counter-revolutionary (and pro-Berisov) Cuba, stayed on, and Mbogo promoted him to be Marshal Leonardo.

For the next fourteen years President Mbogo exercised a maniac's tyrannical misrule. He appropriated a huge proportion of the country's foreign exchange for himself. This foreign exchange continued to flow in because the country could sell a lot of uranium now that nuclear power was back in fashion in the west, after the late 1980s' reduction in both American interest rates and American econuttery. Also foreign aid was being sent south by some entirely decent Scandinavian countries which regarded President Mbogo as a brave resister to the new Russo-American neo-colonialism. These subventions seem extraordinary to us today when anybody can call up on his TC Mbogo's "pillow talk," the bugged tapes showing how he nightly poured out to successive mistresses his dreams and fetishes and plans.

In internal policy within his country President Mbogo's main interest was in devising crueller forms of execution for anybody, or any whole tribes, who in any way opposed him. He by now associated macabre tortures with the dictates of his voodoo religion. In foreign policy Mbogo was at first obsessed with carrying forward the liberation of white South Africa which Lermontov had once planned. During the 1990s the old Union of South Africa broke up, first into the Confederation of South Africa (with separate black-ruled and white-ruled cantons), then into what were really a dozen separate black-ruled and two separate white-ruled states. Among the latter, the Cape of Good Hope, which was becoming a popular spot for telecommuters, prospered more than Transvaal, but all of the fourteen successor states of South Africa did quite well so long as they obeyed the confederation's rule that governments should never spend more than 10 per cent of gnp—and thus should not be capable of threatening anybody.

Still, people in the white areas were richer than in the black areas, and many of the whites were intolerably arrogant. There were black guerrilla bands ready to invade white South Africa, both for purposes of brigandage and on grounds of principle.

President Mbogo's dreams went further than both. In private, and in his pillow talk, he began to call himself the future Lord of the Nuclear Holocaust.

He believed, and with justification, that his country could get hold of a nuclear bomb. It was a producer of uranium. It had inherited knowhow with the build-up of sophisticated Russian weapons for the intended Lermontov expeditionary force of 1989. First-year physics postgraduates could now calculate how to make nuclear weapons, and Mbogo had enough money to hire some criminally insane ones.

His aim as future Lord of the Nuclear Holocaust was to smuggle parts of nuclear devices into white-ruled cities round the world. The first ones were to be planted in the hated white city of Cape Town and along the Johannesburg-Pretoria road. Later nuclear weapons were to be smuggled to Washington, D.C., New York, London, Paris, Bonn, Rome, Vienna, Athens, Moscow, Kiev, Sydney, San Francisco, Toronto. Mbogo also said in his pillow talk—and this certainly proved true—that he had placed a triggerable nuclear device in his own capital. The original plan was to threaten to trigger the devices he said he had placed in foreign cities unless all the world accepted his stated demands, which were to include a Mbogo takeover of white South Africa. But the second plan was far more horrific.

Mbogo told his mistress in his bugged pillow talk that he believed Russia, with American support, was going to mount a gunboat operation against him. In this belief he was right. When the assault was imminent, he intended to go down a nuclear-proof shelter which had radio broadcast facilities. He was going to announce on the radio that the invading Russians and Americans were launching nuclear weapons against his African state. Then he was himself going to trigger the nuclear device in his own capital. Decent anti-neo-colonialist liberals round the world could soon check that his capital was indeed being shockingly nuclearized, and Mbogo trusted that the horror of this would persuade at least two or three of his planters of bombs in places like Moscow and Washington, D.C. to trigger their bombs and do their duty. He would then emerge from his shelter unharmed, and announce that he had been saved by voodoo magic. He expected to be declared Lord of the World, especially as he would be threatening to trigger the rest of the bombs in white cities that had not yet gone off.

The Americans were horrified, but the Russians were relieved, when Mbogo said in this bugged pillow talk that Marshal Leonardo had agreed to help him in his plan. When Russian troop-carrying aircraft started landing in his country, they met no resistance because Mbogo's troops had been moved to his borders, far out of his capital. Mbogo did indeed repair, together with Marshal Leonardo and his cabinet, to a nuclear shelter (later proved to be ridiculously inadequate), and he started broadcasting from there. The broadcast quickly fell silent. When the Russians arrived, Marshal Leonardo was holding Mbogo and the other cabinet ministers at pistol point. Leonardo had been one of the late Andrej Borovsky's agents from the earliest days, and had stayed on in the country to police Mbogo and to place the bugs that captured his pillow talk.

After the overthrow of Mbogo, the two superpowers nevertheless had to engage in assiduous propaganda, so as to convince kindly people in other countries that they were not "gunboat-happy." The two superpowers had a mild disagreement about this. The Russians quickly published the lurid tapes of Mbogo's pillow talk. The Americans felt that his and his mistresses' expletives had not been sufficiently decently deleted, but—as the deposed Mbogo was now in an American mental hospital—they did reveal the patterns shown in his brain under PET scanning, thus publishing to the world what a homicidal maniac the man was. The Russians thereafter wanted open publication of PET scans of the brain patterns of all world leaders, but some heads of government even outside the Third World were not keen on that.

The Russians also now pressed the argument that it is "quite unsafe to allow individual kooks with brain patterns showing them to be capable of violence the freedom to wander around without any computer knowing where they are or checking what they are up to." Even before most countries adopted for internal use the system of requiring both guns and convicted criminals to be bugged so that their movements could be tracked, Russia was trying to enforce this suddenly cheap sort of surveillance on an international scale. Russia worried about several communes of militant anarchists who had settled in parts of the Caribbean and Africa. It demanded close electronic surveillance of what was going on in these places, and threatened gunboat action when its bugging devices there were discovered and ripped out.

This was high-handed colonialist behavior by America's ally, and the woman who in 2004 became U.S. President, Roberta Kennedy, expressed her concern about it in her campaign speeches on the TC. She claimed, "This sort of neo-colonialism must make a revolt of the poor South against the rich North more likely, instead of quenching fires." She pleaded for "a new pattern of incentives to help the poorest countries in the world to get richer at the fastest possible pace."

During the first term of her presidency President Kennedy therefore joined Prime Minister Berisov's milder successor, Ivan Kandinsky, in establishing the Centrobank scheme.

6

2005-8:
The Introduction of
Centrobank

THE INTRODUCTION of the international Centrobank was the last great act of government before governments grew much less important. It was not a conception of policy-making governments at all, but emerged from the first computerized town meeting of the world.

By 2005 the gap in income and expectations between the rich and poor nations was recognized to be man's most dangerous problem. The satellite TC system and two-way cable television channels in sixty-eight countries invited their viewers to participate in a computer conference about it, in the form of a series of weekly TC programs. Recommendations tapped in by viewers were to be tried out on a computer model of the world economy. If recommendations were shown by the model to be likely to make the world economic situation worse, they were to be discarded. If recommendations were reported by the model to make the economic situation in poor countries better, they were to be retained for "ongoing computer analysis" in the next program.

In 2025 it is easy to see this as a forerunner of the TC conferences which play so large a part in our lives today, both as pastime and as the principal innovative device in business. But the truth about this 2005 breakthrough tends to irk the highbrows. It succeeded because it was initially a rather downmarket network television program. This is illustrated by the fact that the two gold-medal-winning telecommuters who were eventually acclaimed for contributing most to Centrobank's birth were Mr. S. C. Hu, the thoughtful and rich retired merchant of Taipeh in Taiwan, and Mr. Bjorn Heglund, the earnest young subpostmaster from the Kiruna district of north Sweden. Neither would conceivably have been consulted if a conference on the subject had been called mainly among the best-educated economists of 2005.

About 400 million people watched the first program, and 3 million individuals or groups tapped in suggestions. Around 99 per cent of these were rejected by the computer as being likely to increase the unhappiness of mankind. It became known that these rejects included suggestions submitted by the World Council of Churches (whose "Charter 2006" was reported by the computer to be likely to increase unhappiness among 87 per cent of the population of the world) and by many other pressure groups. This still left 31,000 suggestions that were accepted by the computer model as worthy of ongoing analysis. As these were honed, and details were added to the most interesting, an exciting consensus began to emerge. Later programs were watched by nearly a billion people as it became recognized that something important was being born.

These audiences were swollen by successful telegimmicks. The presenter of the opening part of the first program was a roly-poly professor who was that year's Nobel laureate in economics, and who proved a natural television personality. He explained that economists now agreed that aid programs could sometimes help poor countries, but sometimes most definitely made their circumstances worse. When Mexico was inflating at over 80 per cent a year in the early 1980s, the inflow to it of huge loanable funds made its inflation even faster and its crash more certain. The professor set Mexico's 1979–81 economy on the model, pumped in the loaned funds and showed how all the indicators (higher inflation, lower real gross domestic product, and so on) then flashed red, signalling an economy getting worse, rather than green, signalling an economy getting better. He followed this with similar examples from several other poor countries in Latin America and Africa during 1950–85. The professor then put the model back to mirror the contemporary world economy of 2005, and played into it various nostrums that had been recommended by politicians of left, right and center, but mostly left. The dials generally flashed red. Then the professor provided another set of recommendations, and asked any viewers who wished to play to tap in their own guesses for the consequent movements in twenty economic variables in the model. Those who got their guesses right to within a set error were told they had qualified for the second round of a knock-out economic guesstimators' world championship. Knock-out competitions of this sort continued for ordinary users of two-way TCs throughout the series of programs.

In the second part of that first program the presenters dared to introduce two political problems into the game. They said that government-to-government aid programs had been particularly popular among politicians during the age of over-government, but there was growing agreement that government-to-government aid was the worst method of hand-out. The excessive role played by governments in many poor countries was one of the barriers to their economic advance, and a main destroyer of their people's freedom. Could anybody think it would have been wise to give aid to President Mbogo?

In consequence, the most successful economic aid programs had been those operated through the International Monetary Fund, which imposed conditions on how borrowing governments should operate. The professor showed that IMF-monitored operations in most years had brought more green flashes from the model than red, which few other sorts of schemes had done. But this involved IMF officials—often from the rich countries—in telling governments of poor countries what to do; and one of the objectives of the initiative called for by President Kennedy was precisely to diminish such embarrassments.

The first questions to be asked in the next few programs, said the compilers, were (1) which countries should qualify for aid?; and, having decided that, (2) up to what limits and conditions?; and (3) through what mechanisms? They promised that later programs after the first half-dozen would examine how any scheme could be used to diminish the power of governments and increase the power of free markets and free people.

The first stage of this computerized town meeting of the world went remarkably well. A consensus quickly emerged that poor countries which agreed to join a club with certain libertarian rules (the principal ones were that markets instead of politicians should set prices; there should be fairly free trade, and fairly free immigration of people and businesses from countries richer than themselves; human rights cases should be referred to an international supreme court) could also have access to the benefits of a new international central bank called the "Centrobank."

The Centrobank should be a body which relied very little on the discretion of its governor, but much more on a computer program. This program should authorize the Centrobank to print enough new foreign exchange called bancor for any applicant country below a certain income per head to allow its internal economic growth to proceed at the fastest possible non-inflationary pace but not by one penny faster. The Centrobank's computer would monitor each recipient country's economy to see if inflationary or other strains were appearing, and would signal that Centrobank must cut off new supplies of artificially created foreign exchange if they did.

Contemporary critics said in triple self-contradiction that (a) this scheme was so insulting to poor countries' governments that few would agree to join it; (b) all poor countries would flock to eat at this trough and there would be an impossibly inflationary expansion of world money supply; and that (c) the anti-inflationary terms proffered from the international central bank were so tough that this would still allow only painfully slow economic depauperization.

Now that the Centrobank has been in operation for nearly twenty years we know that the answer to (a) is that the government of any poor country that does not join Centrobank is likely to be booted out by its people; that the answer to (b) is that, despite this flood of countries into the scheme, newly created foreign exchange for poor countries has in only one year, 2013, exceeded 0.2 per cent of world-wide money supply (WM3); and that the answer to (c) is that progress proved remarkably fast, although that was partly because of the answers that emerged to the second set of questions posed in the next few programs.

The second set of questions which arose after about the eighth program rested on what sorts of purchases should qualify for Centrobank payments. Originally the notion had been that the international Centrobank should open foreign exchange clearing accounts to finance non-inflationary purchases by any persons or any groups in qualifying poor countries. The stated aim was that a poor country should not be prevented merely by shortage of foreign exchange from pursuing the fastest possible rate of non-inflationary economic growth. But under the remorseless logic of the computer a bias was soon introduced in favor of financing purchases by citizens in poor countries rather than purchases by their governments. It became clear that projects by cost-disregarding governments in poor countries led more quickly to inflation than projects undertaken either (a) by penny-pinching native entrepreneurs (who began to appear out of the woodwork in some profusion and in extraordinary places); or (b) by competing multinational corporations on new sorts of performance contracts.

If you ask your TCs today, "What were the main evil consequences of the colonial and immediate post-colonial periods in the poor two-thirds of the world?" two of the top answers will be: "The fact that an entrepreneurial class could not emerge as an important political constituency until the introduction of Centrobank after 2005," and "The fact that until Centrobank no mechanism except uncompetitive government was put in place to meet many of the most urgent demands of the poorest three-quarters of the people." Centrobank's solution to the first of these problems owed much to the proposals from Mr. Hu; its solution to the second problem owed much to the proposals from Mr. Heglund.

Start with why Mr. Hu's proposals for encouraging entrepreneurs were so important. Growth had taken place in Europe and Japan and North America after 1850 because an entrepreneurial commercial class had become a dominant political influence, replacing the aristocracies in Europe and Japan and the *mélange* misdescribed by de Tocqueville in North America. In the immediate post-colonial period in the poor countries circa 1960–2005 power fell instead into the hands of a new class of professional politicians, at a time when they could temporarily do damaging things inconceivable for professional politicians before or (thank God) since.

Their most damaging act was to set "political" instead of market prices. By statutory decree in many poor countries exchange rates and urban wages had been kept too high, food prices to farmers and prices for public utilities kept too low, credit had been allocated by rationing at negative real interest rates, and imports had been rationed by licences that were immensely profitable to the politicians' brothers-in-law who were corruptly granted them. Even in 2005 every single computer program showed that living standards were increased, inflation brought down, and happiness and efficiency advanced, when these policies were abandoned. So did every practical example.

Call up on your TCs the practical example of Taiwan in the second half of the twentieth century; analysis of its success was the basis for Mr. Hu's proposals for Centrobank. Taiwan in

1950–2000 had multiplied its real income twentyfold and its dollar exports four-hundredfold because in the 1950s an invading warlord and his soldiers had been impelled by odd circumstances into *laissez-faire* economic policies against their will; and because Taiwan had thereafter been kept dynamically entrepreneurial largely because of nasty protectionism by rich countries against its exports.

When in 1948 the armies of General Chiang Kai-shek fled from the Chinese mainland to Taiwan, swelling its population overnight, they found an island which relied for over 90 per cent of its exports on rice and sugar. These were two commodities whose sales could not be greatly increased on world markets by dropping their international price. It therefore seemed natural to the incoming soldiers to follow the mistaken policies adopted by so many other authoritarian governments in poor countries all through 1950–2005. For a while they exploited the farmers by keeping internal farm prices too low and Taiwan's international exchange rate artificially high. The soldiers also granted cheap credits to themselves to set up manufacturing businesses.

The results of such folly were the usual ones: food production and exports fell; inflation soared to three-digit figures; and foreign exchange holdings collapsed despite huge American aid. The soldiers met this by restricting imports further to protect their infant industries and their disappearing exchange reserves; this sent inflation even higher. As sugar and rice production used up much land in the overcrowded island, real estate prices in particular went through the roof.

This economic mess was sadly typical of many newly independent countries at the time, but Taiwan was lucky in being newly dependent instead. General Chiang Kai-shek was at this time entirely dependent politically on the Americans, and he unwillingly agreed to propitiate them by accepting their good advice. He moved in the late 1950s pretty abruptly from the then usual developing-country wrong policies (low prices to farmers; protected home market for manufactures but overvalued exchange rate; subsidized interest rates) to the unfashionable and precisely opposite right policies (market prices for farmers and market-determined exchange rates and interest rates; trade liberalization).

The results exceeded all expectations. With its market-determined exchange rate, Taiwan found that its cheap-labor exports of umbrellas et cetera expanded smoothly—until foreign umbrella-makers objected to Taiwan's penetration of their domestic markets; then Taiwan's expansion in that particular product would abruptly stop. So Taiwan grew through its industrial miracle of 1955–2005 knowing that its businesses must find new products for new markets all the time, and that last year's successful firm would often have to close down this year. In consequence of its recognition that bureaucrats cannot know what will be profitable next minute, Taiwan subsidized only one thing apart from its over-large army: its tax and social non-welfare policies were directed to raising savings from 5 per cent of national income in the 1950s to a Japan-beating 25 per cent in the 1980s.

Mr. Hu recommended that the policies furthered by Centrobank in poor countries should be those that had "been furthered by accident in my country, Taiwan," and he suggested some of the relevant software by which the Centrobank's computer model could put these incentives into effect. He was rather too inclined to argue that "anybody who does not follow these policies should not get Centrobank aid," but the process of ongoing computer analysis synthesized most of this into the message, "If you are following Taiwan-type policies, then the computer will allow a much higher level of internal expansion before it flashes the signal that inflation is being fostered so that further Centrobank creation for you must stop." As the co-ordinating Nobel laureate said when presenting Mr. Hu with one of the two gold medals:

His software provided one of the two quantum leaps that turned Centrobank into a success. Although the 1955–2005 Taiwan-type policies hugely expanded national income, the pressure groups in favor of them are entrepreneurs who do not come into being until the policies have already been introduced. In most poor countries that have been following the old and opposite policies of import substitution and price-rigging, the political constituencies in favor of the old policies are by definition more powerful. This is a main reason why these old-fashioned countries remain poor. In some Latin American countries right-wing generals have periodically seized power, and put into effect policies that are supposed to be *laissez-faire*. But these generals generally have to rely for their political mandate on the few old families who already own big businesses in these countries. Even with the best will in the world (which these right-wing generals rarely have) they tend therefore to support and protect yesterday's big capitalists, rather than the grubby entrepreneurs in back rooms on whom growth most depends. Mr. Hu's proposals managed to make Centrobank's computer programs mirror the dependence on entrepreneurs created by historical accident in the 1950–2005 success stories of Japan (which ploughed through yesterday's powerful families in 1945 and had to rely on entrepreneurs thereafter), Singapore (which benefited from not having any farmers or rural classes to exploit), Hong Kong (which did not have any political constituencies, only entrepreneurs) and Taiwan.

Although Mr. Hu was rightly decorated for "enabling Centrobank policies to speak with a Taiwanese accent," the later stages of the first computerized town meeting of the world were carried on more like one of today's many million computer conferences than like the original television network program in which Mr. Hu joined. People after about program fourteen did not put in their views instantly, but after some days' consideration and after checking with the database which showed what was the presumed best form for Centrobank at the moment. The computer still rejected the 99 per cent of proposals made to it that were nonsense; it still incorporated for ongoing analysis the less than 1 per cent of suggestions that seemed sensible and relevant; but it also now introduced a new category. It picked up those contrary views that seemed plausibly sensible, but not suitable for the emerging form of Centrobank's consensus, and put proposers of such ideas in touch with people holding similar views around the world.

From the views of this constructive opposition to "Hu plus 33,179 people's telecommunicated and accepted improvements," one new consensus objection began to emerge. "Under the Taiwanese system," wrote one objector, "the main incentive to entrepreneurs in poor countries is to produce for fairly rich consumers, abroad or at home. If most of the seventy to eighty countries in the Centrobank scheme started exporting cheap-labor umbrellas as Taiwan did in the 1950s, a glut of umbrellas would rather soon appear. It would be better if new entrepreneurs could be encouraged to provide more of the things desperately needed by the poorest three-quarters of the people in these poor lands."

How to do this? It was no good saying that poor countries should follow more egalitarian tax policies so as to direct more of their internal demand to things needed by their own poorest people. In the United States in the second half of the twentieth century, marginal tax rates generally took around one half of earned incomes above about six times gross national product per head. Even this only managed to reduce Gini coefficients, the best measure of wealth inequality, from something like 0.39 to something like 0.34. In Africa in 2000 GNP per head was around $500 a year. Any egalitarian tax policy which promised to halve all incomes above $3,000 a year would have (a) killed all initiative; (b) stirred politicians' brothers-in-law, civil servants and—most important—army officers (who got over $3,000 a year) into instant *coups d'état*. Moreover, no mechanisms existed in these countries to provide cheaply the complicated services the very poor needed most urgently.

This was the problem that benefited from the proposals of Bjorn Heglund, who had long urged that the public services needed in his native North Sweden should be provided competitively by private entrepreneurs on performance contracts, along the lines of experiments which had been tried in the 1990s by various worthy Swedish international aid organizations which "adopted" certain Third World villages. As was said at the presentation of Heglund's gold medal:

> We at Centrobank began to realize that poor countries could best grow richer by selling simple cheap-labor goods to the rich world—a process that did not involve them in using our proffered foreign exchange at all, although it had become possible only after they responded to Centrobank's initial incentives *à la* "Hu plus 33,179." The right way to use their new foreign exchange was often to provide mechanisms *à la* Heglund whereby Western firms are encouraged to make money by providing the services that the poorest three-quarters in the poor world most need.

The time was ripe for this experiment, especially in such fields as medicine. The trend even in the West at this time was to new sorts of Health Maintenance Organizations (HMOs), through which people paid performance fees to physicians and their assistants if they kept them and their families healthy. It was early decided to put the competitive services provided by multinational HMOs into the pool which would qualify for Centrobank payments.

Sophisticated computer measurements of people's health were coming into fashion, and three young doctors just out of medical school at the University of Minneapolis drew the largest single Centrobank payment in 2009 when their HMO, resting heavily on telecommunicated X-rays and long-range computer analyses, plus quickly trained local paramedics and some helicopter-carried Western doctors on call, plus recommended dietary changes and some environmental changes which new staffs personally put into effect (cleaning wells, etc.), brought an extraordinary improvement in the health indices of people over a wide stretch of Africa's desperately poor Sahel. Since the Centrobank scheme rightly meant that you could now get as much money for increasing the health and lifespan of a Sahel camel-driver (which was quite easy) as for increasing that of a Texan billionaire (which was rather hard), these three young

61

doctors became very rich men—and other sorts of performance contracts quickly came in vogue.

This revolution in attitudes and services for the poor of the world meant that commercialism was dashing in where only saints had previously trod. Many of the saints learned from and contributed to the experiment. Consider, from the University of Borovskygrad's database of biographies, the life of Margaret Vogel (1966–2023).

Margaret Vogel was born Margaret Mason in Coventry, England, in 1966. Her parents, who were both doctors, divorced when she was three years old and she was brought up by her mother. She saw very little of her father even before his suicide in 1974. She studied science subjects at school, with the initial intention of following in her mother's footsteps, but failed to win a university place in medicine. She took a year off before re-applying to university, and spent that year in East Africa working for Oxfam, a famine relief organization. There was an unusually severe drought in the area which was in its third and most punishing year while she was there. She watched hundreds of children die of malnutrition and disease because the food she was helping to dole out was too badly organized to cope with demand.

When she returned to England she abandoned her ambition to study medicine and went instead to an agricultural college in Kent, intending to return to Africa once she was trained. She was awarded a B.Sc. in 1988 and went on to do postgraduate research, attached for academic purposes to Kent-cum-Surrey University but based for her fieldwork in Khartoum. In 1990 she met and married Horst Vogel, a forty-year-old West German who had been a Green Movement member of parliament at the beginning of the 1980s, but who was now employed by the Dusseldorf Foundation. He described this as "a body of rich German businessmen who are interested in business-like pursuit of our Green ideals" and summarized in a letter to Margaret before they were married the advantages and disadvantages of business involvement: "The Dusseldorf Foundation puts money into each project according to whether it is satisfied the project is getting results in doing good. It has been generous to my project, and there are gains in having business accounting of what we are doing because we both know that many charities have very fluffy results. But the Foundation is too toady about not annoying the local governments, and both German businessmen and the local governments positively love to order my poor tribesmen about."

Horst's project was to organize supplies of food and other practical aid to drought-stricken populations in the Sudan and Chad. Both countries were in the throes of civil wars that had dragged on for more than a decade, and had settled into a situation of virtually permanent strife. Horst Vogel was arrested in 1991 and 1993 for supplying food to alleged insurgents, but was released on each occasion after a few weeks' imprisonment. Margaret was never imprisoned, though she was removed on several occasions from areas where her team was attempting to operate.

Although she never submitted a doctoral thesis, Margaret told her university that she had completed her postgraduate studies in 1993, and she went to work on an agricultural project sponsored by the Dusseldorf Foundation: an attempt to stop the southward spread of the Sahara by sowing genetically engineered plants that would bind the soil and impede its erosion. The task relied on the active co-operation of tens of thousands of villagers, but it was extremely difficult to convince so many people of such long-term benefits, and they frequently had to be coerced as well as bribed into sowing the unfamiliar plants and then protecting them from grazing by goats. Once the soil in a particular region was stabilized it was necessary to reintroduce useful crops of various kinds: forests for timber, fruits and vegetables for food. In order to make the most economical use of the land, this required considerable central control of ecological management, but this led to wrangles with local populations whose horizons were much narrower than the scope of the plans.

Horst and Margaret each spent the bulk of their time travelling back and forth across huge tracts of territory pursuing their independent missions. They saw each other rarely—usually for no more than two or three days a month, sometimes not for months on end. That was to be the pattern of their lives, but their marriage nevertheless provided an important anchorage for both.

In 1997 Margaret was cut about the left arm and shoulder while trying to defend a stand of saplings against goatherds armed with machetes. She was taken to Khartoum for treatment, but by the time she arrived there the wounds were infected. The arm was saved, but it was badly scarred and remained stiff for the rest of her life. The incident was pounced on by the Press, and the Sudanese government rallied to the support of this local heroine, and in a way she did not relish.

It announced that a number of conscripts who had completed their time in the fight against insurgents would not be demobbed, but instead would be drafted into a different kind of war—the war against the desert. The soldiers were promised that wherever their efforts could redeem land from the desert, they would be paid with parcels of that land. At first, such promises were widely considered to be empty ones, but Margaret Vogel and her team worked tirelessly to convince the soldiers that the reclamation of desert land was indeed possible, and that their best hope for the future lay not in returning to the towns and villages they had left, but in creating land for new towns and villages. She had no particular skill in oratory or in education, but the fierceness of her determination proved infectious.

In 2004 she was seized one night and raped by three dissatisfied draftees. Within a week all three men were found dead, the victims of illicit executions. By this time, Margaret Vogel was a legend in her adopted country and had acquired a certain charismatic authority. She no longer had to fight to obtain cooperation from local people, or to defend the plants that she sowed against the depredations of their livestock.

The rape—and still more the executions—had nevertheless been a horror to her. The Dusseldorf Foundation suggested that she leave the field for a time, in order to join the world-wide computer conference of 2005—the conference which gave birth to Centrobank. Margaret Vogel proved one of the most intelligent critics of the final draft for Centrobank, and found to her surprise that she enjoyed the argument. She feared that many of the multinationals coming into the Third World to "do good out of greed" would try to boss the local people in ways that would cause ructions. But she was interested in those who replied to her, "You think the point of fighting the Sahara is to grow food there, but there will be a glut of food. In Arizona land reclaimed from the desert in the 1970s has a high value as real estate. In 2010, in your Sahara, the demand will be for telecommuters' homes and leisure hotels, as people enjoy the all-the-year-round sun beside the swimming pools in your oases."

Margaret Vogel's company, put together by the Dusseldorf Foundation, won the Centrobank contract for fighting against the spread of her part of the Sahara. But other companies won the contracts for bringing fuller employment and new incentive schemes to the people there. As she and they both proved successful, she was forced to admit that Centrobank worked.

By 2010 people were beginning to migrate into the borderlands of the desert. Vogel Inc. had demonstrated that the land could be rescued from dereliction and made whole again. The local tribesmen now realized that there was a point to such labor, that there were rewards to be reaped. The news that landless men might make their own land spread rapidly throughout the Sudan. The people who already had land or livestock, or some other means of getting enough to eat, would not migrate, but there was no shortage of men who had nothing. Some of the migrants proved very lucky indeed, and were able to sell their hard-won land to developers who wanted to build luxury telecommuter hotels, with that "all-the-year-round sun beside the swimming pools."

A huge advantage of Centrobank was that the Sudanese government had to withdraw from control over the project. Vogel Inc. got money only if it saved land from the Sahara, not by pleasing politicians. The land saved came to be owned by the people themselves. In 2018 Margaret Vogel announced that Vogel Inc. would be dissolved and replaced by a co-operative. The work could now better be done entrepreneurially by the local people in response to market forces. However, while the other white people who had been working with her went on to other projects in various far-flung parts of the world, Margaret stayed in the Sudan. Her emotional involvement with the scheme was too deep to permit her to leave the area, and she considered herself neither young enough to begin again elsewhere nor old enough to retire (she was now fifty-two).

Horst had a less successful time with Centrobank. He did not win the performance contract for the rather ill-defined work he had been doing. The parts of it which were valuable were taken over by competing firms with a commercial incentive instead of Horst's over-politicized passion. Horst came back to live permanently with Margaret in 2006, but he died in 2008 of cancer of the throat. Margaret mourned him, but she had always been wedded more firmly to her work than to him, and she did not feel herself to be alone in the world. Even after she wound up her company, she travelled to other troublespots in the Sudan, helping to solve problems of irrigation, pest control, land management and morale.

Although her intelligence was not exceptional, Margaret's lifetime of experience and her determination that no failure was to be tolerated carried her through all the challenges which arose before her. Though her fame never extended beyond the Sudan, in the area where she worked she was known to everyone and respected as a bringer of good fortune and wise advice. The local people acted on her suggestions and deferred to her judgment, even when they suspected that she might be wrong. She accepted the awesome responsibility this put upon her not because she felt herself uniquely qualified to drive back the desert but because she realized that a chain of circumstances had placed her in the best position to help.

Margaret Vogel died in 2023 of an internal hemorrhage caused by a gut parasite. Twelve thousand people attended her funeral. She was buried in the ground of the house that she had built in 2019 but which she rarely used. It stood, of course, on land reclaimed from the Sahara.

The territory she helped to win back was slightly smaller in area than the land which the expanding desert gobbled up further to the west. She won no particular distinction as a scientist and in terms of the whole ecosphere she accomplished very little; but she helped to relieve the suffering of tens of thousands of people, giving them new lives. Her project demonstrated that in the fullness of time the earth may yet be remade, so that in the parched inferno of the most desolate wasteland there will be one day a fertile paradise, if only we have enough incentives and enough Margaret Vogels to build it.

This story from the Sahel shows how widely the concept of performance contracts was to spread and how dynamically it was to develop. Another ambitious and early field was the granting of performance contracts for creating E. F. Schumacher's 2 million villages. The author of *Small Is Beautiful*, published back in 1973, had preached that the best way to bring help to the 2 billion poorest people in the world was to create 2 million villages (population up to 1,000 each), functioning smoothly with appropriate, hardy, labor-intensive technology. Performance contracts were now put out whereby Japanese and other firms drew money from Centrobank if they transformed life in particular villages in Bangladesh by introducing fuller employment with appropriate, labor-intensive technology.

Other multinationals and hordes of local entrepreneurs drew sub-contractors' fees from these firms if they put labor-intensive export industries into these villages. The trend since 2015 has been for local businessmen to underbid some even of the most famous multinationals. This is true even of the health maintenance organizations. Doctors graduating from Indian medical schools now find it much more profitable to earn Centrobank money competing for health maintenance contracts in backward areas of their own country than by flocking to medical practices in the West.

67

In 2013 the three Minnesota doctors who had become so rich and acclaimed with their success in the Sahel in 2009 lost that contract to two doctors from Arab Palestine who showed they could provide more health cheaper. The Minnesotans objected that they had a lot of capital invested in their helicopters, local clinics, et cetera. This problem was met when Centrobank introduced the rule that the successful new bidder had to pay the old contractor a rent for it, under the "Tibor Liska" system which had first been introduced in a very limited way in communist Hungary back in 1980 when that country tried to reprivatize some grossly inefficient state industries. There was the embarrassment that the new contractor often paid lower wages than the old. This seemed tough, but the only way to get full employment in these poor countries was to stop wage inflation in boom industries there.

The result was that competitive industries spread further and further into the remote areas of the poor South. Sometimes this caused disturbance to the traditional ways of village living. From the database of the Biographical Institute we have extracted the story of Huamanco (1964–   ).

Huamanco was born in a small village where he has spent his entire life. The village is high on the Bolivian plateau of the Andes. Mapmakers place it within the borders of Chile, but that has never mattered to Huamanco and his kin, who have always been as remote from national government as it is possible to be. Political changes in the cities bother them not at all. There are no roads to the valley where they plant their crops. Someone, a century or two ago, must have brought the donkeys which were adopted as beasts of burden, but by the time Huamanco was born it was as though they had always been part of the life of the community. Little else had changed in hundreds, perhaps thousands, of years.

The village probably existed in the time of the Incas and the *conquistadores*, but had not been bothered by either. It was never Christianized, and the Indian blood of its inhabitants was never mixed with that of European invaders. The partic-

68

ular dialect that the people spoke was unknown in the cities of Chile and Peru. The tribe itself was effectively undiscovered, though the villagers made no secret of their existence. Huamanco's people could communicate with the men of neighboring villages ("neighboring" meaning within a hundred miles or so). That was all they needed.

In his early years Huamanco's life, like that of every other member of his community, was organized around the potatoes which were the staple crop of the people. Time was measured by the planting and growing of the tubers, the harvesting, the primitive freeze-drying to make *chuño*, the cooking to make porridge-like *papa seca*. *Chuño* and *papa seca* were the food which sustained the village through the winter months, and which could be transported to other villages nearer to the lowlands for use in barter. The villagers also grew a little corn, and another root vegetable resembling a radish, but they lived at such an altitude that, though the days were warm, the nights were often freezing. It was difficult to make any crop grow in abundance, even though the strains had been adapted to the conditions by centuries of selective breeding.

Huamanco's lot was better than that of many other subsistence farmers in the 1970s. There was always water in the valley. Although the women and children had to travel quite a distance to cut wood for their fires, there was no particular competition for the wood, and the amounts that they cut were replaced by each year's growth. The valley was large enough for the villagers to let some of their fields lie fallow each season, so that the soil was not exhausted. The population of the village was relatively stable although the climate was healthy, because the women suckled their infants for a long time and practiced primitive forms of birth regulation. The people grew enough to feed themselves, with a tiny surplus that was used in desultory barter. The people had no notion of change, no desire for change, and perhaps no need for change. They were as happy as any people anywhere, which is to say they complained perennially about their particular discontents, but accepted their lot with patience and resignation, finding joy and amusement when and where they could. The men were habitual drunkards, being devoted to an evil-tasting alcoholic brew which they made by fermenting potatoes. They had a relatively complicated set of religious beliefs and myths, but the only thing that was really sacred to them was the potato.

When Huamanco was twenty-one, in 1985, the village was visited by an American anthropologist, who settled in the valley with the intention of staying for at least two years. He lived at first in a tent, but eventually persuaded some of the young men to help him build a hut out of stone and clay. Huamanco was one of the young men who helped. At first the anthropologist bought his food by barter, using as goods of exchange metal tools of various kinds. Eventually, he was allowed to work in the fields, and took his share of the produce according to the local custom. He arrived with a rudimentary knowledge of the language, which he said he had learned in a computerized Indian Languages course in Minneapolis. Nobody understood him on his arrival, but he became fluent eventually. When he left, he gave Huamanco his sleeping-bag.

From the viewpoint of the villagers, this was probably the most significant effect of his stay. The tools meant little, because the villagers did not feel that the way they worked the land was inadequate to their needs, but one of their particular discontents—perhaps the one which caused them to complain most loudly—was the cold of the nights. The anthropologist's sleeping-bag was a wonder of comfort by comparison with their crude, rough blankets. Huamanco generously allowed other men to test the miraculous bag, but reserved its main use for himself. This was perhaps the first time that the villagers found something to desire, anxiously and fervently, from the outside world. Unfortunately, there seemed to be no prospect of securing a supply.

Had it not been for the sleeping-bag, Huamanco's people might have had little use for the men who later came to the village, saying that they were fulfilling a performance contract financed by a Swedish international aid organization to offer subsistence farmers advice on how to help themselves to a higher standard of living. The notion would have meant nothing to them in the abstract, but since 1987 they had had something concrete to aspire to. This could mean more sleeping-bags.

The older men were still resistant to any idea of change, but Huamanco and the other young men had learned more than they realized from the anthropologist. Once the matter was explained to them they saw the sense in building a small water-wheel to trap the energy of the streams flowing down the mountain to the valley floor. They saw the sense, too, in sowing genetically-engineered corn adapted for high-altitude conditions, which increased the yield of what had previously been their least abundant resource and gave them a surplus which could be sold. Eventually they contrived—with some technical assistance—to build a windmill to generate electricity. At first they found it difficult to trade for the items that they needed to keep this apparatus going and to make use of the electricity. They were a very long way from the nearest city, and so could only trade with other villages full of subsistence farmers. It appeared, therefore, that what they could most readily produce—food—was not in demand in the markets accessible to them.

This situation changed quite dramatically after 2006 and the establishment of Centrobank. Life in the village changed because the whole pattern of life on the Andean slopes began to alter. As villages closer to cities went over to cash crops rather than subsistence crops, they began to rely for their own food on more remote villages, which found it profitable to sell the food that they grew and to import their own food in turn at a cheaper price from even more distant villages. The men who came to Huamanco's village on what they called "our company's new Centrobank performance contract" said that if the villagers could produce certain metal gadgets they called small components up to a standard tested on their machines, then they could sell them in the city and buy everybody sleeping-bags.

Huamanco was forty-three when the village obtained its first electric lights. By the time he was forty-five everyone had a sleeping-bag. When he was fifty the first battery-operated electronic devices appeared in the village. From then it was only three more years before the village had its own receiving dish trained on a communications satellite. Then telescreens began to spread through the clay-and-stone huts, and the village made its leap from the Iron Age into the age of telecommunications. The children began to learn new languages in order to understand the information which flowed into the village through the screens.

Now that Huamanco is sixty-one he has begun to wonder whether it has all been a mistake. He spends many a cool evening in a light alcoholic haze, remembering the days of his childhood and the kind of life that had seemed so simple and so settled. He has become mistrustful of the gadgets which he helped bring into the village against the opposition of his own father and uncles. He used to be fascinated by their newness, but now they are transforming the village children. The young men no longer have any respect for their elders, nor are they grateful for all that their elders have done.

People laugh at Huamanco now, and call him an old-fashioned fool. They will not listen to his stories of his own youth, cannot comprehend his nostalgic appreciation for times so harsh and remote. It would not have been thus if the people had spurned the performance contractors. Huamanco would have been respected, even revered, as a custodian of wisdom and tradition. He would have known everything that the young people needed to know. Sometimes, Huamanco curses himself for helping to transform the private world of his tribe so completely that he no longer has any real place in it.

At night, though, he is warm in his new sleeping-bag—the third that he has owned. The nights are shorter, too, because of the new light. He can look out through the screen of his TC and see a world of whose existence he had never even dreamed in his infancy. Through the keyboard beneath the screen he can speak to the world. The liquor on which he regularly gets drunk tastes much better than the foul brew his father made. The bread is better, and even the potatoes are bigger. To be a stranger in his own land is uncomfortable, and he would be wary of calling himself a happy man. But he has to concede that there might be far worse worlds to be a stranger in.

The Centrobank age began shortly after new sources of growth had opened for the Cinderellas. This was the time of the rise of the sunbelt states. Most of the countries in the so-called poor South were not in the world's south at all. They were grouped around the Equator.

In the rich countries during the 1970s there had been worry because economic growth was moving to the sunbelts where it was pleasant to live. From about the year 2010 people began to realize that the world's sunbelts were the areas recently called the poor South, and that upper-middle-class living was also cheaper there. So the emigrations began to the countries "where you can even still find domestic servants to employ."

Until very recently it would have seemed crazy to say that a main worry was that in some formerly hungry areas poverty might turn to rather flash prospects too soon, that the Gambia might go down Florida's road. When the Centrobank scheme was put into full effect after the IMF and World Bank meetings in 2006, there were many warnings to the effect that nobody should expect that in the next twenty-five years most of the poor world could have the sort of increase in real incomes that occurred after economic reform in Mr. Hu's Taiwan. Probably the founding fathers of Centrobank should have become more optimistic, by looking at some of Taiwan's neighbors.

Remember that Japan in 1950 had an income per head lower than Malaysia's. Twenty-five years later it had an income per head either slightly above Western Europe's and North America's or slightly below it according to which equally wrong exchange rate you used. Remember that Singapore in the late 1930s was an Indian Ocean port on a par in income per head with Calcutta and Rangoon; after the war it should have been expected to become poorer than they because British defense expenditure, which accounted for much of Singapore's external income, was discontinued. Instead by the 1980s Singapore had soared to West European standards of living because its government followed the free-market policies which Centrobank also enshrined, while until the 1990s Calcutta and Rangoon sank into misery under governments who spent far too much of their poor people's incomes for them. Those early Asian economic miracles before even 1985 came because Japan and Singapore and then Hong Kong, Taiwan, and South Korea enjoyed through more than two decades the 10 per cent per annum economic growth that doubles income in seven years, quadruples it in fourteen, and octuples it in twenty-one.

Of the seventy-six countries that have participated in Centrobank since 2006, twenty-two whole countries and parts of twenty others have enjoyed growth on something like this scale. Two other historic benefits have flowed from Centrobank.

First, a sort of democracy is taking root in place of the old dictatorships. This is not, in the main, because of the promises about human rights to which Centrobank beneficiaries must subscribe. It is because—as the rich North learned some years before the poor South—political life becomes less frenetic when the men booted out of highest office can expect to retire to San Clemente, a *dacha* outside Moscow or the House of Lords, instead of having to hurry to get their brothers-in-law to the firing squad before their brothers-in-law get them there. This happy development seems to take place when incomes per head go above the level attained in North-west Europe in, say, Disraeli's day. That level is now being attained almost world-wide. This does not mean the world has become homogeneous in its standard of life. In 2025 the Indian still has an average income only one-tenth that of the average American. In 1975, when our story began, the average American was nominally forty times richer than the Indian; that is some levelling. The Indian is now above the level of income of the Japanese at the beginning of the 1960s; that could bring some fulfilment.

While Centrobank's first great contribution has been to help to diminish poverty and to abate tyranny, its second has been to help abolish political macroeconomics. When those telecommuters' suggestions were tapped out in 2005, it was considered daring to suggest that a computer model of a poor country's economy was capable of showing when it was proceeding with economic growth at the fastest possible non-inflationary pace, but not one tittle faster. Yet this is now accepted to be true in rich countries as well as poor ones, and we now know that the macroeconomic policies which were the main stuff of democratic politics from the 1930s to the 1990s were disgraceful chicanery.

Politicians would claim that the policies in their manifestos would reduce unemployment or curb inflation, even when scientific assessments showed they would do the opposite. After the success of Centrobank, macroeconomics could no longer be political. People knew it was now scientifically possible to assess whether the next $1 billion addition to annual demand would be more likely to increase or decrease real income, just as it was possible to say whether anybody who jumped off the roof of New York's World Trade Center was more likely to go on up or come down. Electors were not likely to vote for those who proclaimed a jumper would continue on up. Simultaneously, microeconomics have been becoming a matter of how most widely to introduce competition with the production of every service and commodity (with each service and commodity being defined as anything that has any kink in the curve showing its elasticity of substitution with anything else). In other words, economics and most other technocratics (but not the humanities) have in the past twenty years begun to be replaced by *ad hoc* marginal calculations instantly computable at the push of a button on a TC.

7

The Change
in Manufacturing
Employment

WHILE THE THREE GREAT POLITICAL EVENTS of the past half-century were the Borovsky Letter, the establishment of Centrobank, and the decline in importance of governments, the great technological event has been the steady rise in importance of the telecommunications-computer terminal, universally known as the TC. Its significance was perceived as early as 1975, when one prophet was saying:

Eventually books, files, television programs, computer information and telecommunications will merge. We'll have this portable object which is a television screen with first a typewriter, later a voice activator, attached. Afterwards it will be miniaturized so that your personal access instrument can be carried in your buttonhole, but there'll be these cheap terminals around everywhere, more widely than there are telephones in 1975. The terminals will be used to access databases anywhere in the globe, and will become the brainworker's mobile place of work. Brainworkers, which will increasingly mean most workers, will be able to live in Tahiti if they want to and telecommute daily to the New York or Tokyo or Hamburg office through which they work. In the satellite age costs of transmission will not depend mainly on distance.

In 2025 we do not yet carry our access instruments in our buttonholes, and we are too sophisticated to all live in Tahiti, but this was not a bad forecast of the way things would go. In 1975 the telecommuting revolution was poised to change the whole shape of manufacturing industry, then of the new information industries (including education) and finally of society itself.

In the 1970s some 20–40 per cent of the work-force in the three richest areas of the world (the U.S., the EEC, and Japan) were engaged in manufacturing. A typical industry of the 1970s, which lends itself to analysis, was automobile manufacture. In 1979 there were a score of multinationals engaged in this, all headquartered in the U.S. or Japan or the EEC, but there were assembly plants in eighty-three countries. In the three rich areas—which were inhabited by under one-sixth of the population of the world—more than half of households already owned automobiles; outside these three areas, only 3 per cent of households did. While the richest one-sixth of people talked of seeing the end of the polluting automobile age, the other five-sixths were only just about to enter it. It was likely that production would be concentrated more and more in those of the eighty-three assembly countries that lay outside the rich North, but there was little foresight about the way in which this would occur.

In the period 1959–79 workers in the rich countries had become fractious about automobile manufacture. These countries had grown rich because they were initially suited to the Henry

Ford revolution. During the era of mass production engineers sat in towering office blocks arranging how workers down on the factory floor could most economically work with their hands. By the sixties and seventies this had created a problem. Once a country had grown rich and educated, workers did not like being meticulously bossed from the top on how best to work with their hands. From 1959 to 1979, therefore, the workforce in automobile plants in countries like West Germany and France became largely made up of immigrants from poorer lands like Turkey and Algeria. More and more of the workers in American and British automobile plants became workers from the some-times resentful black minority. Labor relations and discipline were not good.

In Japan during the same period more and more cars were produced by what were misleadingly called robots. These early automatons could better have been called general-purpose jigs. Manufacturing plants in the 1960s contained many machine tools which were really special-purpose jigs that had tempo-rarily to be constructed in many chunky shapes and sizes, mainly because a human being cannot hold work against a cutter with the required accuracy and strength. In the early 1970s the Jap-anese filled their factories with general-purpose jigs that could be programmed to keep repositioning work against a cutter with the same nous as a human would show if he were suffi-ciently quick, strong and accurate. By 1976 a Japanese car worker, with the aid of these robots, was producing sixty cars a man-year. A worker at British Leyland (then the least efficient of the European car factories) was producing six cars a man-year. A worker in an American or continental European plant was generally producing ten to twenty cars a man-year.

Fears therefore arose in the late 1970s about supposed huge technological unemployment to come. If a British car factory became as automated and efficient as a Japanese car factory then, in an age of fairly stagnant car sales, pessimists preached that nine-tenths of British car-workers would be made redun-dant. And if foreign factories did not become as efficient as the Japanese, they would go bust. People had been talking of a great possible advance in manufacturing employment in the poor countries of the world, but (it was wailed) there would not be a great increase in employment and wealth in India if automobiles were to be made mainly by robots.

This arithmetic was turned topsy-turvy by the next improvements in robots that took place in the years 1985–95. Early in the computer age people had begun to realize that (a) almost every physical human skill and sensory reaction could eventually be mimicked by a computerized automaton; that (b) developing the necessary software was going to be a painstakingly laborious business involving the planning and programming of a long sequence of tiny step-by-step objectives; but that (c) the happenstance that car-making had originally been organized along Henry Ford lines meant that genuine robots (like the previous so-called robot workers) could be fairly meticulously trained to follow any sequence of movements within its domain; and that (d) the next advances in industrial robots lay with improved sensors for seeing and touching (and interpreting what was seen and touched) before developing sensors for listening (in particular recognizing and understanding commands from humans).

The biggest advances made by the Japanese after 1985 were in improved sensors for seeing and touching. The result was that by the 1990s computerized automatons were better than humans at testing components to see that they reached the required standard. It was this breakthrough that did most to spark the Third World's new role in manufacturing.

The two seminal events in the automobile revolution of the twentieth century were the founding of the Ford Motor Company in Detroit in 1903 and the establishment of the Nissan plant in Kanpur, North India in 1988–91. Japan's own domestic automobile industry had been set up by accepting components from small firms (sometimes workshops with less than half-a-dozen employees) and subjecting them to very stern quality checks indeed. The Japanese were unwilling until the late 1980s to set up overseas plants that drew components from local component-makers: they feared the personal hassle when Japanese inspectors turned down each load of local components, saying "Of insufficient quality." Once the testing was done by computers, this problem became much less embarrassing.

Nissan's plant at Kanpur was established on the understanding that the firm would buy all Indian-made components that passed their computerized tests for quality. Travelling Japanese instructors were very willing to teach tiny Indian workshops how to pass these specific tests, and to leave testing terminals, connected to their mainframe computers, in these workshops for trial-and-error experiments (though the final check before purchase was made in the factory itself). This system has since spread to virtually all manufacturing industries throughout the Third World. After the success at Kanpur founders of small businesses in poor countries could calculate, "If we make such-and-such a component which passes such-and-such a test and can sell it more cheaply than engineers in rich countries—which with our cheap labor we should be able to do—then we will have a limitless market for what we make." The entrepreneur most responsible for helping them to this market was Toshio Nakayama (1917–93).

Toshio Nakayama was born in rural Japan in 1917, and died in the great Tokyo earthquake of 1993 which so sadly interrupted his country's dynamic advance. During his seventy-six years he passed from what West Europeans would regard as a fourteenth-century childhood, through being a twentieth-century high-school drop-out, into becoming perhaps the most important industrialist in the world during the last generation when great industrialists mattered.

He was the fourth son of a Japanese tenant farmer who stayed shrewdly subservient to his feudal squire. For the first ten years of his life Toshio possessed at any one time only a single, humiliating fourth-hand garment (a smock which had belonged to his three brothers before him), ate one staple food (rice, which was less nutritious than a Plantagenet peasant's gruel), and—except in one important respect—enjoyed a general living-standard below that of British, German and French peasants in the prosperous, labor-short years just after the Black Death in the 1340s.

The exception was that his Japanese feudal squire in the 1920s provided a good village primary school. The squire financed the top one-fifth of students from this primary school to attend a local high school. The top boy high-school graduate each year was then financed at university, from which he was expected to pass into the imperial civil service, where the young mandarin would pull strings for his village and squire. All three of Toshio's elder brothers got the university scholarship in their year, aided by the fact that their father was chairman of the tenants' council and urged everybody to bow very low to the squire.

Toshio's family, like many cottage Japanese, had a lathe in the living room. They earned extra income making (in their case) components for radio sets for the Japanese army. Toshio worked excessive hours on the lathe, largely because his brothers always seemed to be about to sit for some crucial exam, and their studies could not be interrupted.

Toshio's studies were interrupted, and he was not particularly good at them. He scraped into high school, but failed the first-year exam there. He felt this to be his first betrayal of his kin. He went to work for his father in the fields, and especially on the lathe. By the time he was seventeen he had expanded the family workshop to three employees, and secured some contracts for making components for civilian radios as well as the army orders. Toshio said he learned in this tiny workshop the principle on which he later founded his huge business empire: "Find out what quality is demanded, then satisfy that quality, and your market is limitless."

At the age of eighteen, in 1935, Toshio was conscripted into the army for the boring war in China. He came back as a signal corps sergeant in 1938, with sufficient of a soldier's gratuity to start a small radio-repairing shop with five employees. During this period he was enthralled by papers written by Professor Matsuo Abe of Tokyo University, presaging innovations like transistors.

At the end of 1941, since he was a sergeant in the reserve, Toshio was called up again—this time for the more exciting Pacific war. He swept south with the triumphant Japanese Army, loudly singing, *"Banzai!"* On the southernmost island that they reached his unit found the enemy airforce ruled the sky over them. Toshio had the good fortune—though he did not think this—to be wounded in an enemy air raid at a time when Japanese ships could still carry wounded soldiers home to the north. Toshio sailed back to an army hospital in Japan four weeks before the Americans invaded the island he had been garrisoning. All his regiment died to the last man. Toshio felt this was his second betrayal of his kin.

In Japan he was deemed sufficiently seriously wounded to be semidemobilized and sent to be number two at a small army radio workshop. The chief technician in charge there was Professor Abe of Tokyo University, who had been relegated to this low job because he was not sufficiently keen on the war. In the spring of 1945 Professor Abe was taken back to Tokyo to perform a secret government task, and he left Toshio in charge. In the summer Toshio left the army base town to visit Tokyo for two weeks to collect sufficient radio stores to stock a new signals regiment to help in the defense of southern Japan. The date was 4 August 1945. The army base town he left was Hiroshima. Toshio regarded this as his third betrayal of his kin.

He found himself with a small warehouse full of radio stores in Tokyo, but with his unit destroyed and nobody interested in his warehouse. He reported to the American occupation authorities when they arrived; but an American lieutenant looked at his ragged radio equipment and said, "Nobody wants that crap, son; as you're a semi-civilian, I'd advise you to keep it and get lost."

The same advice to get lost was simultaneously being given to one of Toshio's friends, but from a much greater height. When General Douglas MacArthur became supreme commander, the Japanese authorities marched a group of pin-striped officials in to see him. "Here," they said, "is a team we have gathered in the past six months to study how you should rule us if we lost the war." The team contained three mandarins, a prominent Japanese economist (who later became foreign minister), an imperial courtier (who had studied constitutional history at Oxford), and as technical adviser Professor Matsuo Abe, who was a graduate of the Massachusetts Institute of Technology. MacArthur hanged the imperial courtier, whom he accused of war crimes; and yelled at the others to get lost, saying they were never to be employed in any official capacity again.

The now unemployed Professor Abe went to live with ex-Sergeant-Major Nakayama in his warehouse filled with unwanted radio parts. They announced they would fulfil some of the civilian orders sent to the lost plant in Hiroshima. From this tiny beginning the two men built up over the next forty years the giant electronics firm of Nakabe, which became the richest manufacturing company in the world.

Nakabe caught and then left each wave in the electronics industry at exactly the right time. Into and then out of transistor radios. Into and out of black-and-white and then color television. Into and out of other consumer electronics. Nakabe did not tarry long in making personal computers in the middle of the 1980s. "This is a field," said Toshio Nakayama, "which is going to become very overcrowded." Nakabe concentrated instead on fitting computers to sensitive robots which could test components for quality. It was these Nakabe testers, with terminals scattered in small workshops all over India, Pakistan, Bangladesh and China, which later helped make these areas into new Japans. It was the main manufacturing development of 1990–2004. "We have enabled small Indian workshops to discover what quality is required," said Nakayama," and now their market is limitless."

Nakayama always wore the same overalls as the humblest of his employees. "I put on this uniform in my Tokyo warehouse in 1945," he said, "and I have been too busy since then to take it off." His paternalism exceeded that of his old feudal squire. "The Americans," he said, "have sadly lost their old ties of church, family and community. In Japan we have created new communities in the workplace, so that the man who sweeps the floor here and I feel we are in the same team, singing the same company song." Nakabe never expanded by buying other companies, in the way that American conglomerates did. "You can no more buy and sell a company than you can buy and sell your mother," said Nakayama. "The Americans and Europeans have never understood that a company is a social entity. Any company which is up for sale is so rotten that it cannot possibly be worth buying."

Although Nakabe executives squandered their expense accounts exuberantly on sake and women and song, Nakayama himself led an austere life. He did not give to charity except within his own firm, but he did finance a lot of uncommercial research. This included the Nakabe Institute of Seismology at the university where his elder brother was by now ex-rector.

This institute reported to him in 1993 that a great earthquake was likely in Tokyo within two days. He sent Professor Abe's son to tell the minister of the interior, but the minister, unconsciously almost echoing General MacArthur, told him to get lost. "Even if your scientists were right, which they aren't, you are inviting me to create the greatest Tokyo traffic jam in history and then watch all the cars disappear into the center of the earth."

Nakayama sent organizing messengers in bean-colored disaster suits to appear on internal television within all his workshops, giving precise information on how Nakabe workers and their families were to evacuate in forty-eight hours from danger areas to safe ones. "We will get only nine-tenths out before the earthquake strikes," he said, "and I will be one who does not leave. It was really my duty to die in the South Pacific or Hiroshima fifty years ago, but now I am privileged to be the captain who may go down on the bridge of this great ship which you my workmates have built."

In the event, 99 per cent of Nakabe workers and their families were saved, but Nakayama was among the lost 1 per cent. He remained calmly in his office in a Tokyo tower block, dressed in a bean-colored disaster suit, and when he spoke to his evacuated employees minutes before the earthquake struck it was clear he was in a state of some exaltation.

Toshio Nakayama felt at the last that he had not betrayed his kin.

The main Nissan factory at Kanpur consisted initially of rows of Nakabe robots and not much else. They turned the components that appeared at one end of the assembly line into completed Datsun cars at the other end, and there were not many Indian workers employed in the factory itself. But then there emerged the next feature of the computer revolution in automobiles: namely, that it made possible custom-built production at mass-production prices.

By early in the twenty-first century computerized sensors on the Kanpur assembly line were collecting information on each car that passed along the line, and sending back to the bank of software contained in mainframe computers in Tokyo such messages as: "This standard car has a chassis strength of such-and-such." The computers in Tokyo worked out that on 20 per cent of cars using Indian roads—those sold for use in the rougher parts of the country—it would be worth marketing a car with a stronger chassis even at some increase in the price. The message would then be programmed into the robots, by telecommunication from Tokyo, "Strengthen the chassis of each fifth car along the line by doing such-and-such."

This obedience to consumer needs exists in every car plant in the world today because of the much better and more customized consumer information available on all our TCs. Most people buying a car in 2025 will key their special requirements into their TCs: "I travel 10,000 miles a year, 1 per cent of them on unsurfaced roads; I don't need my car to be cheaply transportable by aircraft; I habitually use such-and-such a brake pressure; I prefer the following oddities . . ."

The TC will reply: "You can get a customized car which meets all your specifications by putting personalized instructions on the software for all the robots in one of these factories [*choice of twenty-nine*] requesting that the next available car put on the line be modified as you dictate. But that would cost up to $40,000. (Key factories on your TC for price quotations and credit facilities.) For a fifth of that price you can meet most of your requirements by the following standard computer programs at present scheduled for batches D29,000 to D38,000 in June at Nissan Kanpur; batches E17,000 to E26,000 in July at Ford Manila; batches . . . [*and so on*] Key factories for precise specifications and prices."

All this became commonplace after the year 2000. How has it affected employment?

In 1976 the workers at British Leyland (providing 6 cars a man-year) feared that a rise in their productivity to Japanese levels of 60 cars a man-year would cause nine-tenths of them to be sacked. Six hundred standard cars are now produced per man-year in almost any advanced factory. If the British Leyland workers had known this in 1976, they would have feared that by now 99 out of 100 of them would be sacked. In developed countries about 10 of those 99 who would otherwise have been sacked are now employed in the extra work created by customization—writing software programs for the TC so that consumers are better informed and cars better fitted to customized markets. It remains true that in these developed countries only about one-tenth as many people are employed in car-making as had jobs in 1973. They are producing only about as many cars as in 1973. Although many more families have three or four cars, customization means that they last far longer.

In poorer countries the average number of cars produced by each worker in a year is only 200, not 600, because more people are employed in small workshops making components. As they are still paid less than one-third of the average wage in rich countries, this greater employment of manpower is economic. As annual production of cars has increased enormously since 1988 in countries like India (where one family in three now has a car), employment in car manufacturing in the poor five-sixths of the world has risen by considerably more than the nine-tenths by which it has fallen in the rich countries. But into what jobs have the vanished car-makers of the North gone?

A few of them have gone into new manufacturing industries, of a very different kind. We have cited car-making above as an example of a refurbished old manufacturing industry. For a new industry of 2019–25 let us cite the intendedly short-lived example of the Clark-Schmidt Robot Gardener.

In 2018 Maurice Clark was a fifty-three-year-old taking his third undergraduate degree (he had taken the other two at the ages of nineteen and thirty-seven respectively). This time he was enrolled on a computerized learning course telecommuted through the University of Southern California, although he took it while living in his native Australia. Together with two other students telecommuting through USC's database, he devised a system for a robot-driven lawnmower which could also scan soil and assess the possibilities for reseeding. It signalled the videos to be called up on your TC to show alternative uses for the soil in your garden. If you picked one video display as particularly suited to your taste, you keyed its number into the Robot Gardener, and it signalled back, "Put such-and-such a chemical into my tank, and seeds numbers 1234, 5678, 3456 (et cetera), plus software program 29387—both orderable through your TC—into my reseeder."

Clark and his two colleagues put their tentatives ideas for this device on to the researchers' database monitored by the University of Southern California. The entry numbers to this USC database were held by people who had promised to accept the computer's judgment of the value of any additional ideas they might contribute to projects entered on it. In all, 1,213 people—domiciled from Hanoi through Penang and Capri and Bermuda back to Queensland in Australia itself—tapped in suggestions for improvements, of which 176 were accepted by the computer as worthwhile. The payments recommended by the computer for these 176 ranged from $42 (for a cosmetic improvement suggested by an eleven-year-old schoolboy) to one-tenth of the equity (eventually worth several million dollars) for a proposal by a research team from another telecommuting university which proved important enough for Clark to feel slightly guilty about calling the Robot Gardener after himself.

When the improvements suggested by these 176 contributors had been incorporated by Clark into the appropriate software program for making the Robot Gardener, the program was advertised on USC's entrepreneur-browsing program, available on any TC. Entry numbers for the lowest echelons of this can be bought for a very few dollars, but the Robot Gardener was put on a higher echelon because USC's computer had signalled this was a potential quick winner.

One of those who had paid for an expensive entry number into browsing among good "proffered opportunity products" (POPs) was a Dutchman called Carl Schmidt. He had become a successful "arranging producer" in an earlier venture, and now occupied himself browsing through his TC looking for a second bonanza. He made an offer to Clark to take over an option for launch in return for a fairly complicated program of profit sharing, which in practice (because arranging is nowadays a more skilled job than inventing) eventually gave Schmidt much more money than Clark. Clark accepted this, and Schmidt produced a prototype within three days by reprogramming robots in an experimental plant. A video of the prototype was put on consumers' TC channels world-wide the next week, and most of the 400-odd gardeners' TC channels round the world picked it out within days as a "best buy."

Schmidt's video advertisement said, "If you key in your order now with your credit number, you can get a Robot Gardener for a bargain price (applies to the first 10,000 orders only). Tenders are also invited for part of the equity." The advance orders and bids for the equity made it possible to finance assembly of the Robot Gardener for early-bird customers within a few weeks. Contact was kept with those customers, and two minor faults of which they complained were corrected. By the end of 2024 production was taking place in sixty-two countries, and sales in 2019–24 grossed $5 billion. This included production of a cheaper version of the Robot Gardener in the Third World for use in some of the "2 million self-sufficient villages" rather hopefully adumbrated under the Centrobank scheme.

In about fifty of the sixty-two countries production is taking place in robot-using plants with an average of seven to ten workers each. These are small, leased plants. The robots will be reprogrammed to make something else when the Robot Gardener is overtaken by another product, which in modern industry usually happens within eight years. In the remaining dozen countries—those very keen on gardening like the Netherlands and Japan—the factories are managed by workers' co-operatives of about thirty people who run gardeners' competitions through the TC and other profitable sidelines.

Production of the Robot Gardener world-wide employs less than 1,000 people, and the $5 billion turnover in six years has been munificent for them. Even those who have contributed or invested little (for instance, the workers in the reprogrammable robot factories) have earned bonuses sufficient to enable them to take six-month-a year holidays for the next five years or so if they want them. Those who put in early-bird bids for the equity have no reason to complain of their investment, although the fact that they tendered for equity after Clark's research stage and Schmidt's opportunity-search stage meant they had to tender high. The big gainers are those who ran the workers' co-operative in the Netherlands (which proved a particularly successful operation); Clark and his USC colleagues plus those of the 176 original telecommuters who earned equity by contributing early ideas; and Schmidt plus a few associated entrepreneurs who browsed through their TCs and saw an opportunity to program the new product for robot production. All the top people in these three groups are now millionaires.

Note that there was never any intention that Robot Gardeners Inc. should grow into a huge and long-lasting company. Except perhaps in places such as Japan, where they like continuity in institutions, it will fold as soon as its product is no longer near the top of the charts. Clark and Schmidt are already researching and browsing into other possibilities, on separate courses. About fifty of those who succeeded in early participation of this venture hope to become the equivalent of Clark and Schmidt in other things.

At no stage has this enormously successful manufacturing venture employed more than 1,000 people. It is therefore true that the loss of nine-tenths of manufacturing jobs, which we saw has occurred in car-making in rich countries, has also been seen in manufacturing jobs as a whole. Where these countries had 20–40 per cent of their workforces in manufacturing in 1975, they typically have only 2–4 per cent now.

This is not an unprecedented rundown. In the 1890s around half of the workforce in countries like the United States and Britain were in three occupations: agriculture, domestic service and jobs to do with horse transport. By the 1970s these three were down to 4 per cent of the work-force. If this had been foretold in the 1890s there would have been a wail. It would have been said that half of the population was fit only to be farmworkers, parlormaids and sweepers-up of horse manure. Where would this half find jobs? The answer was that by the 1970s the majority of them were much more fully employed (because more married women joined the workforce) doing jobs that would have sounded double-Dutch in the 1890s: extracting oil instead of fish out of the North Sea; working as computer programmers; or as television engineers; or as package holiday tour operators chartering jet aircraft.

The move in jobs in the past fifty years—1975–2025—in the rich countries has been out of manufacturing into telecommuting.

8

The TC
and Education

COMPUTER INCOMPATIBILITY delayed the age of the TC. This seems as incomprehensible today as reading of a planet which discovered the telephone but developed hundreds of different, incompatible ways of making it—some of them marketed by the same company—with the result that while everyone had access to a telephone, most subscribers could not contact the people they most wanted to talk to.

When large computers started to be commercially marketed in the 1960s and early 1970s, there were at first only a handful of computer manufacturers. Technology was advancing so fast that at this stage each manufacturer found there was no way his new generation of computer hardware could be compatible with earlier models. This was natural while technology was advancing from magnetic valves to electronic chips. Unfortunately, the early commercial competitiveness of these companies also encouraged deliberate divergence. A tempting ploy for each big computer company was to make sure that there was just enough compatibility between its current and its next generation of computers, but total incompatibility with rival systems. This ensured that current clients had to come back for more from the same manufacturer. Customers often found during the 1970s that after three years their computer was technically far less powerful than the newest market entry; but, as they had already committed hundreds of man-years to programming their current machine, they had to go back to the old computer's manufacturer and buy the best quasi-compatible update he could offer.

At the end of the 1970s a technological breakthrough occurred which brought both further opportunity and further chaos. This was the microcomputer: computers as a unit went small, and then cheap. You could buy a machine which was recognizably a computer for prices which the mass market could afford. Use and initially incompatibility chaos spread from big business to small business and to schools and homes.

From the beginning of the computer age, managers in industry had felt frustrated because they could not communicate with the experts in their computing departments. They hoped that micros would give them back the opportunity to control their own work. Unfortunately, almost all the micros were harder to program for the things that would be useful to these managers. You could always get the micro to do something for you very soon after you had bought it, but anything at all sophisticated was far more tedious to program on a micro than on a more powerful computing device. In the offices the first micros led to greater computerization of bureaucratic tasks that were mostly already pretty redundant anyway.

In education many rich and some poor countries' governments decided in the early 1980s to subsidize every school so they could buy a micro of their choice, provided a teacher would program it as a device which would teach something. This was a crazy policy. Most teachers were not good programmers, and the smaller the computer the more expert anybody needed to be to program it for a sophisticated use like teaching. Each teacher was, in effect, left to re-invent his own computer wheel. These experiments were thus very boring and very costly.

These early errors by large companies' managers and by government education departments showed that those people who in the early 1980s had the computer buying power were the people least capable of using it wisely. In those days it was still assumed that senior (i.e., older) people were best qualified to make large buying decisions, even in a fast-changing technology which they had never used themselves and whose potential for application they understood only from newspaper color-supplements.

The computer revolution of the late 1980s therefore owed little to the baffled progress of executives and teachers, and much more to the fury of the kids. It was the smaller and younger customers who did most to pave the way for change when hundreds of models of microcomputers came almost overnight to main street stores. These machines were at first not only hardware-incompatible but software-incompatible. In each year of the early 1980s micro owners were presented with a new budget micro which was significantly more powerful and interesting than last year's model. Too often none of the programs you had lovingly made for last year's model could be transferred to this year's. By the second half of the 1980s, when microcomputers had become popular consumer durables in America, Japan and West Europe, owners had split into two factions. The majority still did little fundamental programming of their own, but bought off-the-shelf packages which provided last year's arcade games in your own home, or simple aids to composing music, making graphics displays, word processing, and household accounts. However, a growing section of micro owners, especially teenagers, did their own programming.

Never had a possession presented man simultaneously with such excited pride and initially such infuriating frustration. Excited pride because micros promised the chance to be a cre-

ative inventor in almost any area of human endeavor. Infuriating frustration because a serious program needed so much
work. This frustration was multiplied by the programmer's
knowledge that his products could be readily shared in a matter
of seconds with any friend only so long as that friend had the
same micro model, and of the same year, even though otherwise
next year's improved version would be so much better to use.

As two-way cable TV programs spread, interactive surveys
told of the growing discontent of young people all over the
industrialized world. Politicians had supposed their main source
of frustration was unemployment, but in America and Western
Europe a major complaint was computer incompatibility. Said
one representative youth at this time, "When you have something that you value sufficiently to have worked on it for six
months and you can copy it on to your friend's same-model
micro in a few seconds, but realize that when you upgrade
your machine you will have three months' work to
transfer the same programs, you get very angry indeed with
the follies of your parents' generation."

Big customers agreed with this. One bank president commented, "Perhaps we needed this micro experience and the
fury of young programmers to popularize the truism that every
time a major computer manufacturer launches a new-genera-
tion large computer which is somewhat incompatible with its
earlier-generation computer, the world-wide effect is the waste
of millions of man-years of programming."

The era of computer incompatibility was coming to an end.
Today knowledge once gained need never be lost, and it can
be made available for instant sharing all over the world at the
keying of anybody's TC terminal. Gradually all computers began to be made as compatible as possible, and networks were
marketed which allowed all sets to talk to each other.

This was to have remarkable consequences for the way we
ran our lives. It also had strange consequences for some children of the late 1980s and early 1990s, as the biography of
Giovanni Varchi (1982–   ) demonstrates.

Giovanni Varchi was born in a small town near Ragusa in

Sicily in 1982. His family moved to Milan when he was four years old, and it was there that he was brought up. The Varchi family was respectable—one of Giovanni's uncles was a successful lawyer—but his father Bartolomeo was relatively poor. Bartolomeo had been working in a small family business in Sicily, but moved to become a factory worker in Milan when employment picked up there at the end of the world mini-recession in 1986. Giovanni benefited more than his father from the move: the family grew no richer, but Giovanni received a better education in the city than he could have had in rural Sicily. By the age of seven he had, like so many children of his age at that time, become fascinated by the new technology, and he retreated from the difficult social world into an intimate and almost obsessive relationship with a series of personal microcomputers. He was encouraged in this both at home and at school, where his talent was appreciated.

If he had been born ten years later, he would have passed Prelims at the age of nine and have gone into paid work on writing computer programs immediately. As Italian children in the early 1990s were not allowed to leave full-time education before the age of fifteen, Giovanni spent the next eight years in a state of simmering revolt. He was interested in little else except his beloved machines, but learned English because most contemporary research was reported in that language. His school wanted him to proceed to higher education and university. Giovanni made it clear he would do no such thing, and he defected from Milan on his fifteenth birthday.

He went first to work for a merchant bank in Switzerland, and then telecommuted from there to one in London. His parents were worried to hear that both banks found him a brilliant but exasperating employee. Both quickly recognized his ability, but neither got the benefit of it. The Swiss bank had promoted him promptly from his office boy's job to the computer department. In that department he was asked to plan and oversee some complex systems. He started most promisingly on them, but did not finish what he started. Instead, he got a telecommuter's job to do virtually the same thing for an English bank at a smaller salary. From that bank he departed into the blue yonder, but the English manager said to the inquiring Mr. Varchi senior: "Don't worry, Giovanni will always get a job. He is as clever as a barrel-load of monkeys."

In 2006 Mr. Varchi learned to his distress that the twenty-four-year-old Giovanni was back in his native Sicily. He was running his own telecommuting company, which was nominally a consultancy. He was its only employee. On the surface the company did very little business. It made very modest profits considering the amount of capital which was tied up in its computers. Actually, Giovanni Varchi was by now a multi-millionaire. He had hundreds of bank accounts in different foreign cities, none of which he had ever visited. Most of his money was invested in securities which brought in an income of tens of thousands of dollars per week. This was augmented by an even greater inflow of cash from other sources. Giovanni Varchi was one of the most successful thieves of all time.

He had achieved this distinction by covering his tracks so well that it usually could not be detected that a crime had been committed, let alone how or by whom. He did not rob the companies for which he worked. He used their facilities to get access to communicative links between their systems and others. He began by finding ways to eavesdrop on other people as they used their computer terminals. By studying their procedures he learned how to get access to their programs. Then he would find a non-obtrusive way of removing money to his own accounts. Always he would do this in moderation, creating a small leakage for a short period of time. Always he would cover his tracks by amending records so that it was impossible at a later date for anyone to see how the money had been re-routed.

It is probable that nobody has ever committed quite as many individual acts of theft as Giovanni Varchi. There were many computer thieves in the years 1989–2011, but most took relatively large amounts from relatively few sources. Varchi's distinction is that he was not the telecommuting equivalent of a bank robber, but rather the telecommuting equivalent of a pickpocket. And he was astonishingly prolific in the number of pockets that he picked. Even in 2010, which might be regarded as the peak of his criminal career, no law-enforcement agency or law-enforcement performance contractor was looking for him. Those of his crimes which had been discovered had been identified only as amounts of missing money, whose disappearance was a mystery.

He did not live like a rich man. Probably he did not even know what the lifestyle of a rich man was. It would not be true to say that the motive for his crimes was non-mercenary—he loved being rich—but he had not stolen in order to spend his money lavishly. He was not a greedy man, and was indeed somewhat ascetic in his habits. He could have supported himself easily in the manner to which he was accustomed without ever stepping outside the law. A PET study of his brain reported that his reasons for becoming a thief "may have been largely aesthetic." It probably was not irrelevant that he came from a poor Sicilian background, and thus had blurred notions concerning the ethics of theft, but the respectability of his immediate kin rules out the notion that he was educated into thievery as a way of life.

Like many programming addicts, Giovanni Varchi in his youth saw life as a series of problematic challenges. For him, real life was contained within the relationship between his machines and himself. The tangible world of people, buildings and organic life was a mere extension of this inner world, a manipulated reflection. Other people seemed to him to be shadows on the wall of a Platonic cave. The real core of being was the information that linked their institutions, particularly the computer systems which were the skeleton of their society. It would be tempting to say that in all he did he was simply playing a game, but that would be an oversimplification. It is doubtful whether the concept of a game would have made much sense to him.

In 2012, when he was thirty years old, Giovanni Varchi stopped being a thief and became instead a policeman. It was an easy transition, because in his consultancy work he had been a kind of policeman—nominally, at least—all along. His employers had always asked him to pay particular attention to the security of their systems, to guard against the possibility of computer theft. Because he did not steal from his immediate clients, he had done such work conscientiously, but he had ensured that his own criminal methods always stayed one step ahead of his security measures.

It would be wrong to see Varchi's change of policy as a change of heart, or as a matter of changing sides. He has never repented of his earlier career, and never offered a detailed confession of his activities. They simply became relevant experience, which he allowed new employers to glimpse as an aspect of his credentials. Although he admitted to having been a criminal, he was never charged with any offense in any country—partly because there would have been great difficulty in convicting him, but also because his criminal career really did give him the experience he needed to be a truly expert computer policeman.

Since 2012 his main clients have been law-enforcement performance contractors and the insurance companies which have taken over the functions formerly carried out by national governments in so many communities. He has become one of the men who has managed to keep the information systems on which the world now depends functioning smoothly and securely. He has always remained a freelance operator, and has not even held out for particularly high rewards. In his new role he has challenge a-plenty. His ravenous appetite for absorption into logical and practical puzzles is daily sated. The need to steal has disappeared from his life. He works entirely behind the scenes, mostly in secret. He has never married. Although he sends money to his family in Milan they continue to regard him as a great disappointment and as a test of their emotional fortitude. He never sees them.

Varchi would not have been a worry to his family if he had been born in this century. There has been a sea-change in the traditional ages of man. Compared with 1975 our children in 2025 generally go out to paid work (especially computer programming work) much earlier, maybe starting at nine, maybe at twelve, and we do not exploit them. But young adults of twenty-three to forty-three stay at home to play much more than in 1975; it is quite usual today for one parent (probably now generally the father, though sometimes the mother) to stay at home during the period when young children are growing up. And today adults of forty-three to ninety-three go back to school—via computerized learning—much more than they did in 1975.

In most of the rich countries in 2025 children are not allowed to leave school until they pass their Preliminary Exam. About 5 per cent of American children passed their exam last year before their eighth birthday, but the median age for passing it in 2025 is ten-and-a-half, and remedial education is generally needed if a child has not passed it by the age of fifteen.

A child who passes his Prelim can decide whether to take a job at once, and take up the remainder of his twelve years of free schooling later (after eighty if he likes); or he can pass on to secondary schooling forthwith, and start to study for his Higher Diploma. If he gets a particularly good result at his Prelim Exam (and still more if he does well at his Higher) then he earns the right to extra years of free schooling. In California somebody who gets First-class Honors at all five stages (Prelim, Higher, Baccalaureate, first and second university degrees) earns the right to thirty years of free schooling and students' scholarships, to be taken up at any period of his life he chooses.

The mode of learning for the under-twelves is nowadays generally computer-generated. The child sits at home or with a group of friends or (more rarely) in an actual, traditional school building. She or he will be in touch with a computer program that has discovered, during a preliminary assessment, her or his individual learning pattern. The computer will decide what next questions to ask or task to set after each response from each child.

A schoolteacher assessor, who may live half a world away, will generally have been hired, as a result of PET-pattern compatibility or word-of-mouth recommendation, via the voucher system by the family for each individual child. A good assessor will probably have vouchers to monitor the progress of twenty-five individual children, although some parents prefer to employ groups of assessors—one following the child's progress in emotional balance, one in mathematics, one in civilized living, and so on—and these groups band together in telecommuting schools. In some states children who have failed the Prelim Exam—which now includes exams in emotional balance as well as reading, writing, computer, mathematics, three sciences, civilized living, practical arts—will have remedial assessors in telecommuting schools allotted to them.

Many communes and districts also have on-the-spot "uncles" and "aunts." They monitor children's educational performance by browsing through the TC and also run play groups where they meet and get to know the children personally. Parents in these areas receive especially detailed reports from the "aunts" and "uncles" on their children's progress in emotional balance and civilized living. These contain practical advice such as, "Your child needs to play more with rougher, more interest-differentiated groups of children." Or, "It would be wise to have a PET survey taken of your child's brain patterns, plus a video of him playing baseball, and then call a computer conference in which there will be participation by yourself, your family's health maintenance organization, your child's assessor(s), your local children's uncle and (we would recommend) open TC access to the following bodies—various junior league baseball commissioners (they might be interested in videos of Bobby's undoubted prowess) and a consultancy on shyness in children (because we feel Bobby has problems there)."

Different parents have different views on whether it is best to subject a child to such formal analyses, or whether life in childhood is happier if there is informal mingling in play groups or even old-fashioned go-to-the-classroom schools. Different communes also have different views on this, and if a family thinks its neighbors' choice too formal or too relaxed they will generally move to a community with different tastes and will telecommute to work from there.

Most areas are sensible enough to leave wide choice to the parents, although states and communes differ in the degree to which they enforce changes in a child's individual education system if low results in emotional balance or civics, or repeated failures in Prelims, suggest something is going wrong. It is enforced changes of system which cause the most heart-ache, but the problem has been alleviated since it has become common for one or other parent to take the period of their children's pre-Prelim education wholly or mainly off work, becoming officially Educators for their children.

Some of these parents who have temporarily opted out of employment to be a family Educator also put material on the TCs for other parents to consult. Sometimes this advice is given free, sometimes as a business. It is a business for Joshua Ginsberg.

Anybody who keys the number GINS47286BE7918R3GCAL on his TC will read:

Joshua Ginsberg was born in 1992 in the colony of American telecommuting engineers who settled in the Crimea shortly after the U.S.-CPDR Treaty of Friendship. He has stayed there most of his life, apart from occasional home-swaps, but chose to telecommute to America for his education. He passed his Prelim in 2000 (which was an early age at the time). He worked from 2000–4 as a telecommuter for Citibank of Moscow, and was picked out as its young wordsmith of the year. He then took high-school diploma, first and second university degrees in banking, English, and computer in 2004–11 and returned to an executive job at Citibank. In 2020 he retired to work—probably for ten years—as Educator to his children Julie (born 2015) and Pharon (born 2019).

Since 2021 he has put a parents' advice letter on the TC, usually monthly. It has attracted 323,817 key-ins in these years, nowadays requiring 25-cent entry fee. See schedule for cheaper rates if you accept attached advertisements. The

Ginsberg monthly advice letter is free to paid-up subscribers of the following associations . . .

Ginsberg's entry for February 2025 reads as follows:

Now that two-way portable TCs are nearly universal, and can access libraries of books, 3-D video, computer programs, you name it, it is clear that the tasks of both the Educator and the Communicator are far more stimulating then ten years ago.

One of my recent lessons with my ten-year-old daughter Julie was in art appreciation. In the standard art appreciation course the TC shows replicas of famous artists' pictures, and a computer asks the pupil to match the artist to the picture. Julie said to the computer that it would be fun to see Constable's *Haywain* as Picasso might have drawn it. The computer obliged with its interpretation, and then ten more stylized haywains appeared, together with the question, "Who might have drawn each of these?" I believe that we are the first to have prompted the TC along this road, but it may now become a standard question when the computer recognizes a child with similar learning patterns to Julie's.

Because we are a literary family, creative reading and writing have been an important part of Julie's education. Even in my own early days I found it easier to access books on the TC than my parents did to collect books from the library during their childhood. Since I have been a parent myself I have made good use of the fact that books on the TC are programmable, and when Julie was five or six I would change the names of the main character to those of our own family and Julie's friends. Now that she has advanced to the age of ten, the computer has suggested to her that she should write a fairy story. She did a first draft which the computer discussed with her. It asked questions about the characters to prompt her to add lifelike details, and suggested a list of plot ideas until Julie found one that excited her. We will probably put Julie's completed story on the public TC as her birthday present. We will pay the fee for it to go on the free section first. If sufficient people read it for free without pressing the reject button, the network will put it on paid-for access by its own judgment, and the network and Julie will then share any access fees.

It is sometimes said that today's isolated sort of teaching has robbed children of the capacity to play and interact with other children. This is nonsense. We arrange for Julie and her four-year-old brother Pharon to play with an originally undifferentiated group of children several afternoons a week; it is always their choice whether they want to spend next Wednesday in an organized team game or with less organized tomboy friends. But in work we do prefer to interact with children who are of mutual advantage to Julie and to each other.

The computer is an ace teacher, but so are people. You really learn things if you can teach them to someone else. Our computer has found a group of four including Julie with common interests, who each have expertise in some particular areas to teach the others. The four are now great friends, although they live hundreds of miles apart and have never met each other. We have chosen English-speaking companions for Julie. Our neighbor (also English-speaking) has not. Her child has an international tutorial group (Sasha from nearby Sevastopol, Hiram from Pittsburgh, Amartya from Delhi, and Toshio from Japan). My wife thinks that is "international arty" rather than good educational sense. What do you think?

The TC makes it easier to play games within the family. My parents used to play draughts, halma, then Monopoly and chess with me. They used to try and be nice to me and let me win. This condescending kindness humiliated me, and I always worked frenetically to beat my younger brother (who therefore always lost and dissolved into tears). Today Julie, Pharon and I play halma together against the graded computer, and Julie and I play it at chess. The computer knows

Pharon's standard of play at halma, and Julie's and mine at chess. Its default setting is at that level where each of us can win but only if we play at our best.

Thus Pharon sometimes wins his halma game while Julie and I are simultaneously losing our chess game, and this rightly gives Pharon a feeling of achievement. When Julie or I have lost at chess we usually ask the computer to re-run the game, stopping at our mistakes and giving a commentary. As it is a friendly computer it does a marvellous job at consoling us. Last week it told Julie that the world champion actually once made the same mistake as she had done—would she like to see that game?

I intend to devote the next three letters to the subjects I have discussed here, but retailing the best of your suggestions instead of droning on with mine. Whoa. I stopped to get a biofeedback boost after inserting that, and I have already had a reply from a mum, who has at last got her Prelim-failing thirteen-year-old daughter to show some interest in literature by asking the computer to read books to her in the accents of a pop singer about whom the daughter feels dreamy.

Future suggestions on the TC via the usual access code, please. Payment will be small, but on the following lines. For each three minutes' worth of suggestions that I use, my agent will pay normal access fee (the same as people who don't accept advertisements are paying to get this) multiplied by 2 per cent of the number of people who call up the letter. For the suggestions that I don't use, I'll push the "no payment" button, *not* the reject button. When I search for ordinary material, I often push the reject button to tell the computer that it has sent me an article written by an idiot. It then doesn't charge me, but also never sends me an article by that author again unless I specifically ask for it. Anybody who is paying to read this is by definition not an idiot, so no full reject button for you even if your immediate suggestions seem to me to be daft.

Some people are worried about the attachment of advertisements to semi-educational chatter like this. I don't see the force of these objections. If you don't want advertisements you just tell the computer that you don't want them. In that case you pay more to me. But, even as this goes out, a computer will be assessing what sorts of advertisement are particularly pertinent to the sort of people who seem to be reading it. My guess is that I will be lucky if 10,000 people round the world access into this, and that of those 10,000 about 9,500 will agree to accept advertisements (because for these 9,500 the advertisers will be paying directly to me, so I charge such readers less). This seems to be the free-market system at its best, and enables anybody who wants to try his hand at writing for the TC to do so. No danger of subliminal advertising, because the computer itself now expunges that. I wonder what hopes there might be of getting an advertiser to attach an ad to Julie's fairy story? We will all be thrilled if anyone does.

While the computer's role in children's education is mainly that of the instructor—discovering a child's learning pattern and responding to it—its main role in higher education is as a store of knowledge. Although a computer can only know what man has taught it, it has this huge advantage. No individual man lives or studies long enough to imbibe within himself all the skills and resources that are the product of the millennia of man's quest for knowledge, all the riches and details from man's inheritance of learning passed on from generation to generation. But any computer can today inherit and call up instantly any skill which exists anywhere in the form of a program.

This is why automatically updated databases are today the principal instruments of higher education and academic research. It is difficult for our generation to conceive that only forty years ago our scientists acted as tortoise-like discoverers of knowledge, confined to small and jealous cliques with random and restricted methods of communicating ideas. Down until the 1980s the world had several hundred separate cancer research organizations with no central co-ordinating database.

To some degree, students today become researchers even when they pass from Prelim Exams to sit for high-school diplomas. Most high-school telecommuters, whether aged nine or fifty-nine, spend much of their time browsing through databases and proffering ideas. At this level—and also at first and second university level—the majority of ideas are commercial ones, from students who are trying to make money and reputations that will be useful in subsequent paid employment or entre-preneurship. But higher marks in original-ideas exams are usu-ally earned by those with academic rather than commercial bent, or by those with both inclinations.

An obvious contemporary example of a successful intellec-tual is Mr. Amartya Desai, who won the 2023 Nobel Prize for Literature with his controversial work on translations.

Amartya Desai was born in India in 1984, and moved until the age of fourteen through the traditional Indian education system of the late twentieth century. By 1998 the Japanese were offering telecommuters' scholarships to students in other Asian countries who did well when gaining their local equivalent of high-school diplomas. The young Desai won one of these, and graduated from a Tokyo high-school, the University of Hawaii, and (for his second degree) the University of Southern Califor-nia, all with first class honors. He attended only the University of Hawaii in person, telecommuting from his Indian village for the other courses. He therefore earned for himself the right to fifteen years' further education and students' scholarships at educational databases in Japan and America, encashable at any time he liked. He also, during and just after his first sessions at university, made a comfortable lot of money. He was at this stage a biologist, and won entrepreneurial participation in sev-eral genetic engineering innovations.

By the age of thirty-five in 2019, he decided that he had made enough money and that he now wished to take up his schol-arships, for research into the unlikely subjects of translation and philology. Because he had had to work during his life in the different languages of Hindi, Japanese and English he be-lieved that translations (including computerized translations) often missed the true emotional contents of words. He wanted to translate into English and Hindi some of the best Japanese works that had never won acclamation outside Japan, and into English and Japanese works that had previously won acclaim only in his native Hindi.

He began these activities with "senior scholars' telecommuting status" and some elements of "special scholars' telecommuting status" won during his years as a biologist. Because most new reading and writing are now done through the TC, a computer can keep track of who reads and writes what and when. Free access to these facts is available to other senior scholars when the subject matter is primarily educational. "Senior scholar" researchers can thus trace what the great names in their field are currently reading as well as writing. It is particularly stimulating to keep track of innovative people who look as if they may be about to make great discoveries. The history of science shows that important discoveries generally come from gaining the right facts in the right order. A great discovery is often at the center of many new possible avenues of thought which no one man can follow up. Sometimes these avenues lead to even greater discoveries. The benefits of such sharing have been one of the most obvious lessons of our age, and Amartya Desai was a considerable gainer from it.

Mr. Desai also proved to be a shrewd editor of inward communications. In these days it is easy and free to invite comments on any paper one has entered into the TC, but also easy to be overwhelmed by them. All of these comments are stored. But the computer uses an author's definition of whose comments he would like to read. A wise author will not confine himself to a list of friends or established figures in his field but will seek to include others via a computerized filtering system that uses certain criteria from their scholarship records and PET scans (verified confidentially and with their permission by the computer). Mr. Desai gave himself even more scope by programming his computer to send a personalized thank-you letter to all respondents, graded from "polite brush-off" to "gosh, that's interesting." He then got the computer to catalogue the messages above "brush-off" category in order of worth for perusal by himself at future dates. He was therefore able to filter in work from Ph.D. researchers in philology who had not been heard of before.

He also welcomed comments from all correspondents who had read the three or four papers on his subject which he considered most important. In pre-computer days an assiduous author with this sort of openness could spend his whole time perusing mail. Today's system allows everyone the freedom of choice of whom to communicate with—the receiver as much as the sender. It is possible nowadays to talk to the TC, to have your message instantly transcribed, and sent to Professor Z of Stanford. If Professor Z wants to read it, he can do so a few seconds after you have finished speaking. Mr. Desai proved especially good at organizing his researches in this way. He asked TC viewers world-wide what English speakers among them understood by the word "home," and what Japanese speakers among them understood by the word *"nemawashi"* [the Japanese "root-binding" process of reaching consensus]. It became obvious that these words and emotions had always been wrongly translated into other languages. It would have been impossible to carry out research of this type in the 1980s when people had to write down every message, get it typed, put it in an envelope, take it to a post-box, and hope that the recipient got it a week later if he or she was lucky.

Mr. Desai began putting very interesting stuff on the TC very soon after his research began in 2019. By 2022 the level of entries from all over the world was so high, and the acclaim for his studies so general, that the honor of the Nobel Prize surprised no one.

In 1985, 100 per cent of American boys and girls aged fourteen were in full-time education; by 2025 only 30 per cent of them are, another 55 per cent are in paid work, and 15 per cent are enjoying themselves in leisure. In 1985, 30 per cent of work-seeking Americans aged twenty-four to sixty-five were in manufacturing or other manual employment, 3 per cent were in work connected with education, just under 60 per cent were in what the 1980s guru John Naisbitt already called "other information jobs" (government bureaucrats, private clerks and secretaries, salesmen, accountants, consultants, insurance people, bankers, newspapermen, computer programmers—all of whom were mainly engaged in passing pieces of information around), while 7 per cent were unemployed (nearly all greatly against their will).

By 2025 only 3 per cent of both American men and women in the 24–65 age group are in manufacturing jobs and 5 per cent in other mainly manual jobs. Twenty per cent are in education, mostly just as family Educators and so-called full-time students, but this total includes assessors, communicators of education material on to the TC, and academic researchers—though there is an overlap here with the very large number of commercial researchers or lookers-out for entrepreneurial opportunities who are taking some learning course at the same time. Fifteen per cent are unemployed at leisure (all of them voluntarily), and 55 per cent are still in what Naisbitt would have called information jobs. But one difference is that the information job called government has greatly declined. Another is that most information workers can live at home and telecommute if they wish. So can most educationists and those at leisure. Thus close to 90 per cent of the American workforce in 2025 can telecommute to their daily work from their family homes and the majority choose to do so.

There are others, though, who telecommute but live far from home. Consider the career of Richard O'Shaughnessy (1980–   ).

Richard O'Shaughnessy was born in New York City in 1980. His ambition to be an astronaut was formed early in life, arising as much out of his love for science fiction paperbacks and TV space operas as from any appreciation of what was actually going on in space. By the time he was old enough to take notice, space shuttle launches had ceased to be headline news—their trips into orbit had become routine.

Rick, as he preferred to be known, was born at an opportune moment. The years when American space exploration was a relatively low-key affair were those he spent at school, eventually majoring at college in physical sciences and mathematics. The only significant new space ventures begun during those years were the Space Station and then the Moonbase; this last was at that time mainly an experimental station with no significant industrial activity.

The economic importance of space travel at that time was primarily connected with the business of operating and servicing satellites—mostly communications satellites in geosynchronous orbits. When he applied for astronaut training in 2001, however, the stage was set for a gradual increase in the use of extraterrestrial space, connected mainly with privately financed ventures in the gathering of solar energy plus possibly putting polluting industries some way from Earth. Because he was a civilian trainee rather than a military astronaut Rick was free to sell his own services as he pleased.

From the autumn of 2001 until the summer of 2003 Rick worked as shuttle personnel, and his main business was concerned with the servicing of communications satellites. He was not a communications specialist, though, and had no intention of becoming one. He applied for a job in Moonbase, supervising the establishment of robot factories making small (therefore transportable) but pollutant products. After three months of medical adaptation (which would allow him to live in low gravity without suffering permanent changes in his body of a kind that would make it difficult for him to return to Earth) he moved to Moonbase.

He soon saw that the robot factories on the Moon were not going to be profitable, but he himself was happy in them. He missed space travel but he loved the landscapes of the Moon and life in the base. He married Marilla Mohr early in 2006 and lived happily with her for three years, although the couple declined to join in the slightly hazardous experiment of low-gravity child-rearing. They divorced amicably in 2009 when Rick decided that he did not want to work in an unprofitable

110

industry much longer. He was attracted by a new experimental program aimed at placing solar energy collectors in the Earth's solar orbit.

There had already been a project aimed at establishing solar energy satellites in orbit around the Earth, but this had failed. A main reason was that the geosynchronous orbit was already becoming slightly crowded because of the number of communications satellites and other devices lodged there. The satellites whose task it was to beam power down to the surface of the Earth as microwave radiation could easily be accommodated, but it was impractical to establish the vast sails of solar cells close at hand. The new project involved placing these sails in a kind of train behind the Earth, following the planet round in its orbit, and using a chain of relay satellites to bring beamed power by stages to satellites orbiting the Earth and thence to the surface. Rick O'Shaughnessy became a spaceman again, though the shuttles in which he now rode usually travelled back and forth from the Moon rather than the Earth.

In 2013 Rick decided that he wanted to move on yet again to something new. He took two months' leave, which he spent partly on the Moon and partly on Earth, looking for employment that would suit him. By this time one group of industries on the Moon was making money; not the anti-pollutant industries but those where manufacture by robots was easiest in conditions of low—or, even better, nil—gravity. Rick was a visionary about such industries. Their eventual destination, he guessed, would have to be not the Moon, but space itself: industrial colonies built at distant points in Earth's orbit. He began to look around for a job which did not yet exist—the job of founding an industrial colony at one of the Lagrange Points distributed around the Earth's solar orbit. He was offered a position as part of an expedition exploring the asteroid belt, but turned that down because it was scheduled to take six years. He believed that a Lagrange colony would be founded before 2019.

While waiting for his chance he took a temporary job at Moonbase, and resumed living with Marilla Mohr, though they did not remarry. Late in 2014 he was approached by a group of arranging producers who had a viable list of products that could most economically be produced under nil gravity in a Lagrange colony, and who knew of Rick's commitment to the idea.

Rick became the chief organizer for these people on the Moon. He reprogrammed the robots in some of the Moon's bankrupt anti-pollutant factories, and used some robots to dig up minerals from lunar mines. These lunar mines and workshops supplied most of the materials needed for the construction of the initial habitat at Lagrange Four, the chosen stable point for the establishment of the colony. Some of the payload had still to be brought up from Earth by shuttle, to be collected in orbit, but most of the structure was blasted off from the Moon by mass-driver. Rick took off for Lagrange Four with it.

For two years Rick was in space almost full-time. He returned to the weak gravity of Moonbase only occasionally, and never visited Earth. In 2018, after a routine medical check-up at Moonbase, he learned that his medical adaptation was failing, and that permanent physiological changes were affecting his system. He was told that he could easily be stabilized so that he would suffer no damage while he remained on the Moon or in space, but that if he ever wanted to return permanently to Earth he must submit to more complicated re-adaptation which might mean the end of his career in space.

For Rick there was hardly a choice to be made. Although he had never actually confronted the idea that he might never return to the planet of his birth, he did not find the prospect alarming. He decided to become a spaceman through and through, and accepted that once he was no longer able to work as efficiently as extraterrestrial employment demanded it would be to the Moon that he would retire. Perhaps, he thought, even that might not be necessary—if the work went quickly enough, and the profits began to flow soon enough, there might be a thriving colony at Lagrange Four where he could spend his last years. He committed himself fully to the task of making that happen, and this time he did not become bored or dissatisfied after the passing of a couple of years.

Rick's life would have seemed strange to many Earthbound people. He lived virtually all his adult years enclosed in walls of metal and plastic, in spaces that were often cramped. He lived always in artificial light, except when he could take a vehicle out on to the bleakly shadowed surface of the Moon. He was rarely able to see or smell living things, save for various kinds of algae and meat tissue-cultures. The air he breathed was recycled. So was the water that he drank and excreted. He was rarely hot or cold because all his environments were temperature-regulated. His clothes were always simple and plain. To the Earthbound this might appear a life without luxury; an unnatural life. Rick did not see it that way. He had his own ideas about luxury and nature, and he was living in what was for him the only really enjoyable way.

Sometimes he remembered the science fiction stories that had first set him on the road he had followed, and was amused by the difference between their concerns and his own. Sometimes he would still summon to his screens prose images of adventures on alien worlds or wars that raged across the galaxy. The dreams were still appealing, still fascinating. He valued their sense of distant imaginative horizons, and their casual dealing with the centuries that stretched into the future of mankind.

Although he will never again set foot on Earth, Rick O'Shaughnessy does not consider himself to be estranged from the world of his birth. He has a spaceman's notion of distance, and for him the Earth is always close at hand, even when it is 10 million miles away. He can always see it on a screen, as intimately as he ever wants to look at it. The TC can show him the whole earth at once, or any aspect of life there in any amount of detail. Usually, he considers it unnecessary to dwell longingly over such images, but there is a sense in which it is good to have them available.

In view of the astonishing news that came through just as

this work was being published in mid-2025 (see the final chapter), Rick O'Shaughnessy's colony on Lagrange Four may become a freshly important place. But Rick is already proud of what he is and what he has done. He is a happy man, and intends to go on being one.

9

The Third
Transport
Revolution

TELECOMMUNICATIONS ARE NOW RECOGNIZED as the third of the
three great transport revolutions that have, in swift succession,
transformed society in the past two hundred years. First were
the railways; second, the automobile; and third, telecommuni-
cations-attached-to-the-computer, which was bound to be the
most far-reaching because in telecommunications, once the infrastructure is installed, the cost of use does not depend greatly
on distance. So by the early years of the twenty-first century
brainworkers—which in rich countries already meant most
workers—no longer needed to live near their work. They could
live on the beach of Tahiti if they wanted to, and telecommute
daily to the computers and other colleagues in the New York
or London or Hamburg or Timbuctoo-tax-haven office through
which they worked.

All three revolutions were opposed by the ruling establishments of their time, and therefore emerged fastest where government was weak. All three brought great new freedoms to the common man, but the railways and motor-car manufacture temporarily made access to capital the most important source of economic power. As most men did not like being bossed about by capitalists who could become powerful because they were born stinking rich, they voted to give greater economic power to governments during the railway and motor-car ages. This was economically inefficient, and also made tyrannies more likely and more terrible. The information revolution was fortunately the exact opposite of the steam engine's industrial revolution and of Henry Ford's mass-production automobile revolution in this respect. The steam engine and mass production had made start-up costs for the individual entrepreneur larger and larger, so that in both the steam and automobile ages, to quote Bell Canada's Gordon Thompson in the early 1970s, there was "no way an ordinary citizen would walk into a modern complex factory and use its facilities to construct something useful for himself." But, as Thompson forecast, the databases of the next decades were places into which every part-time enthusiast could telecommute. In all jobs connected with the use of information, start-up costs for the individual entrepreneur in 1975–2025 have grown smaller and smaller. It was "never thus," said Thompson, "with power shovels and punch presses."

In consequence, in the TC Age the most important economic resource is no longer ownership of or access to capital, but has become the ability to use readily available knowledge intelligently and entrepreneurially. This has taken the ground from under the feet of political parties and policies based on a jealous egalitarianism. During the Capitalist Age, politicians had felt progressive when they called upon the workers of the world to unite to fight the idle rich. In the TC Age the cry "Dummies of this land unite against those brighter people" has not stirred electorates as readily as the old class battle cries. Western politicians went on trying for a long while to impose excessive government and taxes, but the bright and entrepreneurial and successful found it a simple matter to emigrate from their rule and telecommute from Bermuda. It seems incredible now that national governments wanted to block such freedom, but a look at the two previous transport revolutions shows reactions as short-sighted as those of thirty years ago.

As railways spread across early Victorian England, the first Duke of Wellington—he of Waterloo—is said to have expressed his displeasure to his peers. "My lords," he warned, "these things will enable the working classes to move about." That was very shrewd of him. The railways broke up the system whereby every yokel was so immobile that he had to be constantly subservient to the most powerful employer in his district, a system that had been nice for dukes and the very upper classes, but for nobody else. The railways also created the United States of America, and did all sorts of other unnerving things like that. The old duke and his kin would have stopped the British railway revolution if they could, but dukes were by 1830 not quite confident enough to dare to stop anything in Europe. It was only half a lifetime since tumbrils full of dukes had rolled to the guillotine in France.

By the time of the second (or automobile) transport revolution, Britain and Europe were unlucky enough already to have bossy but fairly respectable, because half-democratic, governments in place. The first two great peacetime prime ministers in Britain—the first two whom most people can now remember by name—were Disraeli and Gladstone in the 1870s. It was no coincidence that, as soon as they appeared and over-government displaced Adam Smithism, Great Britain started its decline. The first reaction of the British Parliament to the horseless carriage in the 1870s was to pass a law saying that no such carriage could appear on British roads unless a man carrying a red flag walked in front of it. One hundred years later the British Parliament attempted broadly the same policy in relation to cable television.

The horseless carriage law was repealed in the 1880s, but in those dozen years a dynamism was lost, so that economic lead-

117

ership in the automobile age passed from the then great British Empire to the then hick United States of America. The U.S. had the good fortune, in the wake of its Civil War, and in view of its vast distances, not to possess a coherent government at the time. It therefore did possess rumbustious entrepreneurs. Henry Ford opened his motor manufacturing plant in June 1903 with a capital equal to the 1975 price of a small suburban house. He sold his first car that October, and made a profit from then on. Lots of competing American automobile entrepreneurs lost money, but their competition helped put America on wheels.

The United States followed Europe by relapsing into over-big government during the automobile age, but not to quite the same extent. In the late 1870s Gladstone's supposedly left-wing Liberal government absorbed 4 per cent of Britain's gross national product in government expenditure. By the late 1970s Thatcher's supposedly right-wing Conservative government absorbed 44 per cent of it. When the information revolution began, most governments in Europe were spending around 35–45 per cent of their people's money for them. The European governments therefore over-controlled telecommunications from the start.

Telephones in much of Europe had early been put under the control of the post offices, those extraordinary public monopolies which took root even in the United States because, in the seventeenth century, England's King James I and King Charles I had wanted to censor the mail of those, like Guy Fawkes and Oliver Cromwell, who successively plotted to overthrow them. The royal monopoly on letter-carrying created by these frightened Stuart kings meant there was a colonial post office in being when the American colonies revolted 150 years later. Benjamin Franklin won kudos by re-adapting it for the infant United States, where, like so many public monopolies, it became an inefficient porkbarrel from which politicians fed those to whom they owed political debts.

When a North American invented the telephone and an Italian invented the radio, American politicians did not quite have the power to put them under post-office instead of under mar-

118

ket control. Europeans not only put telephones under the control of their post offices, but also created public-sector broadcasting in the image of the first British Broadcasting Corporation (BBC). In cultural matters the BBC first, in 1923–39, imposed on the working classes the old highly moral inhibitions of the European upper-middle classes; the BBC's original director-general, Lord Reith, sacked any staff who became divorced. After about 1960 the BBC imposed on the working classes the new sleazily immoral attitudes of the European upper-middle classes.

The switch from upper-middle-class puritanism to upper-middle-class smuttiness came with the new efficient birth-control devices. Before the birth-control pill was readily available, the upper-middle-class masters of national culture through bodies like the BBC were most afraid that their daughters might become pregnant like proletarian parlormaids. After the pill they were most afraid of not being regarded as trendy. Since most television critics in every country belonged to the upper-middle class, public service television won critics' acclaim, but no single work from this era lives on in high regard of our culture today, except Dylan Thomas's *Under Milk Wood*, a play originally written for radio by a rebellious drunk. The period from 1920 to 1990 was a cultural desert except in youthful popular music, largely because the old cultural centers of Europe put broadcasting into insufficiently competitive hands. The great post-1990 flowering of culture began first in the scattered communes of rejected artists where the airwaves were entirely free.

Despite that, by the time our history starts in 1975, the first stage of the television revolution was already having the familiar and marvellous equalizing effects of any transport revolution. Most American and European millionaires were by the 1970s spending their main leisure hours each night doing the same thing as most welfare mothers; they were sitting in the same sorts of armchairs watching exactly the same television programs. Lovely, lovely.

The second stage of the television revolution, before the real start of the move to TCs, was the switch from broadcasting to two-way narrowcasting. The history books say that the failing countries in this period were those whose government imposed tighter regulations on cable and other narrowcasting, but in fact the new technology rather quickly overwhelmed government defenses in almost every land.

Scotland, for instance, which in those supra-nationalistic times was subject to a British government based in London, was one of the potential telecommuting areas which was only temporarily held back in its dying oil age when the Labor-cum-Alliance government headed by Mr. Neil Kinnock in 1992–5 imposed some pro-public-service cable television regulations. There were good things among the Kinnock dross. One example was the local "jobline"—a very cheap publisher of all local jobs, however temporary or short-notice. People just keyed in their requests for a baby-sitter that night or for somebody to cut the lawn. Soon came "sportsline." Anybody wanting a game of football, mixed field hockey or any other team game next Saturday keyed in their availability. The computer put the teams together, using its knowledge of the players' grades, and found the nearest pitch. Another innovation was the "talkline" for the elderly; the old-age pensioner could advertise for free what were his interests and that he would like a chat, and soon various younger people were paid by the community to chat to them.

These derided do-good public-service experiments speeded the realization that cable television systems, especially when combined with computer terminals, could provide a means of publishing that was cheap, quick, easy to update, intricately indexable between people dispersed between locations, and conversational in style. But it was the introduction of commercial narrowcasting that led the way to the true twenty-first century community.

The new narrowcasters were aided by the fact that telecomputing is much easier than motor-car driving. When the motor came in, there had been the worry that people learning how to drive it would run others over; indeed if the number of automobile deaths had been foreseen, perhaps the man with the red flag would be marching still. But with the computer terminal, experimenters could sit at home playing on their keyboards by trial and non-expensive error. Soon there was astonishingly wide participation in the quite intellectual interactive treasure-hunts and other games which the commercial narrowcast channels carried. Anybody could key in their answers to world-wide quiz games that required out-of-the-way knowledge. Gradually, and more importantly, anybody could participate in the communal and transglobal research experiments on which much of innovative twenty-first-century industry was to be based.

So far in the twenty-first century Scotland has done rather better than England, just as in the late twentieth century Arizona did better than New York. Neither was anticipated fifty years ago. In 1975 much of the population of Scotland lived in or around the sad city of Glasgow, which had the worst alcoholism and some of the nastiest local-government-owned tower blocks in Europe. Population was flowing away from the beautiful highlands and islands, and it was assumed it would continue to do so.

Today most of the rich workers of Scotland live in the highlands and islands. A typical telecommuter is Mrs. Gillian Macleod who keys in figures from her terminal in Brodick on the Isle of Arran to the computer in Saudi Arabia of the insurance company for which she works.

It is extraordinary that more of our grandfathers did not see that this sort of job was the wave of the future. There were four main requirements if an area was to be a success in the Telecommuting Age. They are satisfied in places as far apart as Guam and the Gambia and Queensland and Cape Province and California and Penang, but let us take Scotland as an example.

First, as the prophet John Naisbitt said in 1982, the "languages needed for the immediate future are computer and English." Scotland spoke a variety of one of these. Second, the area had to be a nice one in which to live. Although the Gorbals never was, Scotland's highlands and islands always have been.

Third, it was important that all income earners should adapt happily to the "cafeteria of compensation" schemes that had begun to appear in the 1970s. These allowed the individual employee to decide which mix he wanted of salary, job objectives, career aims, flexitime, job sharing, long or short holidays, fringe benefits or fringe nuisances. After about 1990 the advance in computer power meant that individualization of contracts became the rage. Soon firms with 1,000 staff found that a different contract was preferred by each of the 1,000. It became recognized that any firm which signed a generalized contract with a trade union would attract few workers and would go bust. Some people in the 1980s feared that Scotland's strong trade union tradition would impede its forward path. They muddled the past with the future. In 1975–2025 labor unions have declined in all the areas which had powerful free labor unions before. Free labor unions have been popular and restrictive only in areas which previously had not enjoyed them. The economy of post-communist Russia has been impeded by this.

The fourth pre-requisite was a competitive and quickly changing telecommunications system. Scotland in 2025 is a successful country not just because the next-successor-but-five to cable television's fiber optics is running out of Mrs. Macleod's Brodick back door, but because the salesman of the next-successor-but-six to fiber optics is knocking insistently on her front door to bargain that his new system will link up better with the next-successor-but-four to the old satellite dish.

Governments at first tried to impede and regulate much of this, but an early discovery of the Telecommuting Age was that we could change the way we chose our governments. Until the 1990s we had pretended to ourselves that we could alter our lifestyles by voting on one Tuesday or Thursday every four years whether Mr. Reagan or Mr. Mondale, Mrs. Thatcher or Mr. Kinnock was putting on the tribal demonstration which at that particular moment annoyed us less. After the advent of the TC we found that the most sensible and direct way in which a free man could choose his government was by voting with his feet. The individual could go to live in any area where the government—which could from then on be a very local government—permitted the lifestyle, rules and customs that he liked.

And thus began what became known as the de-politicizing revolution.

10

The Retreat
from
Governments

IN THE 1980s only about forty of the world's 165 countries were democracies, whose statesmen supposedly obeyed their electorates' will. It might therefore be supposed that when the TC Age dawned politicians in these forty countries would be delighted that those who wanted to escape from them should set up their own forms of very local government—communes, monasteries, profit-making local governments run by private-enterprise performance contractors, beach clubs on desert isles covered by insurance policies . . . whatever people wanted. Instead, most politicians tried by every means to hamper these experiments. But free peoples went on with them all the same.

As the TC Age got into its stride, families began to choose their preferred lifestyles by watching videos of those on offer on their screens. Brainworkers, which by then meant most people, could telecommute from wherever they liked. Those doing manual or other jobs that require attendance at the workplace began early to bargain individually for longer holidays during which they could experiment with new lifestyles.

By the early 1990s the world had gotten back to 1949–73's average annual 5 per cent growth in gross world product, which meant that people could double their living standards every fourteen years. But, during this second period of fast economic growth, more and more workers chose to take their own next doubling in the form of six months' holiday a year, rather than in twice the accumulation of the same material goods. A lot of the younger people taking six months' holidays preferred to spend them in new sorts of communities, sometimes pretty odd ones.

Through most of the 1990s governments in rich countries fought against these processes of decentralization and choice, attempting by means of legislation and regulation to maintain centralized political institutions. They put forward three arguments for doing this. First, they said that diminution of the power of central governments would bring economic chaos. This was the reverse of the truth. In the 1970s and early 1980s the main election issues had been the macroeconomic policies of competing political parties; but in the 1990s much of macroeconomics was being proved to have been a mistake. Taxation systems had been retained largely in order to get the money to pay governments for doing jobs which were not needed.

The second political argument was that decentralization might blow the world up. In the gunboat era of the 1990s this was still a strong argument, but when the Centrobank scheme was started in 2006 it became much less so. International crime prevention was increasingly being most efficiently provided by performance contracts. After 2006 there was a popular outcry that the world policeman's role played by the U.S. and the CPDR during the gunboat era should be internationalized, without anybody at first being clear what that could conceivably mean. In 2025 the anti-emergency force of the United Nations—which is the nearest thing left anywhere to an army or

125

navy or airforce—is hired on a performance contract administered by Centrobank. Military expenditure now takes a tiny
fraction of the 4–5 per cent of gross world product it absorbed
in 1985. This transfer to the anti-emergency force did not take
place through any great international conference. It came because owning national armies is absurdly uneconomic.

The third argument offered by politicians for their continued
existence was the need for them to play nanny to their peoples.
The children revolted against their nannies, and the two accounts which follow are typical of the hassles that resulted.

During the 1990s the authorities in Italy, a country cursed
with a proportional-representation system of voting and therefore with a permanent muddled coalition government, took
legal action against (a) a commune which obliged its young
members, on pain of expulsion, to indulge in forced sex with
any member of the opposite sex who asked to have them on
the ration; and also sued (b) a commune which forbade homosexual practices. It was then cross when a private citizen brought
a successful penal suit against a nunnery, citing the European
Supreme Court's decision in case (b) as meaning that Orders
which forbade sexual acts outside marriage were also breaking
the law.

The man who was Italian prime minister that fortnight said
that at least everybody would agree that all these things could
not be right at the same time. The youth of his country showed
they did not agree. Since each member of each community was
merely doing her or his own thing, and since the only sanction
on anybody who disobeyed was having to leave the community,
the libertarian view was that all such prosecutions were equally
silly.

In order to restrict the worldspread of some of these sorts of
communes, governments for a period in the 1990s began to
impose emigration controls as well as immigration controls.
In 2002 a boatload of international (but largely German and
Russian) hippies was stopped by a frigate of the U.S.–CPDR
alliance, on the grounds that they were going to set up a commune on a West Indian island, and that the Federal Govern-

ment of the West Indies (a body that hardly in fact existed) did not want them there. Since the island concerned had been bought privately, this case became a *cause célèbre*, and the American and Russian governments were shocked that businessmen's opinion was on the side of the hippies.

A lot of the most entrepreneurial firms were on their way out of North America and Europe. Restrictions were imposed on these emigrations, and they didn't work. By 2000 most over-bossy central governments were trying to grapple with a blanc-mange. Since entrepreneurial people do not like to be bossed, they moved out of any over-planned economies, which were soon mocked as being residually inhabited mainly by dummies. The CPDR was having some trouble after its long Soviet sleep, as is shown by the biography of Pavel Vishinsky (1960–   ).

Pavel Vishinsky was born in Leningrad in 1960. At the age of seventeen he was employed as a laborer in the steel plant of which his father was director, but he rarely went to work there. He spent most of 1977–82 with what the Soviet authorities called a teenage hooligan gang, but it was not the sort soddening itself with alcohol. Pavel's gang played the black market, and played it efficiently because they operated within the Soviet system. The families of many of Pavel's friends could buy luxury goods at controlled prices in the shops reserved for the privilegentsia. Some of them sold these goods, at much higher prices, to the gang who in turn resold them, at a reasonable profit, to ordinary Soviet people who could otherwise buy luxury goods only if they queued in the ordinary shops for hours.

At the beginning of Andropov's drive against absenteeism in 1983 Pavel sometimes had to turn up at his father's steel plant, but this inconvenience did not last for long. His father saw to it that he drew the wage and ration book of a heavy steel worker whether he attended the plant or not.

In the late 1980s Pavel extended his black-market ventures to other towns, after finding out in each place which goods made for the longest queues. By now he was advising the directors of state warehouses how they could direct unofficial

127

supplies so as to make most money for themselves. Such co-operation meant he no longer had to pay bribes to get trucks to carry the goods he wanted; instead, he was himself paid for carrying them. When the pre-Berisov government dashed for economic freedom in 1991, Pavel was probably the richest thirty-one-year-old non-Georgian and non-Armenian businessman in the new Confederation of People's Democratic Republics.

The Berisov government hoped that businessmen such as Pavel would invest in the huge ex-Soviet factories which they tried to privatize. Pavel Vishinsky kept well clear of that. "Our very large factories will continue to lose money," he said, "mainly because they are too large. They will also have to allow free trade unions, and this will make them lose more money still." This shrewd prophecy pin-pointed a main reason why the CPDR did not achieve a West German Adenauer-style economic miracle, even though most of its states removed most economic controls.

Vishinsky said that the sensible course for a businessman in the new Russia was to "identify opportunities." On the production side, he minuted to his top colleagues at the beginning of 1991: "The old Soviet Union nominally spent 17 per cent of its GNP on the military, but actually used far more than 17 per cent of its best labor and other resources there. This will now gradually come down to perhaps 1 per cent, so money can be made by anybody who gives our able defense industry engineers and scientists the opportunity to do part time entrepreneurial civil work as the defense program shudders down."

Vishinsky put a computer terminal in front of many of the best engineers and scientists previously working in defense. He undertook to market for them the software programs they wrote to enable robots to make new innovative goods that were partly spin-offs from the old Soviet defense and space efforts. These programs and products became one of the CPDR's main high-tech exports.

On the distribution side, Vishinsky argued that, "Nobody in Russia has the slightest idea of how to sell consumer goods, because Russian consumers have never previously had free choice." He therefore imported Western-style public opinion polls and other market-research techniques, and became the acknowledged expert in advising both foreign exporters and Russian producers on market trends throughout the CPDR. "This is easier in practice, though not in conception," he said, "than my old system of measuring the length of queues in Soviet days."

Vishinsky's third insight was to recognize that the new Russia would need what he called "services to help our entrepreneurs in their nursery." For example, agriculture was bound to be returned from the state farms to the peasants. The peasants would need new credit services, but these could not be based on taking away land from mortgage defaulters because the political situation would not allow that. The peasants needed new marketing services, new opportunities temporarily to hire farm equipment at harvest time, various sorts of crop management consultancy through the TC. Vishinsky moved in with all these services at a profit. They provided him with a sound base to sell similar services to poor countries after the Centrobank system started in 2006.

Today he is the richest man in the CPDR, and yet there is not a single large factory that bears his name. He calls his business empire a "confederation of entrepreneurs, providing a mixture of banking and financial supermarket services, management consultancy and marketing know-how—a mixture which the Wall Street houses would be selling too if they were lucky enough to have started from scratch like us."

Vishinsky does not live an abstemious life. He is gregarious and frequently drunk. He gives no money to charity, but is regarded as a great patron of the arts, partly because he has learned to make money out of them. He sponsors communes where the world's greatest artists are free to do their own thing, but he also has a large investment in TC agencies and video recording companies operating out of the communes. He deserves to be called the most successful impresario of the new cultural revolution because he was the earliest to see two features of what was to come.

129

He recognized that the computer would make possible a flood of new artistic insights because of its ability to codify what people felt as they heard or looked at particular things, and also to think the previously unthought. Artists are often lonely people with intense emotions, and it has always been impossible to persuade them to produce things by rote. This is a main reason why the rich, pre-computer mass-market publishing and mass production age of 1890–1990 was a sad cultural desert.

After 1990 Vishinsky used his public-opinion-sampling skills to ask people, "What do you feel when you hear and see what comes next on your TC? Press the R (response) button when the word most nearly encapsulating your feelings appears on the screen." He then made videos analyzing these researches for viewing by the artists in his communes and by wider TC audiences who then telecommuted their own artistic efforts to his samplers. These samplers could invite those whom the computer said were most interesting to come to live in a commune.

Many outsiders said artists would resent the codification of their customers' emotions. Instead, a general reaction was: "Ah, I feel as this segment of people does when hearing or seeing or experiencing something, but I know how to make that particular feeling more intense for myself and therefore presumably also for that segment of the public." This is how the narrowcasting revolution in the arts began.

Vishinsky wrote in a 2000 memo to this section of his staff:

The great artistic innovation in the fifty years before I was born was the ability to record movement and sound. When new forms of technical possibilities for art appeared in the fifteenth century, European art underwent a renaissance. Three hundred years later new types of musical instruments made it possible to move music out of aristocratic salons into concert halls, and the great symphony composers such as Beethoven emerged. Two hundred years later we have gotten this ability to record movement and sound, but why have our movement-age Michelangelos and Beethovens not appeared? Because the old artists had to satisfy small aristo-cratic cliques in Florence and Weimar who had known and refined tastes. Today, although we have these new tech-niques—although it should be possible to hang wonderful moving pictures on our walls, and create new experiences in sight and sound—we have no means of knowing what the audience wants. By techniques of opinion sampling we can discover this, and by techniques of narrowcasting we can deliver it. When a Michelangelo among mobile artists ap-pears, and one will, the first showing of one of his works should be telecommuted simultaneously to the art screens of 10,000 patrons world-wide. They will be giving prestigious dinner parties as they await the moment the screen flashes light. I intend to become a rich pioneer in commissioning and distributing such works.

He is not yet Pavel the Magnificent, but he is Pavel the Rich, and he is helping to set some spirits free.

More libertarian candidates—or depoliticizing politicians—began to appear in North American and European elections after 2000. One of the most widely commissioned news analysts on international TC commented on the eve of the American presidential election in November 2004:

If this third Kennedy (but first female one) to be a candidate wins tomorrow's presidential election, it will mean there has been a large poll in favor of the proposition that few people need bother to vote in future. Analysts say that Ms. Kennedy can win only if 60 per cent of the electorate bothers to punch out their choice on their TCs, versus polls of under 50 per cent at every other American presidential election since 1984. But if she wins two terms on her policy of permitting more decentralization, polls at future presidential elections may be down near 20 per cent—and a good thing too.

Ms. Kennedy's family tradition is on the left of the political spectrum, yet the program of minimalist government for which she stands would have been regarded as right-wing twenty years ago. It no longer is. The principal urge of modern progressives is to fight against government bureaucrats and their constituents, who are trying to keep the country stuck in a pattern of over-government more suited to the pre-telecommunications age. A main part of the battle against bureaucracy is being waged by minority groups, who want control of their own social and cultural institutions. If Ms. Kennedy becomes president it will be a sign that a maverick group of former social welfare recipients has joined with the entrepreneurial class in a new political coalition. . . .

Ms. Kennedy won by a landslide. Most social analysts since then have said it was a good thing that she did. She ushered in an age of acceptance of genuine pluralism. It is probable that the Americans had to do this first. Many people were uncomfortable about the way the U.S. might go after the gunboat age. Under Ms. Kennedy it chose, probably irreversibly, to opt for Centrobank, internationalism, small central government and free dispersal into small communities where everybody could do her or his own thing. Some of the compulsory referendum communes (which enforce some actions that are forbidden almost everywhere else) concentrate on doing things that seem to the rest of us to be very odd, but their members can freely emigrate to do them far away from the rest of us. This has rebuilt social tolerance and trust, which were substantially lost in the 1960s.

Although the TC and consequent telecommuting were the main reasons for the decline in importance of governments, historians agree that there are four other explanations of why by the end of the twentieth century the time for the revolt against governments had come. They were:

1 People had started to realize that 1980s-style representative democracy really meant public-sector imperialism.

2 By 1995 productivity in many government spending departments had disappeared.

3 The computer revolution was beginning to make small entrepreneurial organizations the most successful ventures in

the information industries; and information industries are what most governments had become by the 1980s.

4 Traditionally, the prestige of government had rested partly on mystery, but TV cameras and modern psychoanalysis had stripped that away.

Consider each of these four reasons in detail.

1 *Bureaucracy Is Not Democracy* Until the 1970s the advance to voting democracy had been advertised as bringing to culmination the process by which power had passed from priests to kings to nobles to capitalists to, finally, us the voting people. Instead it became clear during that decade that power had passed even in the English-speaking world to what the contemporary Russian writer Solzhenitsyn called the "political and official bureaucrats." These two groups in these last years of over-government were spending a higher proportion of GNP than ever did the priests, kings, nobles and capitalists during their own peak periods of power, and spending it with less sense of *noblesse oblige* than did the old feudal, squirearchical or capitalist groups in their tame later years. (Call up the Watergate Tapes of 1972–3 on your TC if you do not understand this.)

This was not mainly because the presidents, congressional staffs (of which there were far too many), local government bosses, labor union officials, civil servants, and other political or official bureaucrats whom we elected, appointed or got stuck with were less virtuous than were the supposedly saintly medieval bishops, crusading kings, nobles created out of chivalry, or philanthropic industrialists like Andrew Carnegie who had too much power over our fathers before us. It was because all morality eventually becomes defined as being directed towards the survival of the agent's own group. The reason why we must never allow particular groups to have too much spending power in their hands is that they are certain eventually to have a main and loyal objective of keeping their own bureaucracies growing, because each decision-taker within the system finds that feeding the machine will give him personally a quieter life among those with whom he has to work every day.

133

During the 1970s it therefore became clear that public-sector imperialism was not going to be curbed by electing politicians who promised to curb it. Mr. Jimmy Carter was elected as President of the United States in 1976 on a promise to run against Washington from inside Washington. This was always absurd since "they" cannot be elected to run against "them." You cannot elect a monk to dissolve the monasteries. So the American people turned next to Mr. Ronald Reagan who said (with total sincerity) that he stood for much smaller government than Mr. Carter did. But Mr. Reagan had already served (with equal sincerity) as two-term governor of California. His rule there had left the people of California in desperate need of voting directly for a reduction in their taxes through the referendum known as Proposition 13. His first presidential term ended in 1984 with his administration preparing to put taxes further up.

2 *Public Productivity Declines* The concentration of spending power in the hands of bureaucrats had been sanctified by the presupposition that there were lots of services that could more efficiently be provided by state monopoly than by the market. But in the last third of the twentieth century it became evident that this was no longer true. Even the traditional four basic public services of previous centuries (justice, police, arms, and some modicum of public administration) showed a steep decline in productivity—sometimes greater than 70 per cent—during the period 1965–85; productivity per man in most free-market industries had more than doubled in the same period. For instance, rich countries' manpower in crime prevention rose 30 per cent in 1960–90; but crime rates, instead of falling, quintupled. Their local government staffs in the same period rose by 97 per cent, but the time taken to process citizens' planning requests, instead of halving, tripled. U.S. defense expenditure in 1960–80 rose by 40 per cent, but the index of U.S. ability to enforce respect and peace declined.

This had happened while technological progress (new psychiatric insights for justice, the information-processing revolutions for the police and public administrators, the extraordinary increase in killing power per dollar spent) should have made it especially easy for advanced countries to have enjoyed more effective crime prevention, cheaper public administration and simpler national defense. But there really is no way of saying that crime rates in 1960–90 anywhere did anything but soar in response to the employment of more police, to longer hours in court, to new prison regimes; that the doubling of local government administration staff anywhere led to greater expedition in the handling of citizens' business, instead of typically taking much longer; that gunboat diplomacy was made more terribly swift and sure as the highest technology country in the world spent so much of its treasure, young lives and social cohesion on losing a war to slightly ridiculous North Vietnam and then had its diplomats imprisoned by a thirteenth-century Iranian monk.

Despite this breakdown in traditional public-sector production, the politicians and bureaucrats assumed in the period just after 1965 that extra spending by them would be a good agency for managing many other services, especially health, education and welfare (amalgamated in the U.S. in the HEW Department) and housing and urban development (amalgamated in the U.S. in the HUD Department). During the peak period of expansion of HEW, health costs rocketed, educational test scores dived, and the welfare system crippled instead of aided its clients. During the peak period of expansion of HUD, the inner centers of American cities became terrible places in which to live.

The breakdown of public-sector productivity did not come about because less efficient or less educated people were coming into public service jobs. One of the troubles was precisely that a new class of more educated, articulate and ambitious people had come into them—but were working in an environment where cost-effective methods of production could not be achieved, for two reasons. The first of these was the swift change in technology. By 1970 the decision-maker in any efficient productive system had restlessly to ask: "What is the best quickly-changing and labor-saving technology that I should use to accomplish this task?'' In a state bureaucracy, decision-making power falls into the hands of people who can explain most suavely that anybody who keeps asking that question is being a bad colleague by constantly rocking the boat. In some big business corporations, with layer of management sitting upon layer, decision-blocking power fell into the hands of similar middle bureaucracies. These firms went bust or were taken over by more innovative concerns. But state bureaucracies are not allowed to be improved by death, and therefore continued expanding even in departments where productivity per man had disappeared.

The second reason for the accelerating crisis in bureaucratic production was that each consumer was not being allowed to make his own quantitative choices. In the private sector, a housewife buying food is given the choice: how much food do you want, knowing that this is what you will have to pay if you choose that food from the supermarket? In the 1980s human beings began to see that they would not be free until they were allowed, in the smallest possible groups, to answer the question: how much government do you want, having been told that this is what you will have to pay if you are going to choose government of such and such a quantity and quality (with the quality preferably defined in terms of performance contracts— that is, tax payments are reduced if, by objective tests, performance in the so-called public services does not reach a certain standard)? In the years up to the 1990s there was a conspiracy among politicians and bureaucrats to pretend that human beings could not have this choice in governments, but for a large number of public services in the data-processing age they soon could if they wanted.

3 *The Need to Experiment*   Most old-time government services were really part of the information industry, and by the 1970s this industry was caught up in a revolution far bigger than the industrial revolution which followed James Watt's discovery of the steam engine. Anybody who believed that after this information revolution a voter-employed bureaucracy could con-

tinue to be the main instrument of government was being as daft as anybody who forecast in 1816 that the number of hand-loom weavers would continue to grow and grow.

A startling feature of the information revolution was that successful new producers in it were generally small and always entrepreneurial. Most information businesses even in the 1970s could be set up with a typewriter and a telephone; by the 1990s they needed a TC, but the majority of homes in the rich countries already had that. As John Naisbitt pointed out in the 1980s, many information businesses in the Computer Age were rather like composers of music, and composers of music even in the 1970s were generally entrepreneurs themselves.

Take the biggest public sector industry in rich countries in the 1970s, which was education. In the 1977 elections for the local government of London, only 2 per cent voted for Oliver Stutchbury, who resigned as an ex-Labour alderman from the Greater London Council and ran on a campaign (long preceding Mrs. Thatcher's) to abolish the Council, wisely declaring:

> Nobody knows what the best way of educating the young is. There are no economies of scale or other arguments which can be validly made for requiring children all over England and Wales to conform to the same pattern. What is emphatically not needed is a central policy. What is needed is the maximum variety of different schools and institutions of learning.

Education ministers must have been living in Toytown when they thought in the 1970s that they could continue to give monopolies to whatever sorts of teacher-dominated labor unions and similar institutions fitted their political party's social prejudices best.

By 1985 Mr. Stutchbury's argument was already even more true of most of the other basic public services. Nobody at that time knew even approximately what was the best way of bringing aid to the handicapped, curing or deterring criminals, operating personal social services, or doing the real jobs of town clerks. There were no economies of scale or other arguments

137

which could be validly made for requiring people all over any country or province to conform to the same patterns. What was emphatically not needed was a central policy. What was needed was the maximum variety of different output-oriented initiatives, checked for results all the time, changing as the available technological opportunities changed. That is what has become available to quite small groups of people during the information revolution.

During the 1990s communities sprang up which offered lifestyles based on making intelligent choices of output-oriented "public services" from among the changing varieties on offer. When the central governments said, "You must not run your efficient services but must use our failing ones," civilized people moved outside the jurisdiction of these central governments either to commercially developed communities or else to participatory communes of a sort they liked. In the decaying cities run by old-style voter-appointed local governments, tax bases eroded, tax rates rose, services declined, dissatisfaction grew.

By early in the twenty-first century new forms of ballot-box democracy were emerging even in these decaying old cities. New entrepreneurial and profit-making groups stood at the polls. While the old Republican and Democrat, or Conservative and Social Democrat, political parties clung religiously to their traditional rhetoric, the entrepreneurs advertised that they were in pursuit of profit-making performance contracts. "We will impose property taxes at 10 per cent below present politically-set levels and make a profit from them, and will contract to cut taxes further below that level if crime rates, waiting time for transport, named environmental unpleasantnesses do not fall this year by 5 per cent." The entrepreneurial parties did not instantly sweep the polls in the decaying old cities, partly because so much of the electorate in these places now consisted of people employed by the local government or drawing welfare from it (which was one reason why the cities were going bust); partly because no sensible area goes in a prompt landslide from any particular system to an entirely new one; and partly because the existing political establishment kept voting systems in being which split the opponents' vote. In those cities where local government was most inefficient there were by the early twenty-first century usually not just one entrepreneurial party competing for your vote, but several, all eager for the prize of a performance contract which previous inefficiency had made so tempting. In many cities and states a promise to perform 30 per cent better than the old city council was absurdly easy to fulfil, so great numbers of performance contractors competed at the polls.

This splitting of the vote between competing contractors continued for a time to let coalitions of the old inefficient parties in. But after the year 2010 the entrepreneurial parties started to win local elections in remaining big cities more usually than not. One turning point was when Los Angeles elected to be administered by a Japanese multinational corporation, which offered a particularly daring performance contract. It said that it would return 30 per cent of all local taxes if in the next four years its telescanning devices did not at least halve all street crime. It succeeded in cutting it by 75 per cent.

4 *Politicians Are Discredited* In Japan in the 1960s public opinion polls showed that under 2 per cent of the population believed the promises of conservative politicians, which was smaller than the proportion who believed the promises of professional fortune-tellers. Yet the Japanese continued to elect conservative governments for another thirty years—probably wisely since they brought Japan the fastest advance in economic history, mainly by keeping out of businessmen's way.

This unpopularity of politicians had not been anticipated at the beginning of the telecommunications age. In the early radio days Roosevelt, Hitler and Churchill attracted adulation within their nations because they were effective broadcasters. Two of these men rendered great service to mankind by protecting it from the ambitions of the third, but there seemed ground for fear that broadcast telecommunication would bring in the age of the demagogue.

This fear underestimated the significance of the change from radio to television. If Hitler's speeches had been seen on the screen, more of his people would have seen he was obviously crazy. (Call up the old films of Hitler on your TC now, and apply the competitive psychiatric tests taught today in even a toddler's psychoanalyzing lessons.)

Depoliticization started in the 1980s partly because this was the tail end of the Broadcast-Television Age. It is difficult for us to understand that in the three decades from 1960 to 1990 three-quarters of the adult population in the rich countries were every night watching the same pictures of the same leaders going through the same public relations ploys. It is reckoned that in 1984 the average American saw President Reagan 200 times on his television screen, usually in news reels. In 2025, in this Narrowcasting Age, with so many better things to do, not one American in five recognizes President Taft when he meets her in the streets.

But during that era of only three or four channels per living room leading politicians had no private lives. They therefore turned, more than ever, to have neurotic public ones. In the 1970s the heads of government of the two biggest capitalist countries who won the largest electoral victories (Mr. Nixon of the U.S. and Mr. Tanaka of Japan) had both committed felonies which could have sent them to prison. So had Mr. Nixon's vice-president. The head of the British political party who won the biggest personal swing to himself during a television election in the 1970s (especially among women, who found his television personality calm and manly) was later put on trial but acquitted for alleged incitement to murder a homosexual who said he was his partner.

These were among the politicians who were arraigned. But a gossipy press simultaneously made it clear that earlier Presidents Johnson and Kennedy had also done things while in the world's most important secular job which (if their cover-ups had not been so clever) would have peremptorily disgraced them out of public life. During the 1970s every journalist knew that at least one major head of government had a debilitating nervous breakdown, but it was not regarded as decent to say this even though while sick he could have started a nuclear war. In earlier decades of the twentieth century enormous decisions had been taken by democratically elected men now known to have been incapacitated by illness at the time. Woodrow Wilson in 1920; Roosevelt at Yalta; Churchill in the middle of his last 1951–5 premiership; Eden, who had a terrible tummyache when he invaded Suez in 1956. Lloyd George, Harding and Kennedy were among the many who won most of the public morality vote in their time, although every tickled insider knew they were randy goats. In the poorest countries the situation was far worse. By the beginning of the 1980s a large number of poor countries had dictators who would be psychoanalyzed by any PET scanner today as medically unstable men, who might conceivably blow up the planet.

All through history until this century leaders and princes and kings of nations contained a large proportion of megalomaniacs. We now know that this was a likely hazard or even requirement of the job. Program into your computer the weekly decisions and strains imposed in 1985 on a president of the United States or of *coup d'état*–infested Uganda (these should be tabulated in any history database). Key the computer to a psychoanalytical mode, and it will almost certainly tell you that a normal man under these strains would likely experience many of the grades of megalomania. For the president of the United States in 1985 the probable diagnosis will be only incipient megalomania. For almost any president of Uganda in the years 1950–2005 the probability was one of much more serious illness.

For the first fifty or so millennia of his existence *Homo sapiens* tolerated this megalomania among his tribal leaders. He was led off by strutters on white horses to die in countless wars as a result. When the wars were over, both the conquerors and the conquered wrote in their history books that this sacrifice of brave young men had been glamorous. The history books were written by the survivors.

The nuclear bomb on Hiroshima in 1945 should have seared the message into reasoning men that this toleration of megalomania had to stop. Nuclear warfare robbed man of his margin for error and for a second chance. Once man knew how to make nuclear bombs it was essential (a) to begin to be able to psychoanalyze and depose those who might drop such bombs; (b) to have some sort of international token force to depose megalomaniac tyrants in undemocratic countries; and (c) to reduce the powers of government leaders even in rich countries, so that strain and self-importance among them both declined.

For the first four post-Hiroshima decades, all three of these things seemed to be going the wrong way. Daily exposure to television seemed likely to increase mental imbalance in political leaders. More and more insane tyrants gained control of poor countries, and anybody who criticized this was called "colonialist." The buying power of governments in both rich and poor countries soared; in 1985 the U.S. administration's expenditure was over 36 per cent of GNP, versus 9 per cent in 1929, but it was difficult to say that governments anywhere were spending their money well.

In the succeeding forty years, mankind was saved because all three of these tides turned. The Borovsky Letter helped abolish war. Centrobank helped diminish poverty. And scientific advances helped cheaply to reduce pestilence, drug-taking, famine, and crime.

11

Health
Is
Delivered

IN STEP WITH THE ADVANCE of the TC, the second big technological breakthrough of 1975–2025 has been the biological revolution. In 1975, medical knowledge was everywhere advancing, but three hurdles lay in the way. First, most countries had the wrong incentives built into their systems for delivery of health care. Second, most countries had entrenched bureaucracies which delayed instead of expedited the marvellous new opportunities for relieving sickness and pain. Third, drug companies were encouraged to act as monopolies protecting the things they had patented yesterday, instead of using open worldwide telecommuters' research to find new things for tomorrow.

These hurdles were eventually jumped when new market systems became available that made it profitable to spread efficiency-seeking multinational health-maintenance organizations (of a new kind); when the process of opening up bureaucracies to competition after 1990 meant that those who speeded safety checks on new inventions were rewarded rather than those who delayed them; and when the advance of genetic engineering brought new competition with the drug companies. The booming-then-busting genetic engineering companies themselves soon became ossified protectionist institutions, but by then a new entrepreneurialism had entered into therapy.

As these changes occurred in time to catch and spur the biological revolution, millions of people were saved from unnecessary sickness and premature death. Before then, a few statistics will show how muddled and obstructive many incentive systems had become as a result of both right-wing and left-wing distortions during the last years of world over-government. The United States in the mid-1980s spent $1,500 per head a year on health care. Britain spent $375 per head. Singapore spent $200 per head. All three countries by then had the same life expectancy, with Singapore's increasing fastest. Almost incredibly, Singapore already by the mid 1980s had the lowest infant mortality of the three. Britain had the highest sickness rate of the three, or at least the largest number of workdays lost through workers saying they were ill. Britons also had the longest waiting time before they could get into their rather old hospitals, with suffering people sometimes waiting for years before they could get hips replaced or hernias mended or varicose veins dealt with, which meant they stayed sick a long time in great pain.

America's commercial medical system was by far the most wasteful. Until the 1960s it was also very unfair to the poor. In 1960 the children of the richest one-quarter of Americans saw a doctor about twice as frequently as the children of the poorest one-quarter, and infant mortality among black American babies was three times the whites' rate. In 1960–82 America carried through a genuine egalitarian revolution in the provision of medical care. Those were the years when America's per capita expenditure on health rose from $146 a year to $1,365. By the early 1980s poor Americans were seeing a doctor slightly more frequently than rich Americans, and the rates of surgery had equalized between social classes. Unfortunately, in the process, America's costs of health care had soared out of control. The reason was that America operated its health care under what was called "third-party insurance" plus "fee for service."

By the early 1980s over 90 per cent of the $1 million which was spent in American hospitals every three minutes was paid for by third parties—still usually private insurance (although two-thirds of the premiums were by then paid by employers) with most of the other bills borne by state Medicare for the old and state Medicaid for the poor. Patients in American hospitals therefore soon had an incentive to demand to be treated in the most lavish possible way, since somebody else was paying. American hospitals and doctors also had an incentive to give the most lavish treatment, because they made more money if they did. They might make ten times as much money if they carried out $500 worth of tests which had a 97 per cent chance of diagnosing what was wrong with you, rather than $50 worth of tests which had a 96 per cent chance. Indeed, if a doctor carried out only the $50 worth of tests he was liable to be personally bankrupted through a malpractice suit in the one out of a hundred cases where opting for the $500 would have been right. If you lay dying in a coma in an American hospital in those days, you sometimes had $20,000 worth of medical care pumped into you in your last two weeks. You were not going to wake up to complain; the insurance company paid; the hospital made a profit on the $20,000—and, to be fair, used some of that profit for good works.

Britain's hospitals did not perform extravagant nonsenses like that, but they had gone the other way. In 1948 Britain established the first comprehensive National Health Service in the western world, where everybody was promised he would have the best possible medical care, regardless of cost or ability to pay. In 1949 Britain replaced this by something completely different.

As the NHS had cost 50 per cent more in its first year than

the Health Minister, Bevan, had forecast, the Chancellor of the Exchequer, Cripps, announced the new system in his 1949 budget. He said he would allocate a sum (initially £400 million a year), and then Britons could have the best health care which could be afforded within that figure. For the next forty years British health care was determined by this extraordinary formula. Its quantity was not decided by what customers were demanding, nor by what swiftly changing technology made available, but by how some politician called the chancellor of the exchequer felt on budget day. When it was a Conservative chancellor, he generally felt stingy. When it was a Labour chancellor, he wanted to be more generous; but in practice he was usually caught in an even worse balance-of-payments crisis, so he had to be stingier still. The National Health Service therefore became a method of giving Britain an undersupply of medical care, but then encouraging overdemand for it because there was only minimal charging at the point of sale. The undersupply was therefore rationed by queueing instead of by price.

No competition or advertising as between hospitals was allowed in Britain's socialist medical system. The patient was not told what was the crude curing or killing rate of the hospital or surgeon or other doctor to whom he was virtually assigned. The lack of competition meant hospitals had no experience of what was the most efficient method of staffing or of reducing costs. In the early 1980s British hospitals had far more ancillary workers (porters, cleaning and catering staff) per case treated than hospitals in other countries. As these surplus armies of people were employed within tight budgets, they were underpaid. As they had a monopoly employer (the National Health Service), but were underpaid, they became militant trade unionists. To the horror of Britons and the rest of the world, National Health Service employees started causing great pain to suffering and sick people by some inexcusable strikes.

By the 1980s angry critics said that in socialist medicine countries like Britain, dying patients were wheeled off long waiting lists past pickets of striking porters into under-equipped but over-manned hospitals whose record of infecting rather

146

than curing people was kept a state secret; while in fee-for-service countries, like America, healthy people were whisked into glossy theaters to have dangerous, unnecessary and expensive operations for heart conditions that in socialist medicine countries were treated more comfortably and effectively by sitting at home imbibing drugs, which cautious regulatory bodies like the U.S. Food and Drug Administration had banned.

In 1985–93, almost ludicrously, the two medical systems of America and Britain moved part-way back to adopting the other's mistakes. The supposedly free-market Reagan administration in America reacted against America's runaway health costs by imposing some complicated price controls called DRGs. These made treating poor people for certain surgical operations relatively uneconomic in American hospitals, so the British system (of waiting in long queues, in very great pain) began also in the United States. Meanwhile in Britain the right-wing Thatcher government thought that competition with the NHS should be stimulated by tax concessions for private health insurance. It introduced these without observing from American experience that third-party health insurance plus fee-for-service sent private health costs through the roof. The result after 1985 was a large accession of loss-making business to British private health insurers who therefore started to go bust. The first Kinnock government's Chancellor of the Exchequer, called Hattersley, had said he was a socialist mainly because he opposed private health insurance; he spent much of his chancellorship in the early 1990s pouring out taxpayers' money in order to bail private health insurers out.

It was quite usual in most of the latter part of the twentieth century for politicians to have to reverse course in that way. The service that an ordinary person requires of a health delivery system is to keep him healthy. The incentive given by fee-for-service systems like America's in the twentieth century was, "Treat this patient in the most expensive possible way after he has become ill." The incentive given in socialist medicine systems like Britain's was, "Keep my hospital filled with people who are not really ill because they will be less bother than

147

people requiring a lot of treatment." The incentive for a British doctor under socialist medicine was, "Have mainly fit people on my capitation fee list, and then I will have more time to go out and play golf." Most British doctors were saints enough to resist this.

In France and West Germany the health insurance systems had been started by rather egalitarian social democrats. By the 1980s these had become systems for grossly enriching doctors from the proceeds of huge employers' national insurance contributions (which meant from the most unemployment-creating sort of tax). Under their state-bargained fee-for-service systems, doctors in France and West Germany by the late 1970s got seven times the average industrial worker's wage. The American doctor, under his semi-competitive but still fee-for-service system, got five-and-a-half times it. The British doctor, oppressed by chancellors of the exchequer, got two-and-a-half times it. This cost control should have redounded to the credit of the British system; but it had actually gone too far. A fifth of newly trained British doctors were then emigrating to make more money abroad. They were replaced by doctors from India and Pakistan and Nigeria who had been expensively trained in their own poor countries and were desperately needed there. They were less useful in inner-city Liverpool, where many of their patients could not understand what they said.

The best record for any rich country's health delivery system in the 1970s and 1980s was in Japan. In 1949 the life expectancy of the Japanese had been less than fifty-five years. Thirty years later it was up above top Scandinavian rates of seventy-eight for a woman, a bit less for a man, in the most exciting sudden surge in health standards in all the history of the world.

The Japanese medical system was employer-dominated. If you were a worker in a big company you and your family joined its medical system, and the instruction from the employer to the company hospital was, "Keep my workers healthy." This system included many and regular health checkups, and preventive measures like the wearing of face masks by those with the so-called "common cold" that was an affliction of those days. It also involved some minor wastefulness. Doctors were allowed to make profits from selling drugs, and the blood-stream of the hypochondriac Japanese people became as filled with unnecessary drugs as Manhattan's East River then was with pollutants. But the Japanese big-company health delivery system was dramatically more cost-effective than the parallel health schemes run by the Japanese government and private health insurers. Commissions from abroad and within Japan kept examining why. The reason, some of them rightly reported, was that these health delivery systems in Japan worked much as health maintenance organizations had been meant to work when they were first introduced in California in the 1960s.

In 1985 HMOs had enrolled only 4 per cent of the population of the United States, and enthusiasts were disappointed at their slow growth. An HMO required a fixed fee from each member per year, and then promised to provide all the medical care he needed. In the early 1980s Americans who were enrolled in HMOs went to hospital between 25 and 40 per cent less frequently than Americans enrolled in other insurance schemes. The HMO would examine you, and had an incentive to say if hospitalization was not necessary. As the health record of HMO members was as good as the health record of those in other insurance schemes, it looked as if other Americans were being sent to hospital far too much. HMOs did not flourish in the 1970s and most of the 1980s. They were opposed from both right wing and left wing. From the right wing an HMO doctor was apt to be called a socialist or communist by fee-for-service physicians, and ostracized at the country club. From the left wing the system was attacked as substandard doctoring because HMOs tried to reduce costs.

In 1992 the U.S. Congress adopted a variant of the scheme which Professor Alain Enthoven of Stanford University had advocated in his book called *Health Plan* twelve years before. Enthoven's scheme was that, "Once a year, each family (or individual) would have the opportunity to enroll for the coming year in any of the qualified health plans operating in its area. The amount of financial help each family gets towards the

149

purchase of its health plan membership—from Medicare, Medicaid, employer, or tax laws—would be the same whichever plan it chooses. The subsidy might be more for poor than for non-poor, for families than for individuals, but not more for people who choose more costly health plans. The family that chooses a more costly health plan would pay the extra cost itself." Enthoven thought this scheme would lead to massive enrollment in competitive HMOs as the consumers' best buy. He proved right. HMOs were a fast spreading form of delivery of health care in the rich countries well before the Centrobank scheme in 2006 so successfully spread them to the Third World. Their growth in the Third World produced a new sort of HMO. In America until 2006 HMOs had been employed under a contract, "Try to keep me well"; after 2006 they started to be paid more if they did.

Today most people in all countries, both in cities and scattered communities, rely on one or other sort of HMO contract for most of their health care, though individuals often combine them with other insurance or fee-for-service systems. It was in 1990–2010 that we moved from systems with built-in cost-increasing incentives to systems with built-in incentives for producer competition, consumer choice and cost control. It happened that America was removing the second hurdle out of the way of sensible health care at the same time.

The second hurdle had been set by bureaucracy. America in the 1970s caught the regulatory disease. By 1979 there were 77,497 pages in the Federal Register detailing the health and safety regulations that must be obeyed by all Americans, though nobody could ever have time to read even half of them. They included regulations which obliged a geologist to install a stretcher at his one-man mine, and rules which said that pills for arthritis could be sold only in childproof containers which those with arthritic hands could not conceivably open. But the sternest rules from the Food and Drug Administration (FDA) in the wasted 1970s were those blocking the introduction of new drugs and medical devices.

In the second half of the 1970s tens of thousands of pages of data had to be supplied to the FDA before a new drug was approved. Nobody could possibly read such lengthy reports, but this vetting process made the introduction of many new drugs uneconomic. During the 1960s American wonder-drugs had been appearing in profusion. We now know from our computer analyses of history that millions of people died unnecessarily because the period of over-regulation by the FDA temporarily slowed that down. But it was not possible then, as it is now, to say, "This computer analysis clearly shows we are doing something silly, so let us stop doing it."

By the late 1990s the information revolution had advanced far enough for the tests required on new drugs to be codified. It was possible to say, "If a drug passes the following computer tests, it is safe to introduce it onto the market." The two University of Houston statisticians who devised these computer tests won the Nobel Prize for Medicine in 1996, and never was a prize more deserved. The flow of new American wonder-drugs resumed just in time for the Biological Revolution.

12
Genetic Engineering: Booms and Busts

THE SEEDS OF THE BIOLOGICAL REVOLUTION of the early twenty-first century were sown in the 1970s when techniques of genetic engineering began to spread from experimental laboratories into commercial ones. The Cetus Corporation was a successful pioneer. Companies like Genentech, Genex, Biogen, Celltech and Hybritech followed it into the mass-production of various biological products which had previously been extracted laboriously and at phenomenal cost from the tissues of living and dead organisms.

After the 1970s these companies concentrated on producing cultures of bacteria which had been transformed by the incorporation into their own reproductive apparatus of genes transplanted from higher organisms. These genes were nature's blueprints for manufacturing complex organic compounds of

[152]

vital medical significance. By the early 1980s manufacture had emerged as a four-stage process—isolation, incorporation, transformation and murder.

First, desirable genes had to be located and isolated from the DNA complex where they were naturally present. These were then introduced into a "vector"—a larger unit of DNA—which could be incorporated into a bacterial cell. This was done by introducing the vector into a bacterial culture under conditions that would facilitate the transformation of some of the cells. The cells that remained untransformed had to be selectively killed so as to leave a pure culture of transformed cells which, in reproducing themselves, would manufacture the protein coded by the transplanted gene.

Even in the early 1980s, a ready market existed for several complex proteins. Insulin, used for the treatment of diabetes, was one, but it was soon overtaken in importance by interferon and β-endorphin. Interferon is an anti-viral agent useful in the treatment of virus-induced cancers and of virus infections like the "common" cold and influenza. Previously, it had been difficult to attack these diseases because there was no way to combat viruses once they had begun their invasion of the living cells of the body. Thanks to mass-produced interferon, virus illnesses have been cut back in the past forty years as dramatically as were bacterial diseases following the introduction of antibiotics and sulpha drugs in the 1940s. Today it is rare for people to catch colds or influenza, or, if they do, to suffer beyond the first sneeze.

β-endorphin is the body's endogenous morphine—a natural pain-killer which has displaced other opiate drugs for use as a local anesthetic in minor surgery and in the aftermath of more drastic treatments. During the 1980s there was over-rapid expansion of compounds routinely produced by this kind of technique. A lot of companies brought out hormones and enzymes initially useful in the treatment of diseases of the endocrine system and metabolic disorders. But in the early 1990s it became possible to treat the body's tissues directly, and this kind of drug-taking became to some extent redundant. This was

153

genetic engineering's first period of boom and bust. Today, interferon and β-endorphin are still manufactured on a large scale, and so are the natural psychotropics: the endogenous tranquillizers, hypnosedatives, and so on. But many of the other early genetic compounds have disappeared.

In the early 1980s genetic engineering enthusiasts feared they would be delayed by two factors, one a matter of social impediment and the other a matter of practical technique. The impeding social factor was funk. During the early years of genetic engineering of bacteria, there were many science fictional horror stories about new plagues begun by deadly bacteria likely to escape from experimental laboratories. This was an irrational fear. There was no reason to expect that the kinds of transformation achieved could affect the capacity of bacteria to cause disease or to resist antibacterial drugs. Fears that resistance genes could be transferred into pathogens (disease-producers) faded as people began to understand that manipulations once heralded as categorically new—artificial gene transfers, achievable only in the laboratory—actually take place in nature anyway.

Moreover, commonsense safeguards were bound to be introduced, so that processes of commercial manufacture soon employed attenuated strains of bacteria which were insufficiently hardy to survive outside the hospitable conditions of a breeding tank. In the later 1980s these processes were made entirely hazard-free when *Bacillus subtilis* (bacteria incapable of infecting higher animals) replaced *Escherichia coli* (which can cause sickness and diarrhea in humans).

During the period 1985–90 scientists also broke through the main practical limitation in the way of genetic engineering's advance. They sharply increased the rate of transformation which could be achieved with existing vectors. In 1980 rates of transformation as low as one in 10,000 were common. By the 1990s rates were between one in ten and one in two in living tissue. When dealing with bacterial cultures, the early 1980s' low rates of transformation were not important because untransformed cells could be killed off by the ingenious method of using vectors which conferred immunity to a particular bacterial poison, selectively preserving transformed cells when the poison was later added to the culture.

Clearly, though, such a low rate of transformation set limits on what could be accomplished in terms of transforming the cells of living tissues. Even in the 1980s it was easy to see that it would be more convenient to make a diabetic produce his own insulin by transforming the cells which had lost that ability, but while the rate of transformation was low no such effective treatment was possible. As transformation rates increased in 1985–95, it did become possible. Some of the first successes were seen in the treatment of a wide range of relatively rare diseases, most of which were caused by the lack of a single vital gene. These included blood diseases like thalassemia and sickle-cell anemia; metabolic disorders like phenylketonuria; and some grossly disfiguring conditions. An early success in the mid 1980s was against one of the more common forms of dwarfism. After the early 1990s all these diseases could be treated by the same technique of gene-transplantation. Many lives were saved thereby, and millions of people were permitted to lead normal lives who would otherwise have had cramped ones.

The curing of some disfiguring diseases proved telegenic. Popular television programs showed the cures that had been made. These helped to banish any second outburst of social caution, which might otherwise have swelled up from people who thought the possibility of carrying out genetic engineering on the tissues of the human body was somehow repugnant and dangerous. The urgency of the demand from patients who stood to benefit from the new treatments—many of whom were suffering from fatal disorders and who had everything to gain and nothing to lose—put such thoughts to shame. It would be nice to say that superior analyzing power through the TC helped make the social caution of the 1990s less impeding than that of the 1980s—when delays were imposed against Berkeley's efforts to introduce the first genetically engineered micro-organism into the environment, which was designed to prevent frost damage to crops. Instead, and in truth, it was a few television programs showing great gains in happiness for cripples and dwarfs that did most to force a streamlining of procedures.

Once procedures were streamlined the same techniques of tissue-transformation, which had virtually banished genetic deficiency-disease by the early 2000s, were also applied with happy and dramatic success to various degenerative diseases in which the body had until then gradually lost its capacity to perform certain functions. Millions of people were affected by these diseases, of which the most commonplace was arthritis.

By the first decade of the new century most diseases of this kind could be alleviated, and armies of sufferers and potential sufferers rushed to get treatments that enabled them to retain their faculties and the full use of their limbs for much longer than before. The number of people involved meant that the use of these treatments became the second genetic engineering boom, which was followed by the second bust. Today, beneficiaries receive routine care, but only a quarter as many new treatments are needed each year as in 2008. When there are new treatments in restoring the use of limbs, they can be dramatic. Every TC viewer in 2025 will remember the case of Amaryllis Katoppo.

Amaryllis Katoppo was born on the Indonesian island of Sumba in the first year of the twenty-first century. She was the victim of a fault in embryonic development which left her virtually limbless. She had stunted, almost vestigial, legs and no arms at all.

Her parents had prospered now that Sumba and some other islands of Indonesia had become telecommuters' paradises. The extended Katoppo family owned and operated the sports facilities near Sumba's best beach. They were horrified at their baby's deformity, and angry because they felt that the Spitz-Sampson Health Maintenance Organization of Australia had let them down. A lot of the telecommuters in Sumba telecommuted X-rays of themselves to this HMO because in those pre-Centrobank days there were not yet such good health-care facilities in Indonesia itself.

Spitz-Sampson, aware that their HMO was a growth business and that a scandal would hurt them, sent specialists to reassure the Katoppos that Amaryllis was unlikely to suffer any mental impairment, and that with the aid of sophisticated modern wheelchairs and perhaps prosthetic limbs, she should grow up to enjoy a happy and productive life. Spitz-Sampson pointed out that doctors in several countries had long ago found an unwelcome opportunity to obtain experience in the handling of such cases, because such deformities had been caused in some quantity by a drug named Thalidomide which had been in use as a tranquillizer during the 1960s. Nearly all of the Thalidomide children were still alive, and Spitz-Sampson arranged for the Katoppos to speak to several, now in their mid thirties, in the hope that the family would be reassured about the prospect before Amaryllis.

The Katoppos considered taking legal action against Spitz-Sampson on the grounds that the abnormality should have been detected during Mrs. Tien Katoppo's pregnancy, but they were persuaded that they were the victims of a rare accident of fate. Early scanning of the developing embryo had revealed no genetic abnormality, for indeed there was none. What had happened was an error in the process by which the genetic blueprint was followed in the growth of a complicated body from a single cell. The Katoppos decided to accept Spitz-Sampson's offer to do what they could for their little girl.

Amaryllis learned to talk very quickly, and soon grew into an intelligent, pretty, happy and very determined infant. She needed more care and attention than other children, but the difference was not so very great while she was tiny. A harder struggle began when Spitz-Sampson's medical scientists began to tackle the problem of compensating technologically for her disabilities.

At the age of four Amaryllis was provided with her first wheelchair, whose controls she could operate with her tiny toes. Her first vehicle was simply designed to move about, but this was soon replaced by one which had its own robot limbs fitted; it was at that stage more economical to give artificial hands to the machine than to her. She soon became astonishingly expert in the use of her electronic accessories, which were constantly improved.

By the time Amaryllis was eight years old she was getting along so well with her chairs—which by now resembled small cars, with mechanical arms almost as dexterous as real ones—that the suggestion made by the Kaufmann HMO from Frankfurt, Germany, was almost unwelcome. Kaufmann had won the Centrobank contract for providing health-maintenance facilities on Sumba, although many of the locals and telecommuters still preferred to pay privately to Spitz-Sampson. But Kaufmann's services could now be obtained by native Sumbans for free, and Kaufmann's chief doctors suggested to the Katoppos that research into the development processes of embryos had reached a stage where it was possible to think in terms of putting right the error that nature had made. They thought that it might be possible to make Amaryllis's lost limbs grow.

The Kaufmann doctors explained to the Katoppos that Amaryllis possessed all the genes for making a healthy body. What was necessary was to restore the plasticity that would enable those genes to control the growth and differentiation of new cells, so as to complete the task that had gone wrong in the womb. They made no promises, and admitted that attempts to help amputees re-grow single limbs or even parts of limbs had so far had only limited success. Their hope was that Amaryllis's case might present fewer problems because her tissues had never been traumatized by injury or surgery.

The problem facing the Katoppos was that Amaryllis would be a guinea pig in an experiment. She would have to go to Kaufmann's main hospital in distant Greece for a long time; and once the attempt to restore plasticity to her cells had begun she would be immobilized for several months. There would be disruption of the progress which she was making with her artificial aids. In the end, it was decided to lay the case before Amaryllis, and to let her decide. This was a lot to ask of the judgment of an eight-year-old, but when Amaryllis heard of the possibility of being made whole she would not listen to any suggestion of caution. She demanded that the Kaufmann Health Maintenance Organization should be allowed to try.

The process involved treatment to the vestiges of Amaryllis's legs and to the interrupted joints of her shoulders, so that cells which had differentiated into skin, muscle and connective tissue might be persuaded to turn back into undifferentiated cells that were potentially capable of becoming any type. The resulting cell-bodies, or blastemas, had then to be fed from without by nutrients that would allow rapid cell-division and growth. The developing blastemas had to be stimulated so that the cells differentiated into the right pattern of structure, with bones, nerves, muscles, blood vessels and everything else that went to make up a fully functional limb.

Sadly, Amaryllis was immobilized not for a few months but for nearly two years. The first attempt to make the blastemas regenerate healthy limbs failed, and the re-forming tissues had to be rendered plastic again. Time slipped by while the doctors figured out what had gone wrong, re-tested their methods in animal experiments, and at last decided that they could get it right second time around. Throughout this period Amaryllis was completely immobile, far from home, and in considerable pain. She remained cheerful and optimistic throughout, showing great courage in the face of the first terrible disappointment.

The second attempt went much better, but it takes a long time to grow a whole limb to the dimensions required by a nine-year-old body. With every week that went by, there was the awful possibility that something might go wrong and set the whole project back to square one again. In terms of the virtue of patience, Amaryllis showed she was a veritable saint. Still, the limbs did grow—indeed, the legs became rather longer than her body-size suggested they should be.

Even when she began learning to use her new limbs, there was the possibility that the tissues might not stabilize, and that she might be left worse off than she was when the experiment began. Her learning, though, was rapid. She did not quite achieve the target which she set herself, of learning to walk on her own legs before her tenth birthday, but by that date she was able to use her hands skillfully enough to operate the keyboard on a computer terminal and to build complicated edifices with the construction kit that she was given. Within three months she could walk, and she soon began to run.

She ran very well, and very fast, because the limbs she had been given had been shaped with unprecedented care. It soon became apparent that, though long, they were very good legs indeed.

It was only natural that Amaryllis should rejoice in her new body. Other children grew up taking their endowment for granted, but not she. She had a fierce determination to look after her physique as well as she could. She made herself fit, and kept herself fit, entering into all kinds of sport back at Sumba with a zest that sometimes worried her parents and doctors, who retained the anxiety that the miracle might yet be reversed—that the accident might yet recur. Amaryllis never worried. Her optimism remained unconquerable, and she cultivated what was almost a sense of destiny, sure that the body which had been given to her so late in life must be capable of something very special. She dedicated herself to rigorous programs of training with relentless enthusiasm.

She had passed her Prelim Exam *summa cum laude* while in hospital, and had therefore qualified to go on to an extended period of higher education at any time in her life she chose. Her parents were happy that she should spend her years from eleven to nineteen concentrating on sports, which were the family business. Although she did not coordinate her arms and legs quite well enough to excel in ball-games like badminton and tennis, she could soon stride out faster than any other woman whom she met in Indonesia.

An Australian gold-medal-winner at the Olympics of 2000 was the entrepreneur of a sports complex on a nearby island. He was friendly with the Katoppos, who were in the same line of business, and he took over the coaching of Amaryllis for the Indonesian Olympic trials in 2020. Short notices appeared on Western TCs saying that Indonesia's only qualifier for the

Olympic Women's 800 Meters and 1,500 Meters had been born without arms or legs, but these were generally regarded as some HMO's advertisement blurb.

The 2020 Olympiad, in the modern style, was held at different venues so as to fit in with peak viewing times on world-wide TC. The athletics were in Madrid, which was rather uncomfortably hot for the Russian and Scandinavian girls who were the 800 Meter favorites. At the staggered start for the 800 Meter final, a little Third Worlder with nut-brown body and surprisingly long and lithe legs took off at a startling pace in the outside lane. When the stagger broke at 200 meters, Amaryllis was five meters ahead of the three blonde European favorites, who were watching each other instead of her. At 600 meters a murmur arose because the Indonesian was ten meters up and still going away. Russia's Galina Andreeva pulled ahead of the chasing trio. Round the long bend she approached the leader's shoulder. As the two girls came into the homestretch it was the Russian who was rolling and under strain. The Women's 800 Meter gold-medal-winner was Amaryllis Katoppo. Later she won the silver in the 1,500 Meters, coming second to a United German in a cunning and tactical race. Her subsequent times suggest that with greater experience of competition she would have struck gold in the 1,500 as well.

Amaryllis returned to Indonesia as a national, international and medical heroine. Since then, some controversy has surrounded her exploits. Her case has added to the long dispute about the increasing influence of medical science on the capabilities of sportsmen and women. There has been talk of techniques akin to Kaufmann's being applied to healthy men and women, to build ordinary limbs into exceptional ones, not only in pursuit of sporting achievement but in the making of soldiers.

Any criticism that was thought or spoken, however, evaporated in the face of Amaryllis's charm and vivacity, and in the knowledge of what she had endured in the course of becoming what she was. Health Maintenance Organizations have gone on since then to repair many other bodies that were damaged

161

by accidents, both before and after birth. The techniques made rapid progress after that first successful application. Amaryllis Katoppo gave the main Kaufmann hospital in Greece one of her two Olympic medals, because she felt that hers was a shared triumph.

After the surge of tissue transformation in 2000–10, the next biological boom came in cell hybridization. As early as the 1980s this species of fundamental biological engineering was growing alongside the techniques of transformative genetic engineering. Hybridization allowed commercial enterprises to take advantage of the properties of specialized individual cells, by fusing them with bone-marrow cancer cells in order to produce many duplicates. It had previously been difficult to grow some types of specialized cells in tissue culture because, in becoming highly specialized, the cells had lost their power of rapid reproduction. But all cancer cells have as their primary property the ability to divide rapidly and continually, and the ability to combine the properties of cells by fusion was thus suddenly productive.

The first commercial exploitation of this kind of biotechnology was the multiplication of spleen cells which were responsible for the production of antibodies. By producing multiple copies of cells specialized for producing a particular kind of antibody a substantial supply of a single antibody could be obtained. Previously, antibodies had had to be harvested from the blood of living animals, and it had been impossible to isolate a pure sample of a single type. The new monoclonal antibodies offered scope for much more specific treatment of a wide range of diseases.

The research undertaken by companies exploiting cell fusion techniques speedily became more productive. In the 1980s and 1990s the short-term practical pay-off of this research and development was seen in the development of better techniques of immunization applicable to common diseases, and in the widening of the range of immunoserums in common use. Doctors were no longer just searching for better serums, but were using targeted antibodies. Better protection against some biological poisons—from rattlesnake venom to botulism—was quickly obtained.

The longer-term reward was the insight which study of the process of cell fusion gave into the properties of cancerous cells, and into the switching mechanisms which were responsible for the specialization of the many types of cells characteristic of higher organisms. It was the gradual elucidation of the biochemistry of such switching mechanisms which gave us the basis for an effective attack on cancer.

Cancer is a condition rather than a disease. It occurs when body cells begin uncontrolled multiplication, forming tumors which disrupt the functioning of organs and which may stimulate the development of further tumors in neighboring tissues. Sometimes the cancer is triggered by a virus, sometimes by a chemical compound (a carcinogen) and sometimes it occurs because of some kind of biochemical accident within a functioning cell. In all cases, something has gone wrong with the control system designed to adjust the reproductive potential of the individual cell to the requirements of the tissue or organ in which it is situated.

In the 1980s cancers were treated in a variety of ways, usually involving attempts to destroy the rogue cells without inflicting too much damage on the healthy cells that surround them. Some tumors could be removed surgically, others gradually obliterated by chemotherapy or radiation treatment. In nearly all cases, though, extensive damage was done to the tissue hosting the cancer, and a strain was put on the body's recuperative powers. Inevitably, many cancers recurred. Though the widespread availability of interferon assisted in the treatment of some virus-induced cancers, adding one more weapon to a considerable medical armory, it held out no promise that the whole war might be won. Physicians needed a method by which the cancerous cells could be brought back under control—a way of switching off the cells' tendency to multiply indiscriminately, and thus to rehabilitate them within the host tissue. Once the biochemical gene-switching systems within cells were understood, this became possible.

The near-infinite variety of types of cancer, and the very different problems which face doctors attempting to treat cancers in different parts of the body, have made the war a difficult one to fight. We have not yet banished cancer from the world, and we still discover many cases which eventually prove fatal, but in the past thirty years medical science has won battle after battle in the fight to control this most insidious of killers.

There is one sense in which the conquest of cancer may never be completed. Because so many cancers begin spontaneously—a reflection on the fallibility of such a complex and delicate system as the human body—we may not be able to prevent them from appearing. Despite the high hopes bred in the early 1980s—when emerging knowledge about tissue-specific antigens first made some forms of anti-tumor vaccine realistic—we still cannot immunize people against all cancers in the way that we can against most infectious diseases or many environmental poisons.

In the first quarter of the twenty-first century, however, the capacity of cancer to hurt and kill people has been dramatically diminished. With the aid of regular screening most cancers can be identified, located and made harmless before very much damage is done. New generations of tomographic scanners have given us the ability to locate cancers much more precisely in advance of exploratory surgery, and at a much earlier stage. Treatment can thus be planned more carefully, administered more precisely with the minimum of general tissue damage, and with a much better chance of inhibiting further cancerous growth. Major surgery is now required only in exceptional cases, and the crude forms of radiation treatment and chemotherapy are a thing of the past. Ninety per cent of cancer damage is now preventable, and in countries with effective health maintenance organizations a high percentage is, in practice, prevented.

Research continues into the switching mechanisms which

govern cell differentiation, and which constitute the "sculptor" that shapes an organism from the initially undifferentiated raw material provided by the dividing egg. Despite the lovely victory of Amaryllis in Madrid's sun, the extent to which we can become biological sculptors of ourselves is still limited. We have only begun to learn how to achieve planned cell metamorphosis even in tissue culture, but the potential here is enormous. The use of hybridomas in providing antibodies is still commonplace, but eventually we may expect the process to become industrially redundant as we learn how to work directly upon the body to induce it to produce its own immunities and its own responses to infection and to poisoning. This is, or should be, the fate of all industrial enterprises: they lay the groundwork for their own eventual obsolescence. They achieve great things during their booms. They have fulfilled their purpose by the time of their busts.

In the past fifty years medical techniques have advanced rapidly and steadily, until at the present time it is reasonable to say that almost all the diseases which once afflicted mankind can be fought and beaten. There have also been great advances in our ability to repair the body after it has sustained physical injury. Yet the two most dramatic changes through which it was once thought the genetic engineering revolution might change the whole nature of man have not occurred. We have not developed widespread cloning, and we have not yet made ourselves all live to an uneconomically old age.

13

No Superbabies
and Not Yet
Grandpa Culls

AS THE BIRTH CONTROL PILL spread in the 1960s and 1970s, so that sex became 99.99 per cent for fun, some prophets said that science was bound to home in upon the once-or-twice-in-a-lifetime occasion when sex would be for reproduction. Parents would start to engineer superbabies while they lay in their mothers' wombs. The prospect aroused widespread horror, but pessimists said, "Parents will rightly do almost anything to ensure their child is healthy, and society will not be able to draw the line between that and attempts to make the child more intelligent or more strong or more friendly." In fact, attempts to engineer a fetus even to make it more healthy never took off.

By the end of the 1990s a man who was treated for diabetes or sickle-cell anemia by gene-transplantation and transformation of the relevant body-tissues could be completely cured of his disease. But at that stage he was not able to transmit his acquired immunity to his children, who could still inherit defective genes from him. The techniques available in the 1990s did not permit the reliable and total transformation of the germ cells in the gonads. Even a transformation rate of one in two, though effective enough in restoring the functional capacities of ailing tissues, is inadequate to ensure that a woman whose ovaries are treated will only be able to bear transformed children.

Also, the pattern of incentives had changed. Whereas a man suffering from a genetic deficiency which might kill him was ready enough to demand treatment in spite of hypothetical hazards, he was not nearly so ready to demand that a correction be made in his testes. The balance of probable gain against possible loss looked very different. And by the late 1990s the success of gene-transplantation treatment meant that parents knew that if their children were born genetically deficient, they could nearly always be cured.

At one stage, there was fear that people would nevertheless use gene-transplantation to try to achieve superchildren, either in the womb or by engineering after birth. When various governments imposed rules against this, it was said that ambitious parents would hasten to telecommute from small communes where this engineering was allowed. This did in fact happen to a small extent, tragically for the children born under these circumstances. In communities with changing technology, attitudes and even sports, definitions of "intelligent," "friendly," and "athletic" are changing all the time. But, as a twenty-first-century sage has said:

The qualities that people want least in the modern world are precisely those qualities of stupid arrogance which are most likely to be ordered or implemented by the few stupidly arrogant people who have gone off to superstud communes. Nobody is unemployable in the modern world, if he wants to be employable. But the people who come nearest to being

167

unemployable, and yet are most anxious to be employed prestigiously, are the sad products of the superstuds.

The superstuds therefore never boomed, but quickly bust.

The second fear expressed fifty years ago concerned the growth of world population. Up to 1850 the world's population never increased by more than 0.1 per cent a year. In 1850–1950 this rose to 1 per cent a year, and then the great and happy fall in infant mortality strangely made some people very worried indeed. It was said that world population was now inevitably going to expand by 3.5 per cent a year growth and that this would result in mass starvation by some time in the twenty-first century. A conference on world population was called in 1974 which produced a learned World Plan for Action with the aim of bringing world population growth down to 1.7 per cent by 1985. This plan never needed to be put into effect: by 1974, when the plan was written, world population growth was below 1.7 per cent already, and was falling. The scare had already brought its own antidotes into effect.

Some of these were morally controversial. In 1950 no civilized woman had an abortion anywhere; by 1975 any woman could get an abortion before the next weekend in most big cities of the world. Some of the antidotes were technological; the birth control pill appeared because there was a growing demand for it. But the main reason was that women started to want fewer babies, especially in educated lands. A survey in the late 1970s showed that girls who were still in school at the time of first menstruation said that, on average, they wanted to have fewer than 2.1 babies during their lifetimes. And by the late 1980s most girls were in school at first menstruation, even in poor countries. The significance of 2.1 is that, if the average woman intends to have fewer babies than that, then world population eventually goes down. "Eventually" means "after quite a time." There was still due to be a rise in world population from 1980's 4.25 billion to over 8 billion in 2024 as the babies saved by the drop in infant mortality in 1950–85 passed through childbearing years. And before 1980 new fears arose that population could soar again if people suddenly started living much longer.

This latter fear started the second great world population scare.

Some time in the next two decades [*wrote a prophet in the late 1970s*] some damn fool of a doctor is going to make a breakthrough in curing one or more of the great degenerative diseases. We will then all start living longer, just when the breakdown in three-generational families means that Grandma no longer lives with the grandchildren, just when we have passed the financing of old-age pensions on to governments which in an age of inflation will no longer be able to afford them, especially as longevity increases. It will be necessary to move to euthanasia as fully as we have moved to abortion. Inflation-proof index-linked pensions will soon have to be limited to fixed-term ones, to agreed-date-of-death contracts with a hell of a going-away party on the eve of your ninety-fifth birthday.

This second great population scare has so far proved as bogus as the first one. One reason for this is that we have made a total change in our lifestyles at different ages; with the young going into paid work sooner, the middle-aged learning to play more, and the old studying and working more, especially as telecommuting makes work much less arduous. But another reason is that the improvement in health has taken a rather surprising form. Thanks partly to the spread of HMOs in poor countries, we have reached a stage where very few people die prematurely. Far more people reach the age of three-score-years-and-ten than would have seemed conceivable to an Indian in 1950. But once you have reached about seventy-five, your life expectation after that is not very different from what it has been for thousands of years.

This situation may be about to change, however, and bring some problems with it.

There is no reason, in principle, why we should not find a way to slow the ageing process. Since single-celled organisms

169

can divide and redivide *ad infinitum* without suffering progressive degeneration, we may some day manage to make the cells in our bodies do the same, so that the tissues constantly renew themselves and never wear out. Since 1980 we have discovered several aspects of the ageing process—different patterns of biochemical deterioration which probably should require us to speak of "ageing processes," in the plural. As our DNA molecules replicate themselves and make the RNA (which makes functional proteins), some random copying errors occur. In consequence we accumulate a gradually increasing dead weight of defective molecules produced transiently within cells as a part of normal metabolism. Other molecules, which make up the permanent structures of the body, are affected by molecular cross-linkages.

All these processes are acting simultaneously, with each pattern of deterioration reaching the point of breakdown at more or less the same point in time. So a treatment to counter any one of them in isolation would not have much effect on longevity. In order to extend man's lifespan considerably, all the kinds of wear and tear will need to be tackled at once.

It is easy to see why, given all this, there is no simple elixir of life. Rejuvenation of the tissues of the body is a difficult and delicate business. If and when a treatment for old age does become possible, it is unlikely to be a simple matter of taking pills or having injections. It may be very difficult and time-consuming to administer, and therefore probably costly. That raises problems which have been avoided in the surprisingly egalitarian health revolution of the past fifty years. The discovery of an expensive elixir of life could provoke envy and strife on a scale not previously seen. The poor have always had their mortality in common with the rich, and have taken solace in that fact. Once some men have access to the reward of indefinitely protracted youth, can we expect a 1789 after all? Another bizarre problem is that anti-ageing treatment might need genetic transformations so general that they require the treatment of early embryos rather than mature individuals. That could cause quite a generation gap.

170

In spite of all these caveats, it is probable that a practical method of adding decades to our present measure of youth and virility will be discovered in the twenty-first century. Longevity is something we may legitimately hope for on behalf of our children. Immortality will take a little longer.

It would be pusillanimous to conclude that the people of the world will not be able to cope with the problems this brings. Throughout history people have been anxious about their ability to adapt to the changes brought about in the world by their own efforts and discoveries. Experience has shown us time and again that what has been lacking is self-confidence. No good has ever come of the attempt to declare a moratorium on change; it has never been satisfying, and has rarely been successful in any but the shortest term. Discoveries cannot be unmade. Power cannot be obliterated; whenever an individual or a group surrenders it, it simply passes into other hands. There is no alternative but to take responsibility for the power which our knowledge can give us, and use it as wisely as we can.

The biological revolution has put the future of mankind into the hands of men. Human nature itself is now subject to human dominion. We can amend the inheritance that is in our genes, and are no longer imprisoned by our evolutionary heritage. Our escape is not yet total, but there is every reason to expect that freedom will eventually be ours for the taking. How we will use that freedom remains to be seen.

14

The Forecast
Famines
Become Gluts

IN THE YEARS just after 1975 there were many forecasts of coming desperate shortages of food, energy, some raw materials, and methods of controlling environmental pollution. Instead, all these things became gluts, because freer price mechanisms were sensibly applied and science then homed in on these fields. A third factor was summarized by an economist as early as 1973:

The least useful and least credible sort of medium-term economic forecast today is whatever is at any moment the most fashionable one. The reason for this is now quite logical and rather technical. In modern conditions of high elasticity of both production and substitution, we will generally create a temporary but large surplus of whatever the majority of decision-influencing people five or ten years earlier believed was going to be in most desperately short supply. This is because the well-advertised views of the decision-influencers tend to be believed by both profit-seeking private producers and consensus-following governments, and these two then combine to cause excessive production of precisely the things that the decision-influencers had been saying would be most obviously needed.

Down to the 1990s rich countries—which by then generally had only 3–9 per cent of their work-forces in farming—rigged markets in favor of those farmers, because it seemed politically necessary to woo these 3–9 per cent of voters. Although most of these rich countries were in the less lushly tropical parts of the world, they found these small agricultural work-forces provided far more food than they needed. They built towering butter mountains, undrainable wine lakes, mounds of unsaleable grain.

Poor countries often had 45–70 per cent of their work-forces in farming, and it might be supposed their rulers would therefore be even more intent on pleasing this mass of their subjects. Until 2006, they were not. The rulers of most poor countries were dictators liable to be overthrown by *coups d'état*. Coups were not organized by farmers, but by city-dwellers, who ate food but did not sell it. Dictators therefore kept down the price of food, and their peasants responded by not producing it.

With the coming of Centrobank the rulers of poor countries found it desirable to introduce free-market pricing policies; they did not qualify for Centrobank money unless they did. It is probable that these policies alone would have made many of them self-sufficient in food. But the Centrobank system also made it profitable for rich countries' scientists to devise and sell to the poor countries mechanisms for increasing their food production. At the same time, the revolution in genetic engineering made huge expansion rather easy in crop yields, meat, single-cell protein (SCP), and desert reclamation. Hence the food gluts.

Plant species are inherently more manipulable than animal species. Because plants can reproduce asexually, it is usually easy to produce an individual plant whose cells are all transformed once one has transformed cells in a particular tissue. A whole plant can then be regenerated from these few selected cells. Since the 1990s it has been relatively easy to produce transformed plants which breed true. In the years 1996–9 transformed rice, wheat, and other cereal plants were engineered that were capable of resisting common killers such as pests, drought and frost. By cloning as well as producing new individuals from transformed seeds, stocks of the transformed plants, which were capable of breeding true, could be produced very quickly.

This sort of crop engineering brought especially spectacular yields in the tropical areas where many poor countries were. To combat the pests commonly found in such climates, the plants' newly engineered immunity to the most virulent of them was backed up by the manufacture of bacteria which attacked other species of pests. New, sophisticated genetic engineering techniques ensured these were very specific in their effects and had none of the wider ecological consequences foretold by critics when the experiments in this field began in the 1980s; they also put an end to banshee wails about the effects of chlorinated hydrocarbons and other insecticides on the environment and on the health of nations.

Farming now became a more stable and reliable business, and an economist might have hoped that it would therefore become an unpolitical industry, moving to the areas which could produce food most cheaply. As long as national governments remained powerful, it did no such thing. In the poor countries even the first stages of the Centrobank system helped to create a food glut. They provided an external incentive for the development of food plants capable of growing in places where only dry grass, thorn scrub or cactus plants had grown in the twentieth century. We advanced in those years to the biological systems that allow the fullest exploitation of the land, the soil and the sunlight which streams from the heavens to fuel our ecosphere. We began the business of transforming the surface of the earth by reclaiming the wilderness which was previously inhospitable to man.

As deserts bloomed and food production went into top gear in the lushest poor countries, the seeds were sown of the cereal glut and agricultural slump of 2011–14. Under previous political systems, governments would probably have responded to this agricultural distress by increasing agricultural subsidies. Fortunately, by 2014 computers told governments and Centrobank to cut off agricultural subsidies instead.

Man does not feed on cereals alone, and science was simultaneously creating a glut in meat. There has not been any substantial experimentation in the use of genetic engineering techniques to make heritable changes in human germ plasm. Our superstuds are not creating artificial superhuman beings. Supercattle, however, are being created in herds.

Primitive biological engineering has been practiced in animal husbandry for thousands of years, to persuade cows to produce milk for human use and hens to lay unfertilized eggs. By 1980 the artificial insemination of female livestock, using sperm from the best males of each species, was commonplace; and the first experiments in cloning by separating the cells of early embryos produced by *in vitro* fertilization had been carried out.

Even before the achievement of enhanced transformation rates in the 1990s, much work had been done on the engineering of animal embryos. Because egg-cells are so much larger than other kinds of cells they are much easier to transform. Multiple copies of new genes can be injected into them with a micropipette without the aid of a vector. Experimental transformations of mice were carried out by this method in the early 1980s, but there was initially little control over the number of copies of the gene to be transplanted or over the likelihood of the gene being expressed in the adult animal.

Gradually, in the last years of the twentieth century, a better understanding grew of the mechanisms which determine whether genes are switched on or off, and these difficulties disappeared.

175

The first important innovation was achieved when several species of meat-producing animals were equipped with extra genes. They produced the compounds known as anabolic steroids—the hormones which control the rate at which muscle tissue (i.e., meat) is built up as an animal matures. At first, anabolic steroids were given to cattle, pigs and some Olympic shot-putters in their food, but it was much more economical and efficient to get these patients to breed their own steroids. The animals and athletes that these affected were so heavily built that locomotion became difficult, but it was already commonplace (though controversial) to breed and rear such animals in close confinement anyhow, rather than to allow them to roam free.

The next step was to make economies in the input of raw material to these large animals—i.e., in their method of digesting food. Although cows had the ability even in the 1980s to make use of the cellulose in their diet, the system which they used to do so was highly inefficient. One contemporary scientist commented:

> Cows have a complex system of stomachs which act as fermentation tanks where bacteria break down cellulose into compounds which the cow can handle through its own metabolism. The rate of processing is slow and energy-wasteful, much of the energy potentially present in the plant material being wasted as gas.

During the energy crisis of the 1970s, this led to some gloom among meat-eaters and some agitating from vegetarians. There is a great deal of cellulose in the biosphere, but by far the greater part of it sustains only micro-organisms and some higher organisms (like termites) which have entered into partnership with them. There are three-quarters of a ton of termites for each human being on earth. In the 1980s it seemed to some ecological pessimists that meat production was too wasteful a manner of exploiting the ecosphere. There were suggestions that it would be uneconomical to maintain it.

Thanks to genetic engineering, this fear proved absurd. The

176

efficiency of cattle and pigs in utilizing the energy stored in cellulose and woody plant tissues has been dramatically enhanced. Cows have been given new genes to produce enzymes which enable the animals to metabolize cellulose and other substances directly, without recourse to bacterial middlemen. This has made the feeding of livestock much more economical and much less messy. By the turn of the century it was possible to use artificial enzymes to break down lignin, an undesirable compound generally found in combination with cellulose in waste materials such as paper and some kinds of plastics, so that productive use could be made of these as food additives. This assisted pollution control as well as meat production, and by 2025 the term "waste" has almost lost its meaning because there is a productive use for almost everything.

We have made our food animals into hyper-efficient converters of the inedible into the palatable, but have thereby raised moral problems because the large, heavy, immobile meat animals of today offend many of the most decent instincts of mankind. This revolution helped to speed the development of SCP (single-cell protein).

The years 2005–10 saw frenetic research and development in this field by Western and Japanese entrepreneurial arrangers in food technology. The products were aimed at Third World markets through the Centrobank system. The sales arguments were strong. Young cattle take several weeks to double their mass. Most food plants are a little faster, but are restricted to a particular growing season. Algae and fungi, by contrast, can double their mass in a few hours. Bacteria and some yeasts, under favorable conditions, can do so in less than an hour. Green crusaders proved less worried about immobile bugs than about immobile cows, although there were early fears in the 1980s that the lobbyists who finance them would help see they were excited even about this; witness British Petroleum's lost millions in its problem protein plant in Sardinia which was stifled by environmental fears and pressure from the soya protein lobby.

There were three main problems inhibiting the development

177

of SCP as a human food-source. The first, palatability, had disappeared by the 1990s: food processing techniques were devised which made its texture, color and taste seem luscious to the young. The other two problems—possible toxicological worries and the problem of finding the most suitable food supplies for the growing micro-organisms—were closely linked.

Virtually all the early SCP projects envisaged that the protein-producing micro-organisms would be fed on waste materials. Which wastes? Many early experiments with petrochemical wastes were plagued with problems caused by toxic residues. As many people in the 1980s still believed the world faced an energy crisis, there were complaints when the first successful commercial SCP projects, in Japan and West Germany, used methanol as raw material to produce SCP which was largely used as animal feed. Methanol was not exactly a waste product. It had itself to be manufactured. Ethanol—a more effective raw material—was even more valuable commercially.

For these reasons the projects to develop SCP for human use moved away from the exploitation of petrochemical processes toward the more conventional processing of plant and animal foodstuffs, plus sewage. When fungal protein processes reaped the benefits of genetic engineering in the 1990s, the method was quickly adapted to the production of ultra-cheap protein-rich human foods.

Farmers of the 1990s, successors to the soya lobby, counterattacked by saying that mankind was now eating bugs grown out of its own shit. One remembers the joke about the fastidious old lady in the last century who refused to eat sheep's tongue in a restaurant. "I won't eat anything that has come out of a dirty sheep's mouth; bring me something nice like an egg."

In reality SCP usefully substitutes for processes which happen in nature anyway. All organic wastes are eventually recycled within the ecosphere, entering long chains where they are converted again and again into single-cell protein. What the technological usurpation of the process permits us to do is to speed up the operation.

178

The SCP business is ecologically sound in every way. At no stage is carbonaceous material being taken out of the ecosystem by being converted into a non-biodegradable form. Essentially, this kind of industry is a matter of ecological streamlining. Within the context of the earth's complex life-system it is helping the ecosphere to function more efficiently and more economically. The problem with Mother Nature as a provider of human needs is that she has never had the benefit of good advice from a sensible time-and-motion analyst. Now, at last, we have the capacity to modify organisms that will allow us to act upon the results of such analysis.

If, as seems likely, we will eventually undertake the colonization of the farther reaches of the solar system and send self-sustaining space habitat units outside the system to distant stars, then SCP technology will be vital to the maintenance of ecological stability. Meanwhile it has helped to give the world an even bigger glut of food.

15

Energy and Minerals
Galore, but Bugs
with Everything

ENERGY WAS DRIVEN into glut by the very event which some people wrongly thought heralded a permanent energy shortage. There are several hundred possible ways of releasing energy from storage in matter. The most transportable in the second half of the twentieth century was the burning of the mineral slime called oil, and in the 1950s and 1960s this product was priced too cheaply. If oil gushed from your farm in Texas in 1955 you became a millionaire, but if it gushed from an Arabian desert the Arabs got far less than the Texans for it. This was partly because feudal Arab leaders were not especially keen on their people's simple life being made less feudal by too much money, and the fate which overtook the Shah of Iran once his people became richer suggests the leaders were possibly right.

The main consequence in the West of the underpricing of oil

in the 1960s was that oil was wastefully used. Instead of just being burned in vehicles (for which it was the most economic fuel), oil was also consumed in electrical power stations (for which it was not), and in ridiculously fertilizer-intensive methods of agriculture. Non-insulated houses and unnecessarily heavy automobiles guzzled up this cheap fuel.

One afternoon during a late 1973 war against Western-supported Israel, the Arabs decided to punish the West by quintupling the asking price for their oil. Oil thus went instantly from being too cheap by more than half to being too expensive by nearly twice. The West reacted foolishly to this—initially by trying to keep the price to their own consumers down. The period of so-called "oil shortage" coincided with this foolishness. Once the higher price was fed through, demand proved elastic. In 1973–83 Japan cut its use of oil per unit of gross national product by 45 per cent; and other countries before 1973 had been using oil much more wastefully than Japan. In the United States the switch to capital-intensive nuclear power was delayed in 1975–85 by high eco-nuttery and high interest rates; but after 1985 both came down. Machines were miniaturized, methods of production made less energy-intensive, agricultural systems changed.

In the United States in the early 1980s nitrogen for use in fertilizers that supported grain production was costing America the energy-equivalent of 100 million barrels of oil a year. These fertilizers were not needed for plants such as lentils and soya beans which could fix their own nitrogen. If the genes controlling nitrogen fixation could be transplanted into cereal crops like wheat and rice, there would be huge savings in energy. This genetic engineering problem was complicated by the fact that nitrogen fixation is not carried out by leguminous plants themselves, but by Rhizobium bacteria to which they act as hosts. Rhizobia could not infect cereal crops because certain supporting systems which allowed the bacteria to live in the roots of legumes were missing from the roots of cereals. The problem was therefore not just to transplant the genes for nitrogen fixation from rhizobia to bacteria which routinely lived

181

in the roots of cereal plants—though even this would have been difficult, as seventeen genes seem to be required to sustain the whole nitrogen-fixing biochemical system. The problem was to make cereals and rhizobia friends with each other.

After the early 1990s, with the aid of techniques giving high rates of cell transformation in living tissue, genetic engineers managed to manufacture strains of wheat whose root cells were hospitable to rhizobia and which were capable of exploiting the nitrogenous compounds the bacteria produced. The cereal plants which had been transformed into hosts for rhizobia had to divert some of their own productive capacity to feeding their new parasites and fuelling the reactions which produced the built-in fertilizer. Fields planted with the new strains thus produced less actual grain than fields planted with traditional strains and provided with artificial fertilizer. But, although less wheat was produced per hectare, it was produced substantially more cheaply. The U.S. wheat surplus began to decline as the new crops came into extensive use, but what was produced was produced more economically.

The oil companies also started to use genetic engineering to get oil. They turned to "microbial mining"; the use of micro-organisms as agents to recover the energy of the petroleum locked up in oil shales and tar sands. There were several ways in which bacteria could be used in this exercise, either by producing substances that helped release the oil from its matrix (wetting agents or emulsifiers) or by taking the hydrocarbons into themselves. The latter proved immensely successful, and spread to the mining of many other minerals. Microbial mining therefore helped to banish the false fears of the 1970s that the world might also use up all its reserves of twenty or thirty other minerals and metals.

These fears had been pretty odd, because most of the metals concerned were not actually being used up at all. They were hammered into the shape of a motor car, and then re-used as scrap when the motor car wore out. The real minerals problem which existed until 2006 was political. If a company drilled a mine in some poor country and it was unprofitable, the company picked up the bill. If it dug a mine in a poor country and it was very profitable, the government of the poor country introduced retrospective taxation to steal the profit away. Companies were therefore emigrating to mine even in the Arctic in order to escape the demands of governments in the lush tropical parts of the earth. After 2006 the Centrobank system discriminated against the governments of poor countries which operated in this way. That alone might have returned many metals to glut. But, simultaneously, biotechnological advance made it possible to explore areas where minerals (including oil) had hitherto been difficult to dig out of the ground. Scientists called this "utilizing the fact that various naturally occurring organisms selectively take up particular elements from their environment." Ordinary folk called it "let the bugs do the mining. They won't belong to the National Union of Mineworkers."

Down the centuries the power of selective take-up by lower organisms had been exploited in a desultory way. Some seaweeds take up iodine from seawater and gradually build up such a concentration that it becomes easy to reclaim the iodine from the weed. Bacteria were known well before 1980 which took up cobalt, copper, zinc and many other metals from low-grade ores, and such micro-organisms were used as intermediaries in the processing of such ores. It was easier to let the microbes extract the metal from the ore and then to extract the metal from the microbes than it was to use chemical processes to extract the metals directly. Of particular commercial importance before 1980 was the microbial leaching of uranium ores.

So long as naturally occurring organisms had to be used, the potential of this kind of biological mining was limited. When it became possible to adapt bacteria more specifically for the jobs which had to be done, the business really took off across the world.

The micro-organisms developed by commercial genetic engineers for extracting metals from natural ores were also useful in reclaiming metals from corroded scrap. One of the main problems associated with the technological use of metals is their tendency to oxidize. Until the 1990s it had often been more energy-expensive to recover metals from their oxides—iron from rust, for instance—than from the common ores in which they naturally occur. Biotechnology changed that situation abruptly. The recycling of metals became a much more efficient business.

By the year 2010 the exploitation of oil shales and tar sands using "leach liquor" techniques was well under way. This involved facilitating a flow of liquid through the shale or sand (usually *in situ*, although material was occasionally extracted and transported to leaching quarries). The liquid supplied was a warmed-over "soup" of bacteria capable of feeding on the hydrocarbons in the shale or sand. Initially, this became a substrate allowing the bacteria to multiply; but, more recently, we have seen the development of bacterial species which store much of the materials in oil-vacuoles. Either way, the soup is processed as it is pumped out again, first to extract the enriched bacterial material and then to convert the biomass into useful liquid and solid fuels.

Exploitation of previously uneconomic coal reserves can be carried out in much the same way, but at present this is usually confined to the processing of slag, for reasons which have more to do with pollution control than energy supply. The main impact of biotechnology on the coal industry has been in the purification of easily accessible coal which was once difficult to use because the sulphur it contains is realized in toxic gases when it is burned. Sulphur-loving bacteria, developed by the enhancement of naturally-occurring species, are now used to purify coal and make it safe for burning. At one time environmentalists wailed that the addition of sulphur dioxide to the atmosphere (which ultimately returned to earth as sulphuric acid rain) was the single most dangerous health hazard created by the Industrial Revolution. The threat has now disappeared thanks to the ever-increasing use of biotechnology in sulphur control.

The conquest of pollution has not been quite as complete as

184

the conquest of the other scares. The most successful weapon in this battle has been the price and taxation system. If you pump sulphur dioxide into the air by burning dirty coal, you now, in most rich countries, pay the full price for the damage you inflict on the community by doing so; that gives you an incentive to clean the coal. The same happens if you release into the environment poison from heavy metals—particularly lead and mercury—which had hitherto been locked up in inert ores; and if you let loose organic wastes from the chemical industry.

Down to the 1980s most governments had not used tax systems against pollution, but had leapt erratically from full *laissez-faire* into lunatic bans. These bans blocked the roads to progress, and also spread misunderstanding of what pollution is. It means the release into the environment of compounds which are either toxic or nonbiodegradable or both. The resultant disruption of the ecosphere reflects the inability of local ecosystems to absorb and re-deploy the materials fed into it. Down to the 1980s the only way to tackle particular problems of this kind seemed to be to attempt to trap and isolate pollutants at source. When tax incentives were introduced, entrepreneurs found ingenious ways of trapping them, but they also soon found a better and broader method of pollution control. It has become increasingly convenient either to use biotechnological systems to inhibit production of the pollutant at source, or to use genetic engineering techniques to modify free-living species in such a way that they will mop up and render harmless various kinds of chemical effluents as they are released. Most potential pollutants can now be processed in this way, but that has bred the "second environmental scare."

16

New Pollutants, or a New Photosynthesis?

THE LARGE NUMBERS OF ENGINEERED ORGANISMS which came into use for the purposes of pollution control in the period from 1995–2015 have renewed fears about the hazards associated with the transformation of micro-organisms. Although none of the organisms involved can interact with man or higher animals, and all are thus incapable of causing diseases, so many of them are being released into the environment that there must be some danger of unforeseen knock-on effects. One possibility is that organisms engineered to help cope with industrial wastes might also be able to attack and damage the artifacts produced by the same industries. If we act in order to give local ecosystems the ability to absorb and quickly recycle industrial products which we do not want to have hanging around, we are liable also to equip them with the means to recycle industrial products which we do want to keep. Forewarned of this danger, however, we should also be forearmed against it.

The point about having increased control over the properties of organisms is not just that it allows us to make them perform new and useful tricks for us. We can also incorporate checks and vulnerabilities which allow us to wipe out quickly and efficiently any organisms which become troublesome. Virtually all of the organisms which we now use in microbial mining, in pollution control, in pest control and in industrial processes of manufacture are deliberately designed so that they cannot function without the presence in their environment of partic-ular essential metabolites that they cannot manufacture. We can therefore control where and when each organism can op-erate by controlling the supply of its metabolite. By this means we have kept a tight rein on the distribution and use of the new biological systems which we have created during the last thirty years.

There probably will be times and places in the future when one of these reins will break, because our manufactured or-ganisms are as capable of mutation as natural ones. Some time, the mutants will probably emerge in one or many artificial species which will liberate them from the constraints which we have been careful to build in. There is no reason, however, to panic about this, or to see it as a reason to regress. The greater the extent and sophistication of our biotechnology, the better are our chances of responding quickly and effectively to any small-scale eco-catastrophe, whether it is one started by mutation of artificial or natural species, or by some deliberate act of biological warfare on the part of human terrorists or, conceivably, lower creatures trying to replace man in the battle for evolution, or extraterrestrial beings. To suppress or restrain biotechnology would make us more vulnerable to ecosystemic disruption, not less. Disruption is something which always might happen, whether or not we are using genetic engineering tech-niques routinely to modify and create species of micro-organisms. Familiarity with these techniques is our best chance of defense.

At present, the biological revolution is still in an early phase. A great deal of work is needed to consolidate the gains which have already been made. All of the innovations described so far have come into use on a relatively limited scale. Some have had more spectacular effects than others, but in every case it seems reasonable to say that the most sweeping effects are yet to come. Many applications are still in their experimental phase. The most confident expectation we can have of the future is that the revolution will spread as the Industrial Revolution did before it. The discoveries we have already made will continue to transform the world for centuries to come.

There are, however, some clearly delineated problems which still await solution by innovation. The most dramatic is the need to design an efficient system of artificial photosynthesis. All the techniques in biological engineering which we have so far developed are really mere tinkering. However clever we may be in adapting organisms to our multifarious purposes we are still essentially dependent on the bounty of nature. We have achieved so much in so little time because evolution has been so obliging in providing us with a wealth of materials to work with. We have been ingenious in transferring the abilities of one organism to another and in exaggerating particular selected properties which organisms already had. But we really have done nothing totally new. Our biotechnology is not really ours at all. It is nature's technology, shaped by evolution, which we have partly usurped.

We do have the ability now to make genes: to build up lengths of DNA from component parts. We still use this ability, however, mainly for synthesizing genes whose structure we already know. As early as the 1980s, molecular biologists were working on the synthesis of man-made enzymes; chemically synthesized heredity was already with us; and synthesis of a yeast chromosome had been achieved. We have moved a long way along such roads since then, but not yet into a new universe. No one has yet designed and built a totally new functional gene, utterly unknown within the biosphere, to produce a protein with a property and a purpose that the ceaseless trial and error of the evolutionary process has overlooked.

Our biotechnology, therefore, is still working within the context of the biology which we inherited—the biology of which we are a product. Perhaps, even probably, this is not the only biology which could exist. For every function which is served by proteins there seem to be alternatives. All mammals take up oxygen from the air by means of a pigment called hemoglobin. Some insects also use it; but some use other pigments instead. Almost all plants plunder the energy of sunlight by courtesy of the green pigment chlorophyll, but some use brown pigments and others red. Given this variety one is bound to ask: what if there are other proteins, not yet thrown up by mutational trial within our biosphere, which are more efficient at oxygen-uptake than hemoglobin and better at exploiting the energy of sunlight than chlorophyll?

Sunlight is the fuel which sustains life on Earth. The process by which plants extract energy from sunlight, using that energy to build up complex compounds from simpler ones and thereby storing the energy which animals, including humans, use to grow and move and see and think is the life-process itself. We have always exploited that life-process, but in the past we have been able to do so only by using living plants as our agents. We learned to cultivate them, develop them by selective breeding, and, since the 1980s, to meddle with their genes, but we have not yet learned to substitute something of our own making for the living plant. We have not found or made a more efficient substitute for chlorophyll itself outside the naturally-occurring factory which is the living cell.

Until we can design our own systems which can exploit and re-deploy the energy of sunlight as efficiently as the humble algae does, we humans have no real biotechnology of our own. We have many kinds of solar cells which can extract energy from the sunlight and store it as electricity or as heat, but such devices are very crude indeed when one compares them with the technical sophistication and versatility of living plants.

We are making a determined effort to capture and use a greater fraction of the solar energy which falls upon the face of the earth every day. We are trying to make plants flourish where at present they can eke out only the most precarious existence. The ideal situation, however, would be one in which we did not need to work so hard to adapt existing plants to more hostile conditions. If we had our own artificial systems of photosynthesis we might exploit the desert sun ourselves, without using other organisms as intermediaries. Our ultimate ambition must be to make artificial photosynthetic systems more efficient than those which have evolved alongside us throughout the history of life on Earth. Then and only then will we really be able to claim to be technologically self-sufficient. In 2025 it looks as if that might be one of our children's tasks.

17

The End of One
Drug Crisis
and the False Fear
of Another

IN THE PAST FIFTY YEARS neuroscience, psychopharmacology and other means of fiddling with the human brain have advanced less speedily than many people expected. And the increasingly religious majority of mankind can humbly thank their God for it.

Despite our relative slowness, we have made what our grandfathers would have regarded as some frightening steps towards discovering what many of them thought we were not meant to know. We have found out how to tamper with the chemistry of intelligence, the chemistry of memory, the chemistry of sexual desire and the chemistry of moods. But it cannot be said we have begun to shrink into either a dictatorship of the professoriat or a spiritual straitjacket through the application of our new psychological knowhow, our psychotropic drugs and our SQUID monitors.

There is one main simple reason and one main complicated reason why our understanding of the physiological bases of human behavior has not made the same giant strides as our ability to protect the body from disease. The simple reason is the limitation on experiments. The complicated reason is the increasing scientific probability that man has a soul.

In defiance of defenders of inhuman rights, the greater part of our physiological advances in 1975–2025 has (perhaps unfortunately) been based on experimental work done with animals. Human physiology and biochemistry are little different from those of monkeys and rats: our blood is like their blood, our livers work as theirs do. Animals have different sets of genes, but they share with us a common system of genetic determination. It is true that any technique which we wish to introduce into the repertoire of medical science must ultimately be tested on human subjects, and that we can never be wholly sure that humans will react as rats or monkeys do. But before anything medical is done to a person we usually have reasonably good grounds for expecting that it will work to his benefit rather than to his detriment.

Not so with brains. Animals' brains do have much in common with human ones, both in biochemical terms and in terms of functional organization. There are interesting similarities in terms of thinking, memory and even conceptualization. By and large, though, it is the unique features of the human brain which are of most interest to practical researchers. It is in our behavior that we differ crucially from all other living creatures. It is the power of the human mind which makes us into scientists as well as objects of science. The human brain is capable of much more than the brains of our nearest relatives in the animal kingdom, and some attempts to apply knowledge about animal brains to human brains have made learned people look foolish.

Down to the 1960s and 1970s psychiatry made its main medical advances either from observation of mental impairment in people who had suffered some kind of specific brain damage or from attempts to relieve the condition of people suffering mental illness. There was also some appeasing of hypochondriacs. Conclusions based on such untypical samples proved to be of less general application than was sometimes supposed in that almost pre-computer age.

The more complicated reason which has helped to confound our researches into the phenomena of the human mind has to do with the slippery nature of the concepts which we use for talking about it. The nature of the conscious mind has been a matter of dispute for as long as it has been in existence. When the conscious mind contemplates itself, it finds something very different from what it finds when it contemplates the body and brain. Because of this, most people throughout history have believed in a "soul" separable from the body, and when we reject this notion we have increasing difficulty in finding other terms in which to think.

With the coming of brain scanners and sophisticated computers, the anti-religious minority of mankind hoped scientists would soon be able to draw an analogy between the mind and computer software—the programs that determine the behavior of a machine. Their hopes and the analogy proved rubbish. With proper software, computers can indeed do almost everything the human brain can do and do it faster; but they fall far behind the achievements of the human mind—possibly because they lack the element that theologians call divine afflatus. Computers have not helped the human mind to form a more realistic and comprehensible image of itself, and have instead swung debates about the existence of the soul some way in favor of the theologians. This was unexpected, and Christians in particular are growing bold and almost aggressive about it. "The core of the essential mystery of life," says Pope John Paul IV, "has not been yielded in our TC age to the disappearing humanists." The main moral arguments which developed when brain-scanners and/or psychotropic chemistry were used on (a) drug addicts, on (b) people seeking higher IQs or better memories, on (c) people searching for greater sexual satisfaction, and on (d) lunatics, criminals and politicians were all affected by this recovery of religious self-confidence.

Men have been using psychotropic drugs since time immemorial. Many plant species contain—apparently as non-functional metabolic by-products—compounds capable of affecting the brain in ways that give rise to alterations of conscious experience. Marijuana is a euphoric. Psilocybin (from agaric mushrooms) is a hallucinogen. Ethanol (alcohol) is an intoxicant. Such natural products were used for generations without anyone having the least idea how or why they worked.

With the development of organic chemistry vast numbers of new compounds unknown to nature were produced throughout the twentieth century. The first hypnosedatives (sleep-inducing drugs), like barbital (Veronal) introduced in 1903 and phenobarbital (Luminal) introduced in 1912, seemed welcome. They replaced rather dangerous substances, including opium derivatives like laudanum. But they were the harbinger of a crisis to come.

Greater problems attended the drugs which began to be introduced in the mid twentieth century. They included the pep pills or amphetamines (like Benzedrine), which were first widely used to keep people working despite exhaustion during the Second World War; but which then became fashionable in the 1960s as providers of artificial excitement. Their usefulness was sharply reduced by a let-down effect as the drugs wore off, and by the fact that consistent users faced awkward withdrawal symptoms when the supply stopped.

This was supposed to be mitigated by the next generation of anti-depressant drugs like imipramine (Tofranil), but man was by now entering deep into the business of creating artificial moods. The fashion was extended by minor tranquillizers, like chlordiazepoxide (Librium) and diazepam (Valium), whose relative safety led to their being widely prescribed as a shield against everyday stress. By the 1980s biochemists also reported some success with drugs which were said to switch on and off aggressive behavior, and with drugs which had aphrodisiac effects.

Because the new drugs were invented by professionals in laboratories and utilized by doctors, the impression was created that psychochemistry had come of age as a discipline. It had not. In the 1980s very little was known about the biochemical processes by which these multifarious drugs wreaked their various effects. The question of why Valium had a tranquillizing effect, or why imipramine was useful in relieving depression, remained to some extent a mystery.

Despite this lack of understanding, the drugs were by 1985 being used on a very wide scale. By the mid 1980s more than 100 million prescriptions for minor tranquillizers were being issued annually in the United States alone, along with 50 million prescriptions for hypnosedatives and 20 million for antidepressants. Some 30 million people—one-eighth of the American population—were taking psychotropic medications on a more-or-less regular basis. Most of the other seven-eighths were sometimes using them. At one point it became common for large numbers of schoolchildren to be diagnosed as "hyperactive"—and tranquillized.

This was a crisis, and our fathers took a long time to see it. There was no real sense in which Valium cured stress or the antidepressants cured sadness. They soothed the symptoms, and sometimes sapped energies which were needed to tackle the problems that had made the patients tense or sad.

During this drug crisis period of 1968–98 many popular drugs were seen to have short-term undesirable side-effects, but it was argued that these could be avoided simply by discontinuing treatment. More subtle long-term effects were more difficult to detect. Remember that for 400 years after Raleigh the long-term effects of tobacco remained undiscovered.

Physiological dependence was a more visible problem. It was primarily associated with opium derivatives such as heroin, used medically as pain-killers, but it slowly became clear that amphetamines were also commonly addictive, and that some tranquillizers and antidepressants sometimes could be.

195

In the thirty years before 1990 the constituency of illicit drug users grew at a frightening pace, and governments responded with all the mistakes so typical of those last years of over-government. Heavy taxes had long rightly been placed on the traditional intoxicant alcohol (which was incompatible with driving a motor car) and the traditional tranquillizer tobacco (whose long-term damage to health had been discovered only because it had for a long while existed). By contrast the new drugs were not taxed. In countries with socialist medicine systems they were sometimes handed out free on medicare or the national health service. Nobody knew of some of the consequences of the new drugs because they had not existed long enough for there to be records of them.

Governments responded by setting up huge bureaucracies to check whether the next lot of drugs to come along might have even worse results than the existing set of drugs (of whose consequences they were unaware). This is an unsuitable task for a large bureaucracy, but the bureaucracy inevitably multiplied. All that the multiplied bureaucracy could do was delay the next lot of drugs which by this time generally were designed for market reasons to avoid some of the inconveniences associated with their predecessors. Just as barbital had been preferable to laudanum, and phenobarbital preferable to barbital, and the benzodiazepines (such as Amytal and Seconal) preferable to phenobarbitals, so methyl phenidate (Ritalin) was preferable to amphetamine (Benzedrine) or methylamphetamine (Methedrine). Then imipramine (Tofranil) had still benigner effects. But the bureaucracy's job was to hold all new things back.

Bureaucratic controls were established over laboratories examining new drugs. As security then became nobody's sole responsibility, some of these drugs escaped on to the streets. An early example was the powerful hallucinogen called lysergic acid diethylamide (LSD 25). LSD and marijuana were for a time a cheaper way of getting a high than a heavily taxed bottle of whisky. Young innocents and old fools therefore became hooked on them and on opium derivatives like heroin.

As people became addicted and demand grew the drugs became more expensive and were hit by erratic legislative prohibitions that did not work. The prohibitions were directed especially at pushers, and everybody should have known from experience the consequences of that. During the 1920s the United States had tried to prohibit alcohol in the same way. Predictably, organized crime then took over the marketplace. Pushers became very nasty people indeed, sometimes blackmailing their crazed clients to commit crimes for them, with guns blazing. The clients, desperate for the money with which to buy a fix, also went in for a lot of crime on their own private enterprise account.

By 1985 the drug crisis could be cured only if tax systems could replace bans, if the bureaucracy blocking the introduction of safer drugs could be overthrown, and if science could break through. Fortunately the last two things happened rather quickly.

In America the FDA (Food and Drug Administration) had become a bad joke in the late 1970s, and deregulation had become a popular word. The bureaucracy successfully resisted deregulation which would cost it many of its existing jobs, but it did feel sufficiently embarrassed not to expand further. The organic chemists at the regulatory agencies held on to their jobs, and created new jobs for some organic chemists as their assistants, just when organic chemistry was becoming an anachronism. But there were not many genetic engineers at these agencies. Indeed the old-fashioned bureaucrats wanted to keep these clever people out, lest they leapfrog above them. And happily the next psychotropic surge came with the genetic engineering revolution.

It was recognized well before the 1980s that psychotropic chemicals often had their effect because they mimicked the action of more complicated molecules produced naturally within the body. The action of β-endorphin, the body's own endogenous morphine, was mimicked by heroin and other opium derivatives. β-endorphin is a chemical whose function is to regulate the sensitivity of the nervous system: when produced

197

in quantity it suppresses the reactivity of the system. Heroin, therefore, could suppress pain and give a sensation of euphoric detachment from external stimuli. Problems of addiction were caused because the natural production of β-endorphin involves a system of negative feedback. When heroin is administered from without, the body stops producing its own endogenous morphine. When consistent heroin use is suddenly discontinued it takes some time for β-endorphin production to begin again, and in the meantime the nervous system becomes horribly hyper-reactive.

During the 1990s the advance of elementary genetic engineering made possible the commercial production of β-endorphins. The natural compound replaced morphine and cocaine as a local anesthetic, and began to be widely used in the treatment of heroin addicts. As with methadone and other drugs previously used to wean heroin addicts off the more dangerous drugs, some critics complained there was a problem of substitute addiction—the victims simply became addicted to β-endorphin instead of heroin. But this was a much less pernicious problem.

For one thing, β-endorphin, being a natural compound, had few biochemical side-effects. For another, it was possible to use β-endorphin much more precisely to control withdrawal symptoms while the body's own endorphin-producing system was resuscitated. By 2003 understanding of the system had progressed to the point where it was possible to reset the chemostat regulating the body's own production of β-endorphin, so that the reactivity of a person's nervous system could be more-or-less permanently adjusted.

By virtue of these advances heroin addiction was effectively wiped out as a social problem fifteen to twenty years ago. Governments then sensibly moved from bans to taxation systems—with the highest taxes on the addictive things that did most harm (opium, gin, tobacco, plus some of the drugs which were given free on medicare in the early 1980s) and no taxes on such things as endogenous morphines. Commercial interests made the untaxed things more and more palatable, so that alcohol consumption also virtually disappeared except for certain expensive wines. Today, Palo Altophin is imbibed at parties because it tastes nicer and creates a more social atmosphere than gin, as well as being compatible with driving a motor car (and indeed compatible with doing practically anything provided you check first on a miniSQUID scanner).

After the breakthrough with β-endorphin, it was only a matter of time before biochemists were able to isolate natural compounds produced in very low concentrations within the body which give rise to alterations of consciousness similar to tranquillizers, amphetamines and antidepressants. In these areas, too, aided by intelligent tax changes, artificial drugs were slowly driven out of use by a wholly natural pharmacopeia produced by genetic engineering techniques. This displacement was important in eliminating many of the unpleasant side-effects sometimes associated with these compounds. As is usual with innovations, however, various counter-attacks were mounted.

Some critics complained that one social problem had merely been traded for another. They said that the granting to people of technical control over their own endorphin systems encouraged over-insulation from environmental stimuli, much as central heating encourages people to keep their homes over-warm. Even today a few people argue that over-indulgence in endogenous morphine is helping to sap people's energy, and that there is such a thing as being too contented.

These complaints were as nothing, however, to the next storm that broke. In 2003 advertisements began to appear on TCs proclaiming the imminent arrival of a new generation of compounds such as memoratives which would help people to remember or forget, IQ boosters which could make our children much cleverer than ourselves (perish the thought), and aphrodisiacs which would change the chemistry of sexual attraction.

Several leaders of the newly confident churches said that these drugs promised blasphemous powers that scarce to God were given, and called for prohibition (which would have meant black markets). As we can now see, they exaggerated. Some of these drugs have had unhappy side-effects. It is good that these have been mitigated by sensible taxation, and by the new device of computer checks through credit cards (in some countries some of these drugs can be bought only by credit card which, when entered into your bank statement, marries with your computerized health card so that the sale is refused and your HMO is alerted to give you therapy if you would be a dangerous purchaser of such drugs). But, on balance, the new drugs of 2000–10 have brought more happiness than pain to the world, without changing many ordinary people's lives as much as was once expected.

The memoratives can either enhance or expunge memories. The first of them, magnesium pemoline, worked by stimulating a brain enzyme involved in the synthesis of RNA, one of the elements in the biochemistry of memory-storage. After this enzyme was identified and the gene coding for it was isolated, other enzymes catalyzing the process of memory-storage were quickly tabulated in the same way. Out of this research emerged a series of drugs, some giving a temporary boost to the retentive powers of the memory, some facilitating access to deeper memories ordinarily beyond conscious recall, and some blocking processes of recall so as to blank out the short-term memory and to bring about amnesia.

The amnesiac drugs were expected to be purely medical, and it was thought that there would be little demand for such compounds even on the black market. In two sad respects there was. The amnesiacs provided an ingenious way in which one person could harm another (something for which, alas, there always seems to be a demand); and some people began to look on amnesiac drugs as a gentle form of self-elimination, preferable to suicide.

The doses taken by near-suicides are sometimes large enough to cause permanent impairment, and subsequent treatment with memory-enhancing drugs is then only partially successful.

Should amnesiacs therefore be tightly controlled? The United German Chancellor, Herr Beckenbauer, commented in 2011:

> Most people who in the olden days would have committed suicide today prefer to take amnesiac drugs. Given that those with amnesia can sometimes be rescued—and that, even where one personality is irrevocably destroyed, another can often be built amid the ruins—it seems to me preferable and less messy to allow those who feel suicidal to use amnesiac drugs rather than jump off high buildings.

This German view has not been widely followed. When an amnesiac drug is sold in the United States, other than on a doctor's prescription, it is today very highly taxed; and the retailer will usually insist on a computer credit card check.

More complicated problems arise from the presence in the world of the memory-enhancing drugs. When researchers first went in search of such compounds, students thought diets of them would cause them to sail through exams. Those who got the drugs via bootleggers failed their exams instead.

A good memory is not one which holds everything that is poured into it. The key to efficient memorization is the ability to select which impressions are worth retaining. The best memory is the one which is most adept in the art of forgetting. The sharpest mind is the one which has the happy facility of ignoring all irrelevances. Under memory-enhancing drugs, a student is apt to retain all his sensory impressions in all their confusing profusion. Because of this confusion and profusion, drug-enhanced memories are difficult to use constructively at a later time, and they decay more quickly than memories implanted by force of effort.

Memory-enhancing drugs can be used constructively. They are useful in brief research projects where the attention of the user can be focussed exclusively on material which is both worth retaining and already inherently ordered—that is to say, prepared for use in this way. Also, some pleasures can be more fun if you use a memorative—like playing bridge with a partner who wants you to use a particular bidding system that day.

And some people occasionally value the drug for its inherent aesthetic qualities, much as people once used opium-based hallucinogens, but without the same danger of addiction.

The problems and opportunities that arise in connection with intelligence-enhancing drugs—the so-called IQ-boosters—are different in detail but similar in kind. Insofar as IQ has a physical basis, it is through the speed of information-processing. Drugs which increase the rate of information-exchange between neurones can therefore provide an immediate boost to IQ. This speed of processing is a necessary condition of a high IQ, but it is not a sufficient one. At present we only have drugs which will achieve this effect on a temporary basis, but in future we will probably be able to modify the chemostat which regulates the normal level of the brain's functioning. The main problem will continue to be dosage. There is a fine line between constructive enhancement and an overstimulation which temporarily destroys the brain's ability to function. Manic behavior and epileptic seizures can both be induced by gross overdosing with IQ-boosters, and even safe doses sometimes disturb sensory perception, reduce co-ordination and cause migraines.

The difficulty, once again, is lack of selectivity. The IQ enhancers work on all the neuronal systems within the brain, not just the ones that are involved in the actual business of thinking. A powerful intellect is not the gift of a hyperactive brain. It is the property of a brain which has developed and maintained some particular circuits to a level which we may be tempted to call preternatural.

As with memory-enhancing drugs, IQ-boosters can sometimes be used constructively. It is too cynical to say that they can be wisely used only by people too intelligent to want to use them. There are some individuals of abnormally low intelligence who do owe their incapacity to a general reduction of function in the brain, and who can therefore be helped by periodic administration of intelligence-enhancing drugs. Ordinary people may sometimes gain benefit from the drugs in the quick completion of particular tasks.

Because of the dangers of overdose, IQ-boosters are heavily

taxed except under prescription, and usually computer credit card checks are compulsory. Apocryphal stories circulating in contemporary society, suggesting that such controls mean we are ruled by a secret élite of the super-intelligent who are jealously withholding the secret of their success from ordinary people, are, of course, not to be credited.

The new psychotropic drugs which caused most stir in the media in 2005 were the aphrodisiacs and other sexually exciting compounds. Interest in such drugs extends back for thousands of years. Demand for them generated a good deal of commercial activity even when there was no source of authentic supply. Sometimes even the old witch doctors produced results. Cantharis, or Spanish fly, provided men with an unusually strong and persistent erection, but the condition was painful rather than erotic and the side-effects were nasty. The moral from this can be applied to many of the modern aphrodisiacs. In their way they worked, but people often found that the effects were not what they had really wanted.

Today's aphrodisiacs can be roughly sorted into three categories: attractants, erectants and exultants. Attractants are compounds which are calculated to enhance the sexual attractiveness of the users, and work by subliminal olfactory stimulation. Erectants are safe compounds which have the same effect as cantharis, conferring technical control over the erection of the penis. Exultants are compounds which induce the sensations of orgasm; they are sometimes called orgasmics.

The most efficient attractant drugs are based on human pheromones: hormones secreted by the skin to signal the sex of the secretor which sometimes assist in triggering sexual desire in others. When a child grows up in a normal household, and is equally fond of both parents, he or she is usually attracted in adulthood to the pheromones of the opposite sex; that is how we perpetuate the race. When a boy is too exclusively attached in childhood to Mummy, he can become attuned to the wrong set of pheromones; that is a main cause of homosexuality, which can now often be "cured" if one wants to cure it. As a famous

203

English historian once said, homosexuals do miss a great deal of fun, which never even in olden days provided a good reason for putting them in prison. After their overdue liberation in the late twentieth century, they still did not become every father's dream. Some children passing the age of puberty are now subjected to "corrective" pheromone-sniffing at their health maintenance organizations, and are diverted from being what is no longer called "gay."

In other parts of the sexual jungle, perfumes supposedly containing pheromones were already being marketed in the 1980s, although it was not until later that the actual proteins were identified and isolated. The effects of these chemicals in high concentrations proved something of a disappointment to men and women who had hoped to be able to drive members of the opposite sex wild with desire. In some animals—notably insects and those mammal species where females are in heat for only a brief period—pheromones do work that way, but human behavior is not regulated by olfactory conditioning. Pheromones convey information rather than transmit commands. Anointing oneself with concentrated pheromones typical of one's sex did prove to have some effect in calling attention to oneself, but was not in itself a sufficient basis for the birth of an infatuation or arousal.

A greater utility has been found in anointing oneself with pheromones typical of the opposite sex, which does have a marked effect in discouraging unwanted attentions—they are used by beautiful women who used to be annoyed by wolves. It is probable that the most widespread calculated use of pheromones today is in this vein, which makes the appellation "attractants" somewhat ironic. Biochemistry may yet turn up the technological equivalent of the love potions of legend, but the best guess in 2025 is still that the chemistry of sexual attraction does not lend itself to such manipulation.

The discovery of effective erectants followed quickly from the elucidation of the actual physiological mechanism by which erections are produced. As it proved relatively simple to side-step the physiological let-down effect which usually deflates erections after ejaculation, the marketing of erectants in 2007 was greeted with a wave of initial enthusiasm. A few sexual hobbyists still make regular use of them, but the general boom was short-lived. The drugs maintain the physical capability of erection but not the psychological enthusiasm. The let-down effect is not merely a matter of physiology, but also a matter of cancellation of desire. When in the old days people pleaded that the spirit was willing but the flesh was weak, they were sometimes deluding themselves or their would-be mates. Now the aphorism is (truthfully) reversed.

Even in the treatment of impotence, where erectants have been undeniably useful, they have not been an unqualified success. Their use has proved to be one more example of treating the symptoms without reaching the root cause. Impotence is usually a physical reflection of a psychological problem. Restoring the physical capacity for sexual intercourse rarely makes sufferers any happier with their situation in the long run, and may actually lead to a further deterioration of self-assurance because people resent any dependence on the drug.

The third category of aphrodisiacs, the exultant drugs, are rapidly metabolized hormones which trigger the physiological responses generally associated with surges of joy, sensations of triumph and (sometimes) sexual orgasm. Again, much was expected of these drugs by enthusiasts, although there was a hard fight before they were allowed on the market. The widely expressed fears of addiction cloaked a more deeply felt moral objection to the availability of such drugs.

Once on the market, however, the boom in them faded quickly, for a predictable reason. Most people have always had available the means to induce orgasms in themselves. If thousands of years of masturbation had not made the message clear, fifteen years of exultant drugs have helped drive the lesson home. When we speak of joy, or triumph, or sexual pleasure, it is not the physiological reaction which is important but the experiential content. Synthesizing the physiological symptoms of joy or triumph or pleasure is worth nothing if there is nothing to enjoy, no triumph achieved, no experience in which to take pleasure. Like all shortcuts to happiness and fulfilment, this one not only failed to reach the appropriate destination but led into a small and rather sad psychological wilderness.

In the end, the scientists' substitute for the various imagined forms of amatory magic served to show what a hollow sham amatory magic usually was. The granting of these naïve wishes illuminated their vanity. There are still some people who see this as a failure of psychochemical science, or as a kind of tragedy. In fact it is welcome news, for it conserves the real value of authentic human experiences. It reminds us that it is worth working hard to win pleasure, to achieve triumphs, to capture moments of joy and to make love, because it is really the effort and achievement which make the mere sensations into something worthwhile.

18

Handling the Mad
and the Bad

THE LAST QUARTER of the twentieth century saw two important innovations in machinery for examining brain functions from outside the skull. Before then such monitoring had been carried out mainly by means of the electroencephalograph, a sensitive galvanometer picking up signals by electrodes attached to the scalp. Such instruments revealed various brain rhythms which could be loosely correlated with some mental phenomena. The "alpha" rhythm was apparently typical of the brain at rest, disappearing when the subject's attention was engaged, while the "theta" rhythm seemed to be associated with emotional changes. Most of the interesting data revealed by electroencephalographic scanning, however, was concerned with brain activity during the various phases of sleep. The instrument was not sufficiently sensitive to yield much insight into the working of the conscious mind.

The first important innovation in brain-scanning after 1975 was not concerned with the electrical activity of the brain but with biochemical activity. It arose in connection with the development of the technological art of tomography, the production of X-ray cross-sections through the body. Early tomographs were synthesized by computers from X-ray pictures taken at several different angles, but these were gradually replaced during the 1980s by so-called PET scanners (PET standing for "positron emission tomography").

The new technique involved the introduction into the body, by injection or inhalation, of radioactive isotopes which produce positrons as they decay. Positrons are anti-electrons which, upon meeting their counterpart particles, annihilate to release two photons which travel in opposite directions. These pass straight out of the body, and can be picked up by a ring of sensitive radiation detectors positioned around the subject. Computer analysis can pinpoint the position from which each photon-pair originates, and can synthesize all such data into a color-coded cross-section of any part of the body, showing areas of intense metabolic activity.

From the middle of the 1980s through the 1990s these PET scanners allowed researchers to see more and more clearly which parts of the brain were metabolically most active while a conscious subject is performing various kinds of mental activity: working on an arithmetical problem, speaking, listening to music, and so on. It also became possible to monitor the effects of various psychotropic drugs on the brain, and to investigate anomalies in the biochemical functioning of the brains of people suffering from mental illnesses. Here, therefore, was a technique which involved little or no risk, and which could be used experimentally with relatively large sample populations.

PET scanning revealed that brain activity in schizophrenics and some other mentally sick people could be distinguished from the brain activity of healthy individuals according to characteristic patterns. By the 1990s these patterns were well enough known and understood for PET scanners to become important diagnostic tools in respect of schizophrenia and some other related diseases. The armory of investigation was then supplemented with another kind of machine: a very much refined version of the electroencephalograph. Instead of electrodes of the traditional kind, these new machines employed SQUIDs: "super-conducting quantum interference devices." These are indented rings of super-conducting metal which sustain within themselves a regular magnetic flux that is readily disturbed by external electro-magnetic events. Although these could not be embedded in the scalp like ordinary electrodes because superconductivity requires low temperatures, it was possible by the year 2000 to construct a ring to encircle the head whose signals could be integrated by computer to make tomographs in much the same way as PET scanners did.

By this means information about the electrical activity of the brain could be presented in the same form as information about its biochemical activity. The data thus gained was at first more difficult to sort out than information from PET, but the pictures that emerged were much more detailed. With the aid of these machines, work on localization of function within the brain and on the effects of various drugs was allowed to progress much more rapidly.

Although the flashiest debate aroused by the maturing of SQUID was the battle in 2004 to be allowed to pry into the brain patterns of politicians, the more important human debate, which climaxed in 2008, was about the most compassionate and efficient ways to treat what our fathers called the mentally ill and the criminally deviant, and our grandfathers called the mad and the bad. This was not a controversy between scalpel-happy brain surgeons and sentimental sociologists, between would-be controllers and shocked libertarians. Compared with what people twenty years earlier would have expected, all these four groups had by 2004 changed sides.

When we asked our computer to pick out a typical statement of the 2008 case against "tampering with brains," which also summarized the developments of 1984–2007, it suggested the paper delivered by the Emeritus Professor of Medicine at the University of Toronto, Dr. Charles Simpson, for the teleconference of the World Medical Association in 2008. When we asked for the most complete and nearly simultaneous expression and history of the opposite case, it suggested a paper by the Japanese sociologist Dr. Yasuhiro Nagawa for the Tokyo Colloquium in the same year.

Dr. Nagawa's paper contains several hundred "check your correlations" footnotes, whereby the database dabbler can roam through the crime and sickness statistics of many countries and communes, and himself work out the correlations which show Nagawa's views to be statistically right. We have not included those footnotes in this print-out. We have checked through an appropriate sample of them, and Nagawa's figures stand up every time.

Dr. Simpson's paper contains no figures or footnotes, but is full of a civilized man's expressions of worry and doubt. Since the 1980s the academic trend has been for scholars in the physical sciences to grow more worried about what they are doing. But scholars in the statistical sciences like sociology, with far more facts at their disposal than ever before, have become more dogmatic and hard-nosed in proclaiming which policies do and do not work. Some people may even detect that trend in this book.

If over-government had continued, this could have led to undesirable dictatorships billed as "for our own good." As we can now choose our government with our feet, by going to live in the community whose lifestyle we like, we can imbibe Dr. Nagawa's statistically accurate views but choose to live in communities more influenced by Dr. Simpson's humanity. If we are sensible we will in some degree do both.

Most doctors [*wrote Professor Simpson in 2008*] agree that experiments on human subjects involving gross interference with the brain can be justified only by the desperate hope that extreme suffering might be alleviated for seriously ill

210

patients. As an early example, a generation ago surgeons severed the *corpus callosum* in a number of epileptic patients in order to inhibit the spread of epileptic seizures through the brain.

Ever since then, so-called social scientists have been urging us to do things to mildly ill or supposedly immoral people which are against our medical oath, and which also would not really work in the way which these ignorant people suppose. That pressure seems likely to mount frighteningly in the next dozen years. Usually, we doctors have surrendered too early to those who think that minds and behavior can be cured with drugs and the knife. We have fought back later, but recovered only part of the ground lost.

Thus in the 1980s a campaign led by doctors happily helped to eliminate prefrontal lobotomy as a treatment for schizophrenia throughout North America, and caused restrictions to be placed on the use of electro-convulsive therapy. We knew that the success these treatments sometimes had in alleviating the suffering of patients was often offset by the damage they caused. Such treatments could not be realistically regarded as cures. At best, they represented the medical equivalent of persuading a delinquent machine to function by kicking it. At worst, they might be likened to solving the problem of a club foot by amputation of the limb.

Some people say these complaints cannot be levied against psychotropic drugs, especially now they are being replaced by their natural counterparts. We all agree that the syndromes of certain mental illnesses—particularly schizophrenia, manic depression and chronic melancholia—have specific biochemical abnormalities as their almost invariable correlates. But it is unscientific to say that these abnormalities are therefore the cause of the illnesses.

None of the diseases concerned has been found to result from anything as simple as a deficiency of a particular chemical. In each illness there is a complex failure of cellular function—usually involving the cell membrane—which affects the integration of neurones into an efficient system.

211

Injection of particular drugs can help. Doctors have long known of a treatment for manic depression that involves the use of lithium carbonate, but its toxicity has caused unfortunate side-effects.

Today there is a mounting propaganda campaign that many cases of mental illness might soon be cured by genetic transformation of the neurones which would restore the capacity for self-repair to the cells. In the past few years the genetic transformation of some bodily tissues—particularly the blood, the spleen and the pancreas—has become commonplace as a treatment for inherited genetic deficiencies. But the groundwork for such treatments had long been laid by elaborate experiments on animals, and it is nonsense to say that we can safely proceed to attempt genetic transformation of the brain tissue of complicated human beings after experiments on the tiny hindbrains of rats.

We physicians are entering a period when more intense and more widespread pressures will be put upon us to do improper things like that. The pressures come from social "scientists" who think each correlation is a proof of cause even when it is merely a symptom of an effect in a different species of mammal which is irrelevant anyway.

The pressures from these people will increase in intensity because it is becoming possible genetically to engineer so-called "improvements," as defined by social scientists, in moods, memory, amnesia, intelligence, and sexual satisfaction. Note the importance of definitions here. If some social scientist thinks there is an increase in sexual satisfaction when a man gets a faster erection, then his figures will show that human happiness increases because we physical scientists can now produce drugs which will gave a man a faster erection. But the new drug addict may well get less sexual satisfaction thereby. My main worry here is not permanent impairment of the race because of the machismo associated with careless self-abuse—the drugs will not have permanent effects. But they may in some degree make people calmer at the wrong time, more adept at remembering things they had better forget, more drugged to forget things they would be wise to remember, more skilled at passing IQ tests that are anyway pointless. All of the "wonder" drugs are therefore going to be disappointments. When they are put on today's free markets, after a while they will not sell.

But in the meanwhile we physicians are going to be permitted, and probably told, to do things which the customer does not want, to do things which we know to be dangerous and unscientific nonsense. Worse, the new and wider pressures on us will have little to do with the relatively few extreme cases of serious mental illness, and much more to do with the very large number of cases in the grey areas where it is difficult to distinguish mild mental illness from annoying social unusualness.

The main problem with identifying and classifying the behavioral symptoms of mental illness is that the same behavioral tendencies can frequently be found as occasional aspects of commonplace conduct. Although there are some cases of unambiguous mental illness, there are a great many more cases where somebody is temporarily eccentric, and we are going to be asked to drug away the eccentricity from which genius sometimes flowers. For every indubitable case of chronic depression, there are millions of cases where people get depressed because they are temporarily living in depressing circumstances. For every authentic kleptomaniac, there are hundreds of thousands of petty thieves.

Even if we physicians are not ordered to start tampering with your brain on the third occasion when you cheat in your tax return, even if it is only confirmed criminals with dangerous SQUID patterns whom we start treating with new drugs, those drugs can make those criminals worse. Every scientist except a social scientist knows that the physiological correlates of mental states can be consequences instead of causes. The physiological reaction undergone by an arachnophobe when she sees a spider are clearly responses to a specific perception and a mental attitude. Suppressing that physical reaction would not count as an attack on the cause of the arachnophobe's fear of spiders, whatever that cause might be. It might make her more terribly frightened of something else. In just the same way some of the chemical abnormalities associated with mental states of mania and depression and criminality are evoked as physiological responses to experienced situations. By trying to play God with them we could turn muggers into murderers, or at least their lawyers would argue that we had.

The difficulty of drawing a line between irksomely antisocial behavior and mental illness is explained by the fact that there is no such line. The idea of mental health and the idea of moral rectitude are inextricably entwined. The attempt to distinguish clearly between actions which are the unsullied produce of free will and actions which are partly determined by biochemical imbalance or environmental conditioning is doomed by confusion at the most fundamental level. The decision when or whether to use drug treatments for people convicted of crimes, or children who seem hyperactive, or adults who find life too stressful or too depressing will always remain an arbitrary one.

The libertarian advances of the past decade have been concerned with removing from governments the power to make arbitrary decisions. Now some social scientists are hell-bent on giving back those powers to computer-consulting authorities in the most sensitive areas of individual freedom, and are going to try to force us medical scientists inefficiently to do their dirty work for them.

Dr. Nagawa's paper was written in very different style, as is evident from its first sentence.

This paper will put forward nine propositions. Each of them can be checked independently by the reader through the database on his TC. The appendix lists the entry numbers used to arrive at the particular figures and correlations cited here.

1 Despite the advances of 1994–2008, crime has caused the greatest increase in misery over the past century. If the misery caused by world-wide poverty in 1907 is put at 100,

our TC research (see appendix) suggests a misery index from poverty of only around 8 in 2007. If the misery caused by disease in 1907 is put at 100, our TC research suggests an index of 23 now. If the misery caused by crime in 1907 is put at 100, the equivalent index figure was still around 180 in 2007, having come down from 683 in 1994. In particular areas of particular cities, even allowing for the under-reporting of crime in 1907, the misery index from crime had risen to a fantastic 3,000–4,000 in 1994. This last figure did not merely reflect the increase in reported and unreported crime in the late twentieth century, but also the misery caused by changes in whole ways of life: old people scared to walk alone through parks at night, and so on. In view of the huge increases in opportunities for tracking criminals, for psychiatrically curing criminals, for quick transport of police to the spot, for televiewing troubled streets no longer dim-lit in thick fogs, this rise in misery through crime represented one of the most extraordinary misachievements of the whole period of over-government.

2 Even in 2008 the smallest crime rates are in villages and communes where everybody knows everybody else. The worst crime rates are in big cities where nobody knows anybody else, and where the police have lost touch with one section of the community.

3 During the period up to 1995, when crime prevention was mainly a public-sector industry, the greatest success was achieved by Japan. In 1950–95 Japan carried through the only industrial-plus-urbanization revolution in history during which crime rates went down.

4 Since around 1995 urban crime prevention has been contracted out by most civilized communities to competitive private enterprises. These enterprises have helped bring crime rates down swiftly, though (see appendix) with some spectacularly corrupt failures. The TC allows us to correlate at operational level the reasons for the success of pre-1995 Japan and of some competitive crime-prevention business before and since then.

5   Japan's successful formula stands out clearly from every correlation. The formula was "fairly certain, but generally light, punishment." In 1986 you had a 76 per cent chance of being caught if you mugged an old woman in Tokyo; you had under a 2 per cent chance of being caught if you mugged her in parts of New York. When a crime was committed in Tokyo in 1986, the police arrived on the spot within two-and-a-half minutes on average; the police in New York were often not informed about crimes because nobody expected them to catch anybody anyway. In European and American cities in the 1980s the marginal productivity of an extra detective was nil. The marginal productivity of an extra policeman on foot was high, but this dropped sharply when he was put into a squad car or was otherwise isolated from the community. During 1950–90 American and European police forces increased the number of their detectives and motorized their police forces because these were nicer jobs for these public servants to have.

6   An early success in crime prevention in America came in private leisure areas like Disneyworld and other commercial parks. The objective in these leisure areas was: "Don't have any crime to spoil our customers' enjoyment today." The methods were: to track groups or individuals who look as if they might cause trouble (follow them by some high-school football-coach type dressed as Goofy); plus controlled means of egress from places where money is handled; plus extensive consultation by walkie-talkie about movements of sinister-looking people. These methods have been extended by the competitive crime prevention corporations that are now paid on performance contract. Check any database for relative successes of systems of computerized television surveillance over danger areas for crimes, and methods of narrowing the egress from those areas after crimes are committed. These "nosey-parker" systems are generally given overwhelming approval by referenda in previous high-crime urban areas, and anybody who claims these checks are an intolerable invasion of privacy can move to a smaller com-

mune—many of which let nobody be watched at any time.

The other nosey-parker post-1995 trend has been to attach tracking devices to all guns and some previously convicted people. Some areas still allow all citizens to carry arms, but say that each gun must have a tracker device constantly switched on and bleeping a silent radio message, so that the police know where every gun in their area is at any particular time (and can check which ones have not got their trackers switched on, making them instant suspects after a shooting). Other tracker devices have to be carried by particular people; a requirement for being granted parole is often to be constantly traceable in this way.

7   All the respectable databases show that the least successful legal systems up to 1994 were those based on adversarial games played by lawyers, with rights of the accused not to have their previous convictions recorded, and rights of trial by jury instead of by computer-aided assessment of guilt and of how best and most humanely to stop the criminal doing it again. Under the old over-government system the average time taken by a trial in America multiplied nine times between the late 1940s and the early 1990s, and by 1989 America employed twenty times as many lawyers per million people as did more successful Japan. The conventional American argument was that the twentieth-century American system, relying mainly on over-employment of lawyers, prevented miscarriages of justice. Actually (check through your TCs), it caused more miscarriages of justice than any other system within a democracy.

8   The least successful mode of punishment has been the conventional prison system. In the 1980s these were institutions which achieved an extraordinary economic record by marking up actually negative gross production. Prisons then were creating more recidivists than they were curing criminals. A man sent to prison for an offense was more likely to offend again, and become part of a criminal gang, than a man left out of prison after committing the same offense.

In the 1990s, competitive searches for more scientific cures began. Sometimes these were deceptively easy: witness the man who in 1960–90 had been sent to prison fourteen times for exposing himself—at an eventual cost to the taxpayer while imprisoned of $30,000 a year—and who eventually accepted being admitted to a commune which practiced voluntary nudity. The commune was paid $20,000 for each year when he was kept out of prison. Voluntary farming out of criminals on these contracts, specifying $20,000 for each year they do not commit an offense against anybody else, are now very common, though with constant inspection (including by long distance random televiewing) to make sure these are not slave labor camps. Some communes devoted to love, communal property and good works make a substantial slice of their income by taking in convicted criminals on these contracts, and they have had some astonishing successes.

For those criminals who do not want to be exiled to become partners in rural idylls, there is the alternative of accepting the requirement to carry a track-you-down device everywhere; and there are also some areas which rely on the old public-sector Japanese deterrent of shame. It was common in the 1980s for Japanese police to post pictures at police stations and other places, saying, "Nobuhiro Kato of such an address in such a community and belonging to Mr. Wada's section in such a factory has committed burglary and is on probation." Everybody connected with the young man then felt shame, and worked hard to persuade him not to err again.

9   Even today (2007) the figures show that over 90 per cent of crime is committed by 0.2 per cent of the population. In the high-crime days before 1994, these 0.2 per cent were constantly in and out of prisons. They became the dominant jailbirds there and corrupted any new inmates committed to them. Most of these 0.2 per cent prove to have distinctive brain patterns under SQUID scrutiny. Judges now take account of those SQUID readings in deciding what options of sentence to offer, for example whether probation monitored by a tracker would work. Receiving communes, willing to accept exiles for a fee, demand to read SQUID patterns too.

In future some patients will be able to change their brain patterns by biofeedback training after reading their SQUIDs. It is neither humane nor sensible to say that criminals should be forbidden to use this technique. Some physicians, who think biofeedback experiments should take place mainly under their control, are mounting a campaign to forbid judges to rule that there should be "tampering with the brains of criminals as a punishment for crime." But any biofeedback experiments to change brain patterns will be an option in the range of sentences handed out. Often they will be the option the criminals choose. If such experiments are not undertaken under physicians' control, criminals and their families will increasingly make such experiments outside the physicians' control. The brain patterns associated with criminality are well known, and the families of possible patients are particularly eager to cure them. Some people say the new drugs coming along will make this more frightening, but they should make it easier.

Since 2008 crime rates have continued to fall, and there is no doubt Dr. Nagawa proved a true analyst as well as prophet. The biggest, but accepted, interference with human freedom since 2008 has been the growth of tracking devices, which have to be carried by many convicted criminals and also by some potential (even if unconvicted) terrorists who have been identified by their SQUIDs (sometimes inaccurately). Those devices are carried today by most of the 0.2 per cent of mankind who, according to Dr. Nagawa's figures, commit over 90 per cent of crime. Some of the 0.2 per cent are being cured by biofeedback. Others are being rehabilitated in rural idylls. But it is a comfort to most of us, even if a worry to others, that their computer records are set flashing whenever they move from place to place. These people have not been treated as extensively with drugs as Professor Simpson feared and as some others hoped.

Beside this battle over handling real problems, the earlier row in 2004 about prying into politicians' PET and SQUID patterns seems almost light relief. But it seemed deadly serious at the time. "For the past thirty years," wrote the *New York Times* in 2004, "it has been usual for presidents of the United States to lay bare their income tax returns, so that we can see if they are stealing our money. At a time when it is possible that madmen in high places could incinerate the planet, it must be right that we should be able to see from a SQUID print-out of their brain patterns if they are the politicians we want." In reply to that even the Libertarian floor leader of the House of Representatives during the 108th Congress protested: "In the last Congress every constitutent pressed me to favor tighter and tighter restrictions to prevent the misuse of personal information held in computer databanks. In this Congress everybody is pressing me to vote for intrusions into the privacy of us politicians which would mean no ordinary sinner would dare stand for public office again."

This was one of the last of the great world-wide, got-up-by-the-Press adversarial battles, and it was prompted in part by a controversial gunboat operation in Africa and in part by a bestselling TC tape. Remember that 2004 was in the period when the world was relieved at the U.S.-CPDR peace, but terrified that some Third World nut might start throwing nuclear bombs at his neighbor and pollute the whole planet. The U.S.-CPDR gunboat operations were in progress, and in 2003 everybody seemed to be spreading libels about everybody else's PET patterns, when the Russians and Americans deposed President Mbogo.

This coincided with the appearance of a best-selling TC tape, *The Warlords, 1914–2004*. The first section of this tape traced the outbreaks of world war in 1914 and 1939 to medically explicable misdecisions by the inbred royal houses of Europe (such as the physically and emotionally crippled Wilhelm II), by politicians who were under stress through having to pretend they were pillars of upper-class morality when they weren't (such as Asquith, Woodrow Wilson and Lloyd George), by some military men whose deduced SQUID patterns (devised *post facto* for that tape) could be compared by the reader with SQUID patterns available on TCs to show the brain patterns of the clinically insane. Then came frightening medical analyses of the people who ruled in 1920–45—such as the syphilitic Lenin and the impotent Hitler—and the tape allowed the reader to explore typical SQUID patterns attached to the different illnesses of every Allied leader present at Yalta.

The second section of the tape then reported the even more destabilizing illnesses, nervous breakdowns, addictions to alcohol or other drugs, and weird sexual drives of seventy-nine people who, it claimed, could in 1944–2004 have plunged the world into its final nuclear war. The tape included charts which falsely guessed what the SQUID print-outs from all these pre-SQUID Age brains might have been, and spread a fear that, for most of the age of maximum danger, the world had been partly ruled by madmen. Even today it is possible to call up this tape and compare the alleged SQUID patterns of one late twentieth-century American president with the published SQUID pattern of one of the twentieth century's most reprehensible computer fraudsters, and find a very significant correlation.

There were grains of truth within these fields of nonsense. The world in our fathers' day was filled with too many official secrets acts and diplomatic corps. Both of these were dangerous devices liable to destroy the world. Diplomats would say to visiting jouranlists, "Although that judgment is right, I trust you will not be writing it about President Lunaticci, because its appearance in a newspaper in our country would anger him into acting against our country's interests." Although most newspaper journalists (as distinct from some broadcasting ones) rightly told diplomats where they could stuff such warnings, it is surprising that diplomats did not see what they were doing. They were prolonging a system whereby presidents stayed in office who were unbalanced and emotionally insecure enough to wax cross when they read rude things written about themselves—instead of, like most of us nowadays, calmly becoming interested.

Today it is general to send a print-out of one's SQUID to anybody with whom one has meaningful business dealings. For instance, the authors of this book telecommunicated their

SQUIDs to those whom they were going to interview, and as a normal courtesy most of the interviewees telecommunicated their SQUIDs back. It is easier to have a direct intellectual conversation if one knows the other discutant's brain pattern in advance.

A TC recall check for the past eighteen months shows that 94.7 per cent of those who have stood in recorded elections world-wide so far in 2024–5 have filed their SQUIDs with the electorate, and many of the missing 5 per cent were presumably "didn't bothers" since elected officials now make few important decisions anyway. But in 2004–6 people were much more excitable in their debates because, although the new drug culture had begun, the proper and calming use of biochemical monitoring devices, permitting the extension of biofeedback techniques, so far had not. It was only after 2010 that we moved towards being a world of Greek Stoics.

It was known even in antiquity that the mind could take conscious control over some bodily processes that normally operate automatically. The achievements of Eastern mystics in this regard were much celebrated in the last quarter of the twentieth century, especially by young people in the upper middle classes of the West. By the 1980s the benefits of meditation were widely touted in Western universities and some churches. Most people, however, could make little or no progress in this regard until the advent of the new forms of electroencephalograph.

The improved SQUIDs and PETs of 2000–10 enabled people, for the first time, to get back information about the effects within the brain of their conscious efforts triggered by certain events. Once people could see on a screen whether the alpha rhythm was present it became easy for some of them to produce or cancel it at will. Even something as basic as the alpha rhythm has implications for consciousness. There is now scientific evidence on our screens of what the Eastern mystics knew—namely that conscious control over that rhythm has a marvelous calming effect.

At first, the complexity of the devices which replaced the

electroencephalograph prevented their widespread use in biofeedback training. *Circa* 2010 the most common use was still
among the so-called "biofeedback freaks" who patronized the
expensive Stoic schools which had invested heavily in such
equipment. The fashionable thing to say then was that only a
minority of people could ever benefit spectacularly from such
techniques. Some exceptional individuals took to it much more
readily than others, while many people could not even get started.

Until 2012, moreover, biofeedback was not successfully ex-
ported to the poorer countries on the Centrobank system. Indeed in some Buddhist areas priests agitated against new
opportunities for scientifically induced calmness on what might
be called Luddite grounds, even more passionately though less
nobly than Western low-church religions had once agitated
against alcohol and other rival opiums of the people.

This "snobs' monopoly" in biofeedback is now disappearing
as the latest devices—especially the new blood-analyzing machines which are sensitive to designated organic molecules,
including the endogenous tranquillizers, stimulants and
hypnosedatives—make it easier (and cheaper) for even some of
the dumbest of us to enhance our conscious control over the
production of these compounds within our own bodies. The
future possibilities look limitless. Ever since intellectual (as
distinct from emotional) philosophies and religions began, it
has been argued that calmness of mind is within the scope of
self-control. Perhaps now we can look forward to a time when
it really will be, not just for a favored few but for nearly everyone who wants it.

Probably many people will not want it. The healthy human
mind cannot be reduced to a set of simple chemical and electrical operations. Some people, like Professor Simpson, say this
is also true of the chemistry of mental illness; and they are
partly right. Individual minds are remarkably resilient in with-
standing attempts to control their operation narrowly and specifically. We should be very grateful for this, because it is in
this resilience that our capacity to be free individuals lies.

Because we have seen and survived a revolution in psychotropic biochemistry, we are today relatively contemptuous of the supposed threat that advances in psychological science pose to our individuality. It was not always thus. Eighty years ago the threats seemed more real and baleful. It was plausible then for the Huxleys and Orwells to harbor anxieties about a coming Brave New World of total mind control; a world where everyone could be tranquillized into docility, and people's ideas and beliefs carefully molded by conditioning. It was easy then to imagine that every new drug, every advance in the understanding of how the human brain works, could put methods for the psychological manipulation of the many into the hands of the few.

In the mid twentieth century many nightmarish visions were produced of future societies which were totally regulated: visions of over-governed countries whose people were reduced to automata because psychological science had given birth to an awesomely powerful technology of psychological control. It was imagined that the mental capacities of individuals could be determined at will by the manipulation of embryos and the drug-assisted education of children. It was feared that intelligence levels might one day be pre-set; that structures of ideas could be built within the mind in order, reflecting predetermined designs; that the emotional life of individuals could be orchestrated with drugs and electronic signals; that behavior could be engineered by subtle command and by the environmental reinforcement of conditioning by reward and punishment.

The people of that era had some grounds for fearing this. They had seen the power of conditioning in shaping the behavior of rats, especially in the direct electrical stimulation of the pleasure centers of rats' hindbrains. It was not then understood that humans' behavior is organized along lines different from the behavior of rats. Most rats really are creatures of conditioning, virtual living automata. People feared that they could become likewise. The Jesuits used to claim that if a boy was theirs during his first impressionable years, he was theirs forever. Too many people gave credence to this claim even while the Jesuits sank slowly into historical oblivion.

When the Chinese communists in Korea tried to brainwash their own ideology into the minds of American soldiers, people paid far more attention to the few partial successes than to the legions of failures. When electrodes were implanted in the brains of human subjects, it was the few occasions when one or two individuals reported sensations of strong pleasure that claimed the attention.

It is true that individuals are to some extent the simple product of their genetic endowment and their upbringing. Most mature individuals do possess some of the beliefs and ideals drummed into them when they were young. It is equally true that this is not the whole story. If it were, moral education would work far better than it does, there would be no such thing as a generation gap, and there would be no such thing as progress.

In the end, we can take most comfort not from what we have done, but what we have gloriously failed to do. We have failed to find ways to mechanize people. We have failed to rob them of their humanity. We have become happily confident that, no matter what our continuing analyses of the working of the human brain may tell us, the power of self-determination—the freedom to be what we choose—cannot be taken away from us. That is one of the glories of this age of under-government.

19

On Home Swaps
and Hegel

WE COME TO THE EVENTS of the past decade, 2015–25. Contemporary history is raw and thus inaccurate stuff. The events picked in this book as important from 1975–85 are not those that people reckoned most important at the time. Our grandfathers turned neurotic about strange vogue words each decade—Watergate, Vietnam, environmentalism, planning, sexism, unilateralism—which seem as irrelevant to us as the customs of the Mamelukes. It may be that these final two chapters are misleading journalism, while we hope the preceding chapters have been history. But we have picked out four happenings as the most important features of 2015–25. The last three can be given the grandiloquent names of "The Unravelling of the Previous Hegelian Antithesis"; "The Internationalization of Taxes and Welfare and the Consequent Coming End of the Nation State"; and "The First Messages from Somewhere Else."

The first important happening may seem more mundane. It is the growth in home swapping.

Home swaps took place even in the 1980s at holiday periods, but they were anxious undertakings if you did not know your co-swappers well—and if you had to stick to the dozen or so families whom in those lonely suburban days you did know well, your choice was hopelessly limited. In the past decade people have been able to key into their TCs details of the swap they would like to make—anywhere in the world and for any period. The TC churns back a list to choose from. A video camera makes an inventory of your home as you leave it, and at the end of the swap makes a matching inventory; the TC charges the ex-swapper for anything that needs to be restored to its original state; insurance companies cover the transaction with fees based on past experience of particular swappers or of their category groups.

With these services available, Central Europeans and Russians from the CPDR have proved particularly prone to wanderlust. In 2024 nearly 10 per cent of Germans spent less than three months of the year in their own homes, and over 3 per cent lived in more than six countries during the year, telecommuting from each to their ordinary job.

Most people prefer to put down firmer roots than that, but many now take expert advice on when to experiment in uplifting them. A typical example is the house swap for ten months in 2018 between the Macfarlane family in the South Island of New Zealand and the Hirsch family in an open-area housing community just outside New Orleans.

The Macfarlane family had considered itself close-knit. The thirty-eight-year-old mother had recently been the breadwinner, telecommuting to the Tokyo bank for which she worked as an English-language loans officer. The forty-one-year-old and very house-proud father had retired for the period 2012–18 to be Educator to the two children, now aged thirteen and fifteen; unusually, both of them were going on straight to higher education, but would be doing this directly through the TC and the father was no longer needed to aid them.

Mr. Archie Macfarlane was therefore going to return to his old job as a TC salesman for custom-built goods. He had started as salesman for the bespoke tailoring to which almost everybody has returned: the customer points a video camera at herself, it feeds information on her measurements into the computer, which instructs the computerized cutting machine to make a suit exactly fitted to the customer's bulges. But Archie Macfarlane then went to work for a Hong Kong hypermarket in the Confederal Republic of China which took orders from customers for custom-built household equipment: "I want a self-propelling vacuum cleaner which I can set to cleaning the eight rooms in my house. This is the video plan of my rooms, with the furniture placed as shown in the accompanying videograph to scale. Tell me if a vacuum cleaner can be made with programs that will make it automatically clean each of my rooms if I telephone instructions through to it." Archie Macfarlane would collect these orders from his TC, calculate what prices would have to be charged if the item was totally custom-built; then telecommute back to the customer saying, "If you are willing to accept the following modifications the price can be cheaper because . . ."

As this was quite a well paid job the Macfarlanes' living standards would rise quite substantially when the father as well as the mother were again both teleworking. The family therefore arranged for one of the now fashionable family TC conferences with psychoanalysts and lifestyle counsellors. They thought they were merely asking, "Now we are going to have a higher income, how can we best spend it in order to maximize happiness in our already happy and self-satisfied family?"

The report from the counsellors on lifestyles was rather a shock. They said the two Macfarlane teenagers were too self-centered and shy to be as happy now or as successful in the future as their talents allowed them potentially to be. Their outdoor recreations (golf, rock-climbing, angling, owning racing pigeons) were all too individualistic. The Macfarlane family played regularly in family two-ball golf foursomes, but in reality these games now irritated all of them. The children showed greatest enjoyment when playing over-competitively with their parents against other families, but they at present only did this in games via the TC (duplicate bridge against other families on the TC, with the computer shuffling the cards; or a game where all four family members shot at screen space invaders while families in Singapore and Cape Town shot simultaneously at the same targets). The children would be happier if they lived near children of the same rather bright ability and age as themselves—and in a community where families regularly played each other in active games such as informal four-person volleyball teams.

Mr. Macfarlane would also be happier if he could regularly play in a tennis four with men of his own approximate ability. Professionally, if he was to be successful as he returned to TC salesmanship even of custom-built goods, he needed to become more gregarious for a while. Mrs. Macfarlane had shown by her answers to questions that she would like a period of enjoying various facilities not available in their part of New Zealand—for instance, she would like to be able to eat out occasionally at French restaurants.

All four would be better rounded people if they lived for a while in a less tidy house. If the father started a new telecommuting job in his present house, he would keep on doing too much housework. The children needed to be encouraged to engage in more horseplay, because at present they were too neurotic about not scratching the furniture.

The counselors suggested the Macfarlanes were a household that would gain from a house swap of at least ten months, and programmed the Macfarlanes' TC to suggest several alternative swaps with families who wanted to make the reverse changes. The swap they eventually accepted was with the Hirsch family who lived in an open-plan housing community near New Orleans. In these communities people open up parts of their homes so that others can use and share special facilities that individual households otherwise could not afford. Examples are swimming pools, tennis courts, hobby equipment like photographic darkrooms, and lots of pay-TC subscriptions. These open-house areas are often monitored by what are sometimes called big-brother TV sensors—which virtually eliminates undesirable behavior by visitors, since not only does the sensor by an agreed program automatically invoice them for any damage, but it can eventually cause their community club status to be downgraded, which is a more pragmatic penalty than any fine. Also, insurance companies have learned that TC-monitored open-home areas are good risks for fully comprehensive insurance.

It happened that the Hirsches' community had just voted by referendum to opt for a rather cheap and therefore strict insurance; one where the company specified the program to be used by the big-brother TV sensor, which included stiff automatic billing and downgrading or disqualification procedures, in return for a low premium per adult (plus 80 per cent per teenage) head. The insurance contracts accepted by referenda differ widely, because motives for operating within such a community also differ. Some households run such open-home areas as a mini-business; others as the most economic way of having two swimming pools per ten houses; others for the joy of being a social center where by definition you meet people with similar interests.

The Hirsches had reached a stage where both parents and both children (then aged nine and eleven) did not fit in with the community club very well. Mr. Joe Hirsch was a slightly scatterbrained researcher who wanted to spend the next few months working hard through the ordinary TC on a project that could then become ripe for entrepreneurship. He was distracted by the constant noise from his four-a-side volleyball court and splashpool. Mrs. Marjorie Hirsch complained, "We are never going to teach our children the virtue of some tidiness so long as we live so communally." The children were threatening to be underachievers; it was obvious they should both go into a period of paid work after Prelim instead of going straight on to secondary schooling, but there was a danger they might not pass Prelim until well after the age of twelve. They needed a period of quiet working through the TC, with their mother as Educator. Most of the children in their immediate open-home area were slightly older than they, and the young Hirsches were not always welcome in the team games. They might recover their self-confidence in more isolationist pursuits for a while. Because of his lack of self-confidence the elder Hirsch boy had been guilty of some minor vandalism, and his community club status was in danger of being downgraded now that the new automatic insurance contract was coming into force.

There were some difficulties in fixing the details for the Macfarlane-Hirsch house swap. Mr. Macfarlane drew attention in the video-inventory to the fact that there was one small stain on one carpet, while some of the Hirsches' carpets seemed more stain than carpet. It is also true that neither family stayed in its new environment when the ten months were up, though significantly each moved then to a lifestyle between old and new. The Macfarlanes came back to New Zealand but nearer a city. The Hirsches moved to California. Today both belong to open-home-area clubs, but ones less intense in facility-sharing (though wider in geographical range) than the club in New Orleans. The elder Hirsch boy owns the champion homing pigeons on America's west coast.

Note that these two families, whom the TC rates as typical for 2018, both returned towards the center from their previous lifestyles—the Macfarlanes becoming less hermit-like, the Hirsches less communal. This return part-way towards old habits has been a second main trend of the past decade, and Hegelians can feel smug.

The most accurate prophet of what has been happening in our time would have been an over-simplistic Hegelian from two hundred years ago. G.W.F. Hegel (1770–1831) argued that at any one time the prevailing historical forces or ideas (the "synthesis" or ruling culture) are inevitably generating their opposite (the "antithesis" or the counterculture). The resulting struggle between the two leads each opposing force to absorb some features of the force it is fighting against, and so a new synthesis emerges; it then generates its own antithesis, and the cycle starts over again.

Much of the period 1970–2010 was what one might call a period of antithesis: people were revolting against the previous synthesis of accepted ideas, habits and constraints. This period of antithesis was given different names by the brightest observers of the 1970s and 1980s. Herman Kahn talked of a "multiple trend" towards the "erosion of traditional levers." John Naisbitt listed ten megatrends. Alvin Toffler espied a "third wave" which "develops its own super-ideology to explain reality and to justify its own existence."

Hegel had taught that, after each period of antithesis, a new synthesis is created by some (but not total) revolt against the period of antithesis itself. Let us see which of Naisbitt's Megatrends (or Kahn's eroded levers or Toffler's third waves) have been surging back in 2015–25, and which have not.

One of Naisbitt's stated Megatrends in 1982 was "from Either/ Or to Multiple Options." Before the 1980s, he said, "Either we got married or we did not (and of course we almost always did)." Naisbitt quoted sociologists who feared that in the 1980s one-third of American marriages would end in divorce, so that by 1990 at least thirteen separate types of household would outnumber the conventional family (that of husband-breadwinner, wife and two children).

Among the new types it was estimated that a quarter of American children in the 1980s might at some time have polyparents, some of them living in what Toffler was calling "an aggregate family, in which two divorced couples with children remarry, bringing the children of both marriages (and the adults as well) into a new, expanded family form." Overlapping with this, Naisbitt reckoned that "more than a third of American children born in the 1970s will have spent part of their childhood living with a single parent (and the emotional and financial consequences of this trend will be commensurately large)."

For the children born in the 1980s these things did indeed happen, and the young people's revolts of 1995–2004—the attempts of hippies to take over West Indian islands, the swing of votes that eventually brought in President Roberta Kennedy and so forth—sprang partly from them. How therefore does our TC pick out as more typical of the last decade two such traditional 1950ish nuclear families as the Macfarlanes and Hirsches, one with working wife and househusband and two children, the other the same but for the spouses having swapped roles?

Modern developments have brought the family back together again. With the TC, both spouses often work from home, as in the old farm and homestead days. They usually consult lifestyle counsellors before marriage, sometimes lovingly together, but sometimes surreptitiously without the other partner knowing. Lifestyle counsellors can predict with horrid expertise which marriages have a more than average likelihood of ending in divorce, but they can also advise on what lifestyle would maximize the danger for any particular couple, and what lifestyle would minimize it. The study of how to keep marriages together in a way that will make both partners happy has become a well computerized science.

Sexual relations with somebody other than one's spouse are no longer, as in part of the twentieth century, generally deemed a reason for break-up, save by quixotics. Sexual taboos belong to the era when delightfully making love could embarrassingly also mean making babies. Children are now born when they are wanted. In childhood they are not treated as permissively as in the 1980s when Daddy saw them only a few hours a week, and could not understand why Mum did not find their constant clatter the most invigorating fun. But—again as in homestead days—they see their parents at work in the TC room and are generally themselves given something useful and remunerative to do at a very early age. By the age of twelve today's children will usually go into fully paid employment. Toffler noted in the 1980s: "The alienation of youth today flows in large measure from being forced to accept a nonproductive role in society during an endlessly prolonged adolescence." This alienation has disappeared, and it has made families more close-knit.

One of the other megatrends that Naisbitt listed in 1982 was

233

"From institutional help back to self-help." In the previous fifty years, he said, Americans had delegated their children to the schools, their health to their doctors, their souls to their business corporations, their spending responsibilities to their governments. Now, he thought, they were going to claim all these back. Again, in terms of 1985–2014, he was clearly right. How far has there been some Hegelian swing back since 2015?

In education, there has been no swing back at all. Parents steadily take over more responsibility for the TC-monitored education of their own children. Far more fathers retire temporarily to be Educators for their children's formative years than anybody would have conceived in 1985, and slightly more even than in 2015. Probably, the next swing back will be to mothers as the more usual Educators. In the 1970s children's upbringing was too much Mother's affair. In the 2010s it has been too much Father's.

In health there has already been some Hegelian cycle. We do not trust our family doctor as explicitly as in 1970, but do not have as many nutty private diets and jogging fetishes as in 1985. We get our health scientifically monitored by a health maintenance organization, and decide whether to follow its advice, with full statistical knowledge of each doctor's past killing or curing record.

In our relations with the successors to business corporations there has in 2015–25 been some small swing back toward what was regarded as normal in 1985 but odd in 2015. Few people are as intent on singing corporation songs as they were in Toshio Nakagawa's day, but compared with 2015 there is now again a greater desire to "belong" to an enterprise. In an earlier chapter our TC picked out the Clark-Schmidt Robot Gardener as one of the most successful of 2025's business ventures. It will not be alive in five years' time, because some other venture will have out-innovated it. But it is probable that more of its workforce will in some degree stick together than on the demise of a similarly successful venture of 2015.

Our TC tells us that one of the most successful new business ventures of 2014 was the Cohen-Patel lifetyle counseling pack-

234

age. At its peak this venture employed 2,000 workers. As Cohen-Patel is completely out of date, it employs none now. Our TC reports that only about 10 per cent of the original workforce are today in jobs that they attribute to having been in Cohen-Patel then.

When the 1,000 or so workers now involved in Clark-Schmidt find that new competition makes it advisable to close down, the majority of them will go to a week's break-up party at some pleasant spot like the Big Island of Hawaii. There they will pick up their end-of-venture bonuses, and form networks. The manual workers, who will probably use the bonuses to take an extended holiday, will club together and say, "This team of us will be in the market for more manual labor in six months' time; that team in twelve months' time." Those from Clark-Schmidt who want to try to be entrepreneurs or innovators or researchers next time will have the TC entry numbers and work-preference schedules of each of these teams. There will be agents employed by other entrepreneurial managers at the break-up party who will themselves take details of the teams formed from this successful venture and will be offering new opportunities for some of them to do something else together.

Although no Clark-Schmidt Robot Gardeners will be made in 2030, it will be surprising if more than half of the workers are not congregated in twenty or so successor ventures, which will probably keep ties with each other. Some people think that in this way the business corporation is being reborn, although no longer on a boss-worker basis. Students of Naisbitt will remember that one of his other ten Megatrends was "from hierarchies to networks."

Obviously, however, the most interesting Hegelian question is whether there will be any swing back from the most significant trend of 1984–2014: the retreat from big government. The answer in 2025 seems to be that we are re-strengthening local government compared with 2014, but that the speedy internationalization of tax systems and the slower internationalization of social security systems presage the end of the nation state.

20

Voices
from
Somewhere

THE MOVE BACK to some stronger forms of local government in 2015–25 should not be exaggerated. There are fewer totally anarchic or otherwise oddball communes than ten years ago, but many more communities have adopted insurance contracts as their main instruments of government. The choice is between having the cheaper but tough-on-vandals sort of contract which caused problems for the Hirsches because of young Nat's peccadilloes, or less fussy contracts where premiums for everybody are higher but the general atmosphere of the community is more relaxed.

People in any community choose which sort of contract to adopt by voting in referenda through the TC or by moving out of communities where they think the insurance rules are too lax or too nosey. Referenda are much more sophisticated than in 1975. Those voting in them do not just listen to a short, shouted argument on the TC between advocates of two alternatives. If the referendum is on what insurance contract to buy, many different contracts will be put on offer. Community members can key into their TCs specific questions about each, such as, "What would happen under this contract if an eight-year-old boy did such-and-such . . . ?" A computer (not a salesman) collates what would have been the savings or additional penalties under each contract if last year's experience and events were precisely repeated. Every vote cast for any contract therefore has the opportunity to be a well informed one.

Naturally, referenda do not apply to insurance contracts alone. They can apply to almost all matters on which public money is spent. If there are local government elections now, the three competing parties are usually those who say (a) "We will stage and obey intelligently mounted referenda on the following wide range of subjects"; those who say (b) "We seek to be elected to make decisions for you, and think the staging of these constant referenda is becoming a bore"; and (c) profit-seeking companies who say, "Let us run this local government on performance contract—we will charge you only this level of local property tax for this level of service, and if the service we provide falls below what we have promised we will give you part of your tax money back."

It is tempting to report that there is a steady swing towards one or other of these three parties. Instead there has recently been a different swing in different places at different times as people get fed up with the relative inconveniences of each. But it is true that those who say, "We will govern you" have a less satisfying time than in the days of public-sector imperialism. In most areas, and at all layers of government, referenda have long since laid down maximum proportions of GNP that the public sector can spend. Credit stops are put on the bank accounts of governments if they look like exceeding this, so that government servants can see that if they exceed their spending limits their salaries will not be paid. Few people today stay in any government's service for long, and this is a huge advantage.

Most public servants are very junior people in the communities they serve.

There are still some functions for upper layers of government to perform, but the indications from 2015–25 are that these are becoming increasingly automatic and internationalized. Two particularly important trends here are in immigration policies and tax-cum-social-welfare policies.

There has been an international attempt to help ensure relative freedom of immigration. The swing to decentralized democracy after 1990 increased the danger that people already living in nice parts of the world would say that nobody else could move into them. By international agreement it is no longer legal for any area totally to ban immigration or to impose totally restrictive zoning laws. The battle has concentrated on which are the permissible ways to wriggle into partial bans on immigration and which are the unpermissible ones.

You can restrict immigration if you live in either a fully or a "co-operatively" commercial development. In the latter, the houses and land on the estate belong to a company in which the present residents hold shares. Governments cannot say that a man must allow anybody to be free to build a house in his own garden, even when it is fairly obvious that he and his neighbors are colluding against newcomers in a way that puts all their own real estate values up. The counter which has been found to this is that nearly all regional and national governments now impose property taxes which vary with a property's value—and which generally also have a superadded tax on that part of property value that emerges from local building restrictions. This makes it superaddedly expensive to live in exclusive private estates.

If the commune of Nobs Hill tries to escape this superadded property tax by making a unilateral declaration of its independence from regional and national government—as is its right in any civilized system—then regional and national governments charge an economic (i.e., high) price for all regional and central government services sold to it. As this includes a charge for use of surrounding TC infrastructure, this makes life on a unilaterally-declared-independent Nobs Hill more expensive still. In practice, most "rich men's communes" now hold referenda on how far they will contract in or out of accepting the same fairly free immigration rules as surrounding areas do. Most of them now escape excess infrastructure charges by contracting in sufficiently to accept rulings from the rather sensible Regional Supreme Courts which have sprung up over the past two decades.

These Regional Supreme Courts were an American invention, but they have operated in a Japanese legal mode. Cases before them are searches for consensus rather than arguments where lawyers are paid high fees for clever adversarial speeches. The judges check through their TCs to find what the quantifiable results of their rulings would be. Recent court decisions have made it permissible for communes to charge 30 per cent higher insurance premiums for new entrants than for existing inhabitants; in California, Chief Justice Wu ruled this is reasonable, "Because the co-operative habits of the present residents may have made a cheap contract profitable to the insurer, and neither party can be certain that some particular newcomer might not disrupt these." But supreme courts practically everywhere have made it illegal for local areas to put difficulties in the way of cashing welfare checks, for the plain purpose of keeping "scruffy foreign welfare recipients" out.

As early as the 1970s there was a trend towards internationalization of the top rates of income tax. All countries found then that if they levied top tax rates above about 60–65 per cent on the very rich, then the rich departed for sunnier climes. This emigration accelerated enormously when telecommuting began. But it did not seem for a long time as if there could be any similar move towards internationalization of welfare payments for the poor.

Most of the things deemed to be "public goods" in public-sector-imperialism's twentieth century—such as sanitation and public parks—were not public goods at all. Garbage collection became much more efficient when it passed out of the hands of politicians and public-sector trade unions into competitive performance contracts. Battersea Fun Fair, run by the parks department of the London County Council, proved much less enjoyable for everybody except muggers than did Disneyland, founded by Mickey Mouse. But support of the poor is a public good, albeit an awkward one. Only rich communities can afford it but only poor communities will give a large majority vote for having it.

In the first decade of our history—from 1975–85—there were worries about the coming "entitlements crisis" for old-age pensioners, and the growing "welfare burden from the poor." In 1975 the Elizabethan Englishman or Gerald-Fordian American retired on his sixty-fifth birthday with a state old-age-pension which he thought had been paid for by his "national insurance" or "social security" contributions during his working life. Actually, only a tiny proportion had been paid by those contributions. Most was paid by the taxes put on those still in work, on the principle that, "If you pay grandpa's pension now, your grandchildren will pay yours later." Social security systems expanded during the decades 1940–90 when two former props of the old—the assumption that savings held their value and that households remained three-generational (with granny, mum and children)–had both eroded because of inflation and the growing belief that granny should be cared for by the state.

For the informed thirty-five-year-old in 1975, the prospect for when he would be a grandpa looked frightening. By the time he was sixty-five, in 2005, medical advances would probably mean that he could live to about eighty-five, in 2025, but during those assumed twenty years of retirement—2005–25— it looked as if the non-earners (his fellow retired contemporaries and the youngsters at school and college) would in many rich countries put a grave burden on those who were earning money in work. The number of Americans over sixty-five had risen from 4 million in 1900 to 24 million in 1980, and was then (nearly rightly) projected to reach 55 million in 2030. An old person in 1980 cost three times as much in medical care as a young adult; he or she was a heavy user of other social services which had lately begun to be provided by welfare states in profusion, and the situation seemed likely to worsen dramatically as the children of the baby boom years, born in or after 1946, came after 2011 in a rush to the pension rolls. Remember that at that time it was also assumed that more and more people would spend the years from five to twenty-four in full-time education. The great bulge of people born in 1946–57 seemed destined to reach retirement just as old folk were no longer regarded as respected senior citizens but instead as a frightful fiscal drain.

It was therefore widely forecast that in 2005–25 those employed would refuse to have their earnings taxed heavily enough to pay grandpa even his fully "entitled" pension. In 1980 an article in *The Economist*, called "Grandpa Goes Mugging," urged the United States to "Cut transfer payments to the well-off old," because arithmetic showed that "more than the whole of each year's output rise is already being promised to Americans who have retired or are retiring from working. There is less than nothing extra available for anybody else." *The Economist* thought this could strangle incentives for working. Similar fears were being expressed right across West Europe, Japan and Australia.

We now know that most of this fear was misplaced. Because work at the TC is rather relaxing, and because we take most of our education later in life, more than 65 per cent of both today's seventy-five-year-old and today's fourteen-year-old citizens of the United States have paid work (versus virtually none from either age group in 1985). By contrast, a much smaller proportion of 2025's thirty-five-year-olds are working on any one day, versus about 70 per cent of them in 1985, because today's thirty-five-year-olds are more likely to take time off to be educators to their children, or to have a long holiday after some successful venture, or to go back via the TC to college.

If the index-linked "entitlements" program for the old had been continued during this period of return to work by the elderly American, grandpa would indeed today be stinking rich. So entitlements have not been continued. Each American cit-

241

izen who reaches sixty-five this year—the people born in 1960—will instead qualify only for the pension (now called senior citizen's supplement) actuarially bought by her or his previous contributions. Because the inflationary recession of 1975–85 had by 2005 been replaced by falling-price boom, this supplement is quite generous. So most of today's poor are not old people, and none of them is a citizen of North America or Europe or Japan or Australasia or even the CPDR. About 10–15 per cent of citizens of these countries belong to families that draw some welfare benefits, but most of their neighbors regard them as lucky.

Even in the 1980s the "welfare burden" for the poorest in countries like the United States was not as large as conservatives wailed. While total government transfer payments (especially to the elderly) took more than 10 per cent of America's GNP in 1980, genuine welfare payments to the poorest took under 3 per cent of America's GNP. It was rather ridiculous that there should be clamor that this bare 3 per cent should be cut down. Today almost all rich countries have got rid of their previous government transfer payments like old-age pensions (except those actuarially earned by past savings) but they have increased welfare payments or minimum incomes to the poorest by negative income tax schemes. These schemes intensified for a time the North-South gap: the worry that the Third World countries would continue to be unable to look after their really poor, even if the rich nations began to manage to do so.

These worries, like Asia'a and Africa's poor, are still with us, but new hopes are emerging that they may not be for long. Let us look at today's apparently grimmest comparisons—at, say, the difference in income between the United States and India.

In 1985 income per head in the United States was a bit over $12,000 a year. In 1985–2025 real income per head of United States citizens has increased at an annual average of around 3.5 per cent; this means that in forty years it has quadrupled to around $48,000 in terms of 1985 prices. Because prices have slightly more than doubled in the meantime (wholly because of price rises in 1985–2005; since then in most years prices have fallen), nominal income per head of United States citizens in 2025 is almost exactly $100,000 a year. This gives a gross national income for the 270 million United States citizens of a bit over $27 trillion.

While a rich American in 2025 with an income above $500,000 a year pays the almost internationally universal top marginal income tax rate of 30 per cent, a poor American has the right to have his total income made up through America's negative income tax system to around $40,000 a year (equivalent to $20,000 a year in 1985 prices). This figure of $40,000 may be cited here too glibly. It varies with the number of dependents, and disposable personal income per head is different from GNP per head. Key into your TC to find today's different allowances for dependents, and also the rather muddling way in which definitions of both personal income and GNP have altered over 1975–2025.

But a reasonably fair comparison is between this $40,000 (or $20,000 in 1985 prices) and the $6,500 a year which was the average drawing per beneficiary by the totally unemployed under state insurance schemes in the U.S. in 1985—an average that also rides roughshod over complications about dependents and so on. In summary, Americans now allow their voluntarily idle to draw some money from the state so as to put their real incomes up to about three times the state income which was drawn by an involuntarily unemployed American in 1985. There is no harassing of the unemployed to "Take any reasonable job you are offered or lose unemployment pay" as there was in our grandfathers' time.

Many people say this is too generous ("The idle American today has a real income 75 per cent higher than a hard-working American got in the early 1980s"), while others say it is still stingy ("We have only trebled real incomes for the poorest Americans during forty years when we have quadrupled them for everybody else"), but the bank has not exactly been broken. As only about 11 per cent of Americans (just under 30 million) live in families which draw any negative income tax, and as less than half of them draw it up to the full amount, the cost of these negative income tax welfare payments—which are by far the biggest remaining expenditure of the U.S. Federal Government—today amount to under $1 trillion a year or less than 4 per cent of GNP.

Now consider India. In 1985 it had a reported GNP which was under $300 a head a year or around 80 cents a day. Since Americans with under 80 cents a day in 1985 would have starved, while Indians survived, there was already something bogus in these figures. The cost of surviving was lower in India, which was later to have important implications for immigration. In 1985–2025, because of its post-1990 expansion, India has achieved an average 7 per cent per annum growth in real GNP. This has doubled its real income every ten years, therefore multiplied it by sixteen in the past forty years. As its population was still rising until 2014, though it has stopped rising now, its real income per head has risen only just over tenfold, instead of sixteenfold. That has got its income per head up to a bit over $3,000 in terms of 1985 dollars. As its prices have slightly more than trebled without significant devaluation against the dollar, the average Indian in 2025 has an income of around $10,000 against the average American's $100,000.

The very few rich Indians earning over $500,000 a year pay the same top marginal income tax rate of 30 per cent as the richest Americans. If they were charged more, they would emigrate, to telecommute from outside the Indian tax net. But this allows the minimum income for the Indian negative-income-tax recipient to be something less than $2,000 a year, versus the average Indian's $10,000 and the welfare-recipient American's $40,000.

The obvious incentive for the welfare receiving American has been to go off to some beach in India, where he is nearly four times as rich as the average earning Indian, where he can employ servants and can live high off the hog. For rich countries like the United States, this emigration seems admirable, although it is a reversal of their history. In the late nineteenth century the Statue of Liberty called from the west to the old world to send America its poor, huddled masses yearning to breathe free. In the late twentieth century America suffered because its poor (such as welfare mothers with too few husbands and too many children) huddled in the inner cities and other areas least suitable for any children to grow up in. These welfare recipients and inner-city public servants became the majority local population in places like inner New York and voted that the city should bankrupt itself by raising welfare payments and index-linked pensions for inner-city public servants ever higher.

In the early twenty-first century America has been happy to send its nominally poor, like its hippies and its handicapped, eastwards to second-class holiday resorts like Burma's Ramree Island. Since 2010 it has been arranged that welfare payments from the American, European and Japanese treasuries can now be paid into banking deposits which are drawable upon by American, European and Japanese social security recipients' credit cards anywhere in the world.

Is this going to help make the Third World richer and happier or is it going to spur bitter resentment there? The race is on to see it leads to international depauperization, and there are hopeful signs. It is true that an upwardly mobile Indian, striving successfully to get nearly twice his region's normal living standard, say $20,000 per head for his family, can resent a welfare-drawing American who lives on a beach near Bombay drawing twice that Indian's income for deliberately doing nothing at all. As Herman Kahn said of upwardly mobile blacks who hated hippies in San Francisco in the 1970s: "One is busting a gut to get what the other is throwing away."

But it is a saving grace that most of the poor emigrants from the rich countries are now themselves rather gentle and cultivated folk. Some are people who have decided to take their $40,000 a year and retire out of what they call the West's TC rat-race to sit contemplating their navels in the East. Some are handicapped people, genuinely grateful that they can afford to pay Indian servants to push their wheelchairs round Ramree. A few are Americans or Europeans who say they will draw their

$40,000 a year, and go to do good deeds in the poorest areas of the world. Some of these busybodies do tend to be resented, as some of the old colonial missionaries were. But, in general, relations between the rich countries' poor emigrants and the poor countries' still poorer inhabitants are remarkably good.

In places like Ramree some of the foreign welfare-receiving community are now the sons and grandsons of America's expatriate poor. This was expected to cause legal problems— especially in view of the many intermarriages with locals. "American expatriates" cannot go on receiving for ever welfare benefits from an America they have never seen. In practice, most of these second-generation emigrants have chosen to integrate themselves back into working through TCs as tele-commuters who can stay American citizens, especially since employment opportunities are now growing faster for English-speaking telecommuters to America from the 7-per-cent-a-year expanding poor countries than in the 4-per-cent-a-year expanding rich ones. But it is clear that we are approaching a period when there must be a sea change in the whole concept of nationality.

At one stage, nationality implied that geographical proximity was the main link between peoples; in the TC age, when we telecommute and talk to our grown-up families by satellite, it is absurd to suppose that it is. There is still a "language barrier," but a diminishing one. In conversation, people like to use their native tongue, but most material put on the TC can be keyed for reception in a different language.

Next, the assumption was that those belonging to a "nation"—even if living thousands of miles from what used to be its shores—shared common law and taxes. Today taxes have become pretty well internationalized (people would move out of high-tax areas if they were not) and we have achieved a sort of internationalization of law (people move out of communities whose customs they dislike, and the authority of the consensus-seeking regional supreme courts has been rather surprisingly accepted). The remaining concept of nationality rests on two things.

246

First, a mush of cultural and emotional and nostalgic ties. These enjoyably flourish. At the televising of the Olympics I thrill if I can cheer home an athlete wearing the rose of England, even though we have not inhabited the same continent for years.

Second, the claim to belong to one nation rather than another is a hangover from the twentieth century's welfare states. Although a pensioner now receives merely what he has actuarially put in, the difference in welfare entitlements is still enormous. If you can somehow legally call yourself an American, then you are a member of a club where the poorest one-eighth receive up to $40,000 in welfare a year. If you have to call yourself an Indian, then at the bottom of the pile you can receive only $2,000 in welfare a year.

It might seem surprising that two groups of people put up with this. First, why do the richer seven-eighths of Americans allow a tax equal to nearly 4 per cent of their incomes to be drawn from their bank accounts to support the poorest or hippiest one-eighth of Americans whom they devoutly hope they never see? Answers: it is a sort of insurance, a sort of family tie, and not very much money. But it is true that the seven-eighths of Americans round the world plainly do not want much more of it. It is significant that the $40,000 has not been increased for five years. Unless inflation returns, it may never be increased again.

Second, why do the Indians put up with this? Answer: what could they do? When there was poverty in Europe it must have been infuriating for the sweating proletariat that there were charities called "retired gentlefolks' homes," though these were not in fact the institutions which revolutionary mobs were most eager to pull down. Anyway, people have nowadays understood that poverty is not conquered by pulling down institutions. It is conquered by building up institutions like Centrobank. And here an important development lies at hand. Next year (2026) will see the twentieth birthday of Centrobank. It has done wonders because it has allowed developing countries to draw newly created foreign exchange up to the point where this increases output without sparking inflation. As many of these

247

countries have gone above the average level of real income which qualified for Centrobank help, the Centrobank system has been extended to smaller communities than countries—including in recent years to some very small communities indeed.

To celebrate the twentieth birthday next year, there is now a project for a second town meeting of the world. Nobody can say whether this might be as successful as the first, but the opening presentation will be as controversial. Conferees will be asked to vote first on the proposition that the $40,000 a year drawn by American welfare recipients is sufficient to allow an adult a "liberal life." If this is agreed, the presenters will point out that we are within two decades of this income being attained by the average citizen in poor countries. The average Indian's income is $10,000, but at its present average annual 7 per cent growth India should quadruple this in around twenty years. China will pass this $40,000-a-year average before 2040, and even laggard very poor countries should follow later in the 2050s or 2060s. However, the very poorest people in these developing economies will still be far below the "liberal life" line. The poorest Indian at present gets $2,000 a year. This would have to multiply twenty times over to reach the "liberal life" level. Even if India continued with 7 per cent annual growth—which it will not do, because working Indians will soon start taking longer holidays—a multiplication by twenty would take forty-five years.

The object of the TC conference will be to ask conferees for suggestions on whether this period of forty-five years could be cut by an internationalization of welfare after average incomes in the main poor countries pass well above $40,000 a year. Latter-day equivalents of Mr. Hu and Mr. Heglund will be asked if they can suggest ways in which incentives for work might not be damaged if, by some time in the 2060s, we could be providing a welfare minimum at something like present American welfare rates for every voluntary drop-out or handicapped person in the world. This would involve some increase in top people's income tax rates, but with a huge prize in view.

248

If it could be achieved the last real reasons for differentiation into nation states (apart from pleasant emotional ones) would have ended, and the remaining curse of world poverty would be abolished. In the last few steps of all of man's long journey from endless toil and hunger to the very threshold of comfort and ease, we have in the past fifty years achieved unexpectedly smooth acceleration. In the next forty years we and our children may cross that threshold. The solution of the economic problem seems at hand.

Until the extraordinary news of the past three weeks, it had been intended to stop this book at that point. But since 9 June 2025, there has begun to filter in the most startling tidings in the history of our planet.

It was just over 100 years ago, with the establishment of the British Broadcasting Corporation in 1923, that radio messages began to emit from the earth which provided regular news bulletins on what was happening, and threw into the ether intelligible discussions of what sort of a people we were. It now appears that there is one or more inhabited planets round some star or stars which are 100 years of two-way radio contact (i.e., fifty light-years) distant from us.

Since 9 June a stream of radio advice has begun to be heard, geared to a people who are assumed by the sender(s) to have the technology, social organization and limited understanding of psychology which we had on Earth in the middle 1920s. The object of these messages is to instruct us in the best ways of technological, social and psychological advance. This was to be expected.

Across the 100,000 light-years of our little Milky Way galaxy alone, there are more than 100 billion stars. About one in 200 of these looks as capable as our sun of having at least one life-supporting planet moving round it. Way back in the 1960s scientists calculated that there are probably more than 500 million other Earths. Two-thirds of these should be more advanced than our planet. The Earth, at only 4.5 billion years old, is about one-third of the age of the galaxy. It has taken just over 4 billion years for life on Earth to evolve from primitive microbes to modern technology. If one of the planets born at the same time as the galaxy evolved at the same pace, it would have reached our stage of civilization 8 or 9 billion years ago. Since then it will have moved on, presumably at an accelerating pace. The mind boggles at where it could have got to.

Although those interpreting the messages received since 9 June do not think they are listening to a planet which was born at the beginning of the galaxy, it is clear that those sending these messages live in civilizations which have themselves received instruction over the ages from other planets further out; a chain which perhaps stretches back even through other galaxies to some ultimate source whose nature is going to cause theological argument. The problem before those sending us these messages seems similar to those which would face us if we were able to transmit advice to an unseen civilization which appeared to be at about the social stage of Rome under the Emperor Augustus in A.D. 10, but with the knowledge that what we said would arrive about fifty years later in A.D. 60 (by when unfortunately, although we would have no way of knowing this, Rome was under the Emperor Nero). It is as if we were to send a message to Rome under Antoninus Pius in A.D. 140 which would arrive in the time of the Emperor Commodus in A.D. 190.

We would rightly be chary about sending such messages because we would not want to signal to a Nero or a Commodus the secrets of today's nuclear fission and mind-bending drugs. Indeed, these beings' problem is twice that. They heard from us fifty years before, and signal to us fifty years on.

There is a theory that our new mentors may be only temporarily optimistic. Those communicating with us now have but recently heard of the Treaty of Locarno. The latest statesmen they know are Coolidge, Briand and Stresemann. Some think their transmissions may stop in about six years' time, as they hear an Adolf Hitler has arrived.

There is a more hopeful view on why these messages are arriving now. At any stage until very recent years, at any stage during the long era of over-government and of man's inhumanity to man, the information now coming in would have been misused. In the late twentieth century it would have been sequestered by some governments as an "official secret" to increase their power over their peoples. In the early twentieth century it would have been used by colonial powers to strengthen their rule over their unwilling subjects.

In the past fifty years we have escaped from that era of over-government and that sort of colonialism into an age where we will have open TC debates and intelligent referenda on whether we can be adult enough properly to use the extraordinary new information coming through.

Perhaps that is why the messages are being permitted to come to us.

Index

Index